Kitezh

the Russian Grail Legends

Kitezh

the Russian Grail Legends

by Munin Nederlander

translated from the Dutch by Tony Langham

Foreword by John Matthews

The Aquarian Press
An Imprint of HarperCollins*Publishers*

The Aquarian Press
An Imprint of HarperCollins*Publishers*
77-85 Fulham Palace Road,
Hammersmith, London W6 8JB

Published by The Aquarian Press 1991

1 3 5 7 9 10 8 6 4 2

© Uitgeverij De Ster — Breda 1988
English translation © The Aquarian Press 1991

Munin Nederlander asserts the moral right
to be identified as the author of this work.

A CIP catalogue record for this book
is available from the British Library

ISBN 1 85538 037 4

Typeset by Harper Phototypesetters
Northampton, England
Printed in Great Britain by
Mackays of Chatham, Kent

Contents

Acknowledgements

I would like to thank the many people who have helped me in the preparation of this book, particularly my wife, Alja Wormgoor-Werz, and my friend, Bas van de Bosch. Without their help this book could not possibly have been published. My wife accepted that in relation to the size of this work I had to devote a disproportionate amount of time to it: working on the manuscript proved to be very arduous.

The beginning of the commentaries on the Kitezh legend and the Russian bylini contained in this work, which are taken from early Russian history, is based on an article by the Russian publisher Valentin Tomberg in the German magazine *Antroposophie, Wochenscrift für freier Geistesleben*, 13th year, no. 12, 22 March 1931. In that article, which is reproduced here in translation, the Kitezh legend is identified as the central legend of the Slav culture. It was Tomberg who first identified it as such. Therefore I would also like to thank him.

My greatest thanks go to the benevolent spiritual forces that have guided me. I dedicate this book to everyone it will concern.

Foreword

I first became aware of *Kitezh: the Russian Grail Legends* in 1988, when Dolores Ashcroft-Nowicki drew my attention to the large volume she had acquired while teaching in Holland. Knowing of my interest in the Grail and in Russian legends, she showed me the book, and together we decided to recommend its translation and publication in English by the Aquarian Press. Happily, this has been achieved, and the book you are holding is the result.

It tells a strange and fascinating story, drawing some exciting parallels between the Russian legends of Prince Vladimir of Kiev and his Knights of the Golden Table and those of Arthur and the Round Table of Camelot. Although there are almost as many differences as there are similarities between the two cultures, the overlap between the two mythic cycles — between Camelot and Kiev — are indeed remarkable, and open up possibilities for deeper exploration still, which I myself hope to achieve during the next few years.

Of the great and mysterious city of Kitezh itself, little is known. It was supposedly founded in 1168 by Georgi (Juri) Vselodovich, a distant cousin of the same Vladimir around whom the cycle of tales referred to above first constellated in the Middle Ages. At some point, however, it vanished, rather like Arthur himself, and from that moment it became a place of legend, a withdrawn paradise to which only the elect could find their way.

This too is reminiscent of the Arthurian tales, in which the knights of the Round Table go in search of the Grail, the final resting place of which is the holy city of Sarras, far to the East. In these Western European Grail legends the Quest-Knights ride out in search of what they perceive as an *object*, which can heal the earth. In those of Eastern Europe the Grail is manifest as the earth itself, and the heroes of the Golden Table of King Vladimir experience its mystery in a symbolic relationship with their native earth through the presence of the invisible city of Kitezh. (This supplies the missing element of an actual Grail Quest in the Russian legends.)

Munin Nederlander suggests that in a future time, mirrored by the past,

9

all people will be able to enter the spiritual City irrespective of their nature. This belief lies at the centre of his book, which sets out to prove that the ancient mysteries of 'Mother Russia', as embodied in Vladimir and his Botaryi (Knights), reflect a future arc of history in which these symbolic stories will be re-enacted, but in a spiritual dimension.

This is all in keeping with Anthroposophical teaching, and 'Munin Nederlander' (the name can be interpreted as meaning 'Memory of the Low Lands') is first and foremost a student of Rudolf Steiner's intricate and fascinating vision. The book is written in a curious mixture of naivety and sophistication which characterizes much Anthroposophical writing. The almost transparent mysticism is balanced by the precise and detailed commentary. The two interact to form a unity of surprising strength, and though the book is at times difficult to follow in terms of detail, it is very well worth the occasional effort for the gems of wisdom and insight this produces.

One of the most important aspects of the book are the translations (many for the first time in English) of the great cycles of heroic songs known as *Byliny*. These contain a fascinating account of a past heroic age, very little removed from that of the ancient West. The many parallels are evident, even at a superficial reading, and some are traced in the present book in extraordinary detail.

At a time when the Eastern and Western halves of the European continent are speaking to each other for the first time in many generations, this is indeed a timely and important book. It shows some of the ways this dialogue can be opened up to create a new spiritual unity between the USSR and the rest of the world. It is my personal hope that this is allowed to develop unchecked, and that further and deeper explorations of Slavic and Russian myth and spirituality are permitted to continue. The outcome can only be of the greatest value to both East and West.

John Matthews.
London, 1990

Introduction

This publication is the first part of a treatise on the Slav Kitezh legend, in commemoration of the thousandth anniversary of the existence of Kiev Rus. It provides an interpretation of:

1) 'The legend of the holy city of Kitezh', an ancient Slav text from Kitezkaja Legenda, published by V.I. Komarovic, Moscow 1936 (prose);
2) 'The legend of the invisible city of Kitezh and Lady Fevronia', the libretto of the opera *Kitezh* by M. Rimsky-Korsakov, written by W.J. Belski in 1905 (verse).

These are two versions of the mysterious Russian legend about the ascension or descent of the sacred city of Great Kitezh into the *Svetli Jarr*, the brightly shining lake. Both versions of this legend are simply called the Kitezh legend.

The interpretation is carried out firstly in relation to the Slav *Bylini* (heroic epics) about the Round Table of (the Brotherhood of the Grail) of King Vladimir, the Red Sun of Kiev. It is also seen against the background of early Russian history, which can be considered as an organic unit with a foundation in the honorary request of the Slavs to the Varangians for order (the so-called Slav-Rurik Call, and the Varangian Answer to this). These indicate how the Kitezh legend is related to that of the Bylini. It is also interpreted in the light of Western European spiritual science. The reader is assumed to have some knowledge of the teachings of Rudolf Steiner, and of theosophy, anthroposophy and Rosicrucianism. For this purpose, the Bylini stories are summarized in this book, virtually all taken from Boris Raptschinsky's book, *Russian Heroic Sagas and Legends* (Thieme, Zutphen, 1923), together with commentaries which are also based on Western spiritual science.

With regard to the facts in the outline of early Russian history, and the two subsequent historical periods, I based my description on standard works, such as *Ancient Russia* from the Parool-Life series, and Ph. L. Barbour's *Dimitri*.

The Kitezh legend will be identified firstly as a Slav cultural legend (cf. Faust as the Germanic cultural legend). Secondly, it will be seen as a Utopia (the Utopia 'Philadelphia' from the Apocalypse) or as the 'social conclusion' in the form of a Christian communist state, the quest for the Grail by King Vladimir's Round Table.

Western European spiritual science, particularly anthroposophy, emphasizes that early Russian history (including the reign of Dimitri Donskoi) should also and particularly be seen as a mythological outline anticipating Russia's future history. Clearly, a similar idea applies to an even greater extent to the mythological side of this history, i.e. to the Kitezh legend, and in relation to the bylini. Therefore the interpretations and commentaries will constantly indicate that the content of the bylini and the Kitezh legend (like the history of Kiev Rus) is related both to Russia's past and future.

The introduction and the emphasis on this idea inevitably raise the question of the character of 'modern Russia', i.e. Russia as a land conquered by the Mongols, a Tsarist empire, and a communist Soviet republic.

The history of Kitezh and its interpretation will show that:

1) Present-day Russia emerged from the Slav Call for order and some unasked for (incorrect) answers to this — an unasked for answer on the part of the Mongols, an incorrect answer on the part of the Anglo-Saxons, and an unasked for and incorrect answer from both. It will also show that its character (the character of a non-Christian communist state, in a threefold sense) is based on this.
2) The force is active in 'modern Russia', which is represented by the so-called Demetrius essence. This links Russia's early and future history, Kiev's former and subsequent Round Table, and above all the Christian communism of the ancient and future Kitezh.

I hope that this treatise will contribute to the correct Varangian Answer to the Slav–Rurik Call for order in the sense described in the Epilogue.
Baarn, Whitsun 1988

1.

The Kitezh Legends

The Legend of Kitezh: the Slav Church version (The legend of the Holy City of Kitezh)

Introduction

The original Slav Church version of this legend can be found in the book *Kitezkaja Legenda* by the Russian historian and linguist V.L. Komarovic, published in 1936 in Moscow. *Kitezkaja Legenda* consists of the basic Slav Church text of overlapping and interrelated fragments, an extensive interpretation of the text in twentieth-century Russian, as well as a map of the area where the cities of Great and Little Kitezh were supposedly situated.

This translation of the legend, like the German translation of the anonymous Russian original, is completely faithful to the Slav Church basic text. The texts shown in brackets were provided by the Russian student N.N., who translated the text into German. The texts shown in double brackets are my own additions or clarifications.

Basic prose text

The book was written, according to tradition, on the fifth of September of the year 1138 (6646).

ONCE UPON A TIME there lived the exalted true believer and great prince, Georgi Vsevolodovich, the son of the exalted true believer and great Prince Vsevolod, who was christened with the holy name of Gavril, the miracle worker. This exalted true believer and great Prince Vsevolod was the son of the great Prince Mstislav, and the grandson of the exalted King Vladimir of Kiev, the supreme ruler of the whole of Russia who resembled the Apostles. Prince Georgi Vsevolodovich was the great-grandson of the exalted true believer and great King Vladimir. The exalted true believer Prince Vsevolod was the first ruler of Novgorod.

After some time it happened that the people of Novogorod became agitated about the following problem: 'How can our Prince, who is not christened, rule over us, who are christened?'

A delegation was sent and drove him away. He fled to his uncle, Jaropolk, in Kiev, and told him why he had been driven away by the citizens of Novgorod. When his uncle had heard his story, he gave him a castle. The people of the city of Pskov asked him to rule over them, and this is how Vsevolod came to rule over Pskov. During his reign he was blessed with holy baptism, and was given the name Gavril.

In Pskov he led a devout life and was held in high esteem up to the day of his death on the 11th of February of the year 1163 (6671). He was buried by his son, the true believer and great Prince Georgi.

His holy powers brought about many miracles.

Praise be to Christ, our God and all the saints,

Amen.

At the request of the people of Pskov, in the year 1163 (6671) the exalted true believer Prince Georgi Vsevolodovich ascended the throne of his dead father, the true believer Prince Vsevolod, baptized with the name of Gavril.

The exalted true believer and great Prince Georgi Vsevolodovich went to visit the true believer, Prince Michail Chernigovski. When the true believer and great Prince Georgi arrived to visit the true believer Prince Michail, he bent down before him and uttered the following words: 'Greetings, O true

14

believer and great Prince Michail! May you excel in your devoutness and Christian belief. Endeavour to resemble in all ways our great-grandfathers and our great-grandmother, the true believer and great Queen Olga, who was converted to a belief in Christ, the chosen one, the pearl of great value, and to a belief in his holy Prophets, Apostles and holy Church fathers. Endeavour to resemble our just great-grandfather, Tsar Konstanin, who was like the Apostles.'

The true believer Prince Michail replied: 'Greetings to you, true believer and great Prince Georgi Vsevolodovich! You come to me with well considered advice and without envy. You speak with a different mind than our grandfather Sviatopolk, who wished to reign alone and therefore killed his brothers who were true believers and great princes. He ordered that Boris be pierced with a spear and Gleb stabbed with a dagger. Throughout the years of their rule he betrayed them by means of flattery and the infernal lie that their mother was on her deathbed. And because they, like their peaceful prophet Christ, were well intentioned lambs of God, they did not defend themselves against their hostile brother. However, the Lord raised up his followers, the true believers, princes and miracle workers, Boris and Gleb.'

The great princes Georgi and Michail embraced each other, and celebrated a solemn feast and were joyful.

Then the exalted and great Prince Georgi addressed the true believer Prince Michail: 'Grant me permission to build houses and citadels of God in the cities of the holy land of Russia.'

The true believer and great Prince Michail answered: 'As it is your wish, you will build houses of God to the glory and honour of the holiest name of God. And you will be rewarded for your devout wish on the day of Christ's return to earth.'

For many days there was a solemn feast, and when the true believer King Georgi wished to return to his home, the true believer Prince Michail ordered his servants to prepare the official consent to build the churches. He endorsed it with his signature.

When the true believer and great Prince Georgi started his journey back, the true believer Prince Michail accompanied him and took his leave with dignity. The two princes knelt down before each other and the true believer Prince Michail handed him the consent.

(*Another version continues from this point.*)

The true believer Prince Georgi took the consent from the true believer Prince Michail, and bowed down before him. Then the former also bowed down.

Georgi travelled through many cities, and when he arrived in Novgorod in the year 1164 (6672), he ordered a church to be built in honour of the Assumption of Our Holiest Lady, the Mother of God, the Virgin Mary.

From Novgorod he travelled to his own city of Pskov, where his father, the true believer Prince Vsevolod, baptised under the name of Gavril, the miracle worker of Pskov and Novgorod, had died. From there he travelled on to Moscow, and in the year 1164 (6672), he ordered a church to be built in honour of the Assumption of Mary, Our Holiest Lady, the Mother of God, the Virgin Mary. From Moscow he travelled to Pereslavl Saleski, and on to the city of Rostov.

At that time the great and god-fearing Prince Andrei was in the city of Rostov. On the 23rd of May 1164 (6672), the true believer Prince Georgi ordered him (?) (not clear in the original Russian) to build a church in honour of the Assumption of Our Lady in the city of Rostov.

During Prince Georgi's sojourn there, deep ditches were dug for the foundations of the Church. During these excavations the immortal body of Leonti was found, the servant of Christ, and miracle worker and Archbishop of Rostov. The power of that living body led the people of Rostov to be converted to the Christian faith, and they were all baptised, great and small. The true believer Prince Georgi was extremely joyful about this. He thanked God who had granted him such a valuable treasure. He offered a prayer of thanks and ordered the God-fearing Prince Andrei to travel to the city of Murom to build a church there in honour of the Assumption of Our Lady.

The true believer and great Prince Georgi himself travelled from Rostov to Jaroslavl on the banks of the Volga. He took a boat and travelled down the Volga. In Little Kitezh, on the Volga, he stepped ashore.

(Another version continues from this point)

All the people of that city requested the true believer Prince Georgi to bring to their city the miraculous holy statue, the icon of the Holiest Mother of God of Feodorovsk. Before fulfilling their wish, he sang songs of praise in honour of the Holy Mother of God. When he had finished, he wanted to carry the holy statue into their city, but was unable to move it from its place.

When the true believer Prince Georgi saw this as the will of the Holy mother of God, he ordered a convent to be built in her honour on the spot she had chosen for her image. The true believer Prince Georgi continued his journey not by water, but overland.

He crossed the rivers Uzol, Sandu, Sanogtu, and finally the River Kerschenec, and arrived at a lake called Svetlojar. He observed the beautiful and spiritual area, and at the request of the people he ordered a fortified town by the name of Great Kitezh to be built on the shores of Lake Svetlojar. The setting was magnificent.

On the opposite shore of the lake there was a holy oak forest. On the advice and command of the true believer and great Prince Georgi Vsevolodovich, ditches were dug for the foundations of the city, and a church was built in honour of the establishment of Christ's Cross. (This was on an Orthodox Holy Day.)

Subsequently another church was built (The Assumption of Our Lady), as well as a third church (The Annunciation). In addition, he ordered portraits to be painted of all the saints. The city of Great Kitezh was 100 sazen wide (1 sazen = 2133 m.) and 100 sazen long. As the site was not large enough, Prince Georgi ordered that it should be extended by another 100 sazen. The city was now 200 sazen long and 100 sazen wide. Building commenced on this fortified city of stone in honour of the prophet Jeremiah and his followers in the year 1165 (6683).

Three years later, on 30 September 1168 (6686), it was completed in honour of the holy Martyr, Gregory of Armenia.

Then the true believer Prince Georgi Vsevolodovich travelled to Little Kitezh and ordered the distance between Little Kitezh and Great Kitezh to be measured. It amounted to 100 poprist (church measurement: 1 poprist = approximately 23.33 km).

When the true believer and great Prince Georgi Vsevolodovich learned this, he offered a prayer of thanks to the Lord and to the Holy Mother of God. Then he ordered a historian to chronicle events. The true believer and great Prince Georgi Vsevolodovich held a Mass and sang songs of praise for the Holy Mother of God of Feodorovsk.

After the Mass, he sailed in his ship to his father's city of Pskov, which was also situated on a river. The people of Kitezh took their leave of him and kissed him farewell with great respect.

When the true believer Prince Georgi Vsevolodovich arrived in Pskov, he passed many days in prayer, fasting, and meditation. He gave many alms to beggars, widows and orphans. About 75 years passed after he had founded all those cities and churches, and it was the year 1239 (6747).

That year it was God's will, and because of our sins, that the dishonourable and godless Khan Batu entered the holy country of Russia. He laid waste and burnt down many cities and churches, slaughtered many people, struck down small children and raped young girls. There was great lamenting.

When the true believer Prince Georgi Vsevolodovich heard this, he wept many tears, prayed to the Lord and the Holy Mother of God, and assembled his warriors.

With his warriors he set out to fight the dishonourable Khan Batu. At the moment that the two armies encountered one another, there was a great battle and much blood was shed.

When the true believer Prince Georgi had only a few warriors left, he fled from the dishonourable Khan Batu. He fled down the Volga to Little Kitezh. There the true believer Prince Georgi stood firm against the dishonourable Khan Batu for a long time, and prevented him from entering the city. At night the true believer Prince Georgi secretly left Little Kitezh and fled to Great Kitezh.

In the morning the dishonourable Khan stormed the city of Little Kitezh with his hordes and conquered it. He killed the inhabitants, but because

17

he could not find the true believer Prince Georgi, he decided to torture someone. When the victim could no longer endure the torture, he betrayed the road to Great Kitezh.

The dishonourable Khan hastened thither. When he arrived at the fortified town, he overran it with his hordes and took Great Kitezh on the shores of the Svetli-Jarr. On the 4th of February the dishonourable Khan Batu murdered the true believer Prince Georgi Vsevolodovich and left the city. This brought to an end the power of the true believer Prince Georgi Vsevolodovich.

'This is what Batu thought he had achieved, or at least, this is how he saw it.' The city of Little Kitezh on the banks of the Volga died out, and Great Kitezh on the shores of Lake Svetlojar no longer existed.

Similar events also took place in history as recounted in the biographies of the Holy Fathers, and as described in the book 'Monasiki', and in the Book of Hermits, the alphabetical biography, The Book of Jerusalem and in the Book of the Holy Mountain.

These books give corresponding accounts of the lives of the Holy Fathers, though the holy places often differ. For that matter, there were as many monasteries with as many Holy Fathers with different lifestyles as there are stars in the sky. It is no more possible to write down all those names than it is to count the grains of sand on the seashore.

The holy prophet King David, inspired by the Holy Ghost, writes in the Book of Psalms, inspired by God: 'The just man flowers like a date palm and multiplies like a cedar of Lebanon which was planted in the house and garden of Our Lord.'

Inspired by the Holy Ghost, the holy Apostle Paul wrote in his letters: 'The wolf in sheep or lamb's clothing who lives beneath his dignity is not worthy of the world.'

These words were also uttered by the holy St John in his teachings on the third week of fasting.

(*End of this version.*)

A similar account was also passed down to us from Mount Sinai by the holy Anastasi. In addition, our respectful father, the great Ilarion, describes the saints in the same way as the Scriptures mentioned above. All in all, it is clear that there are hidden cities and monasteries. When the Antichrist assumes world dominion, the people in mountains, caves, and subterranean abysses will flee. Then God, who loves man, will not abandon people as they beg for salvation with burning zeal, great emotion and tearfulness, for the Lord will do everything for mankind. According to the divine words of the Saviour in the Holy Gospels, all who wish to be saved will be saved.

Six years after the murder of the honourable true believer and great

Prince Georgi Vsevolodovich, and the interment of his sacred mortal remains, Khan Batu penetrated the rest of Russia to wage war. The true believer Prince Michail Chernigovski went to fight against Khan Batu, together with his boyar Fyodor.

When their warriors engaged in battle, a great deal of blood was shed, and the dishonourable Khan Batu killed the true believer Prince Michail Chernigovski, together with the boyar, Fyodor. This took place on the 20th of September of the year 1242 (6750).

In the fifth year after the murder of the true believer Prince Michail Chernigovski, the dishonourable Khan Batu murdered the true believer Prince Mercurii Smolenski on the 24th of November of the year 1247 (6755). In the year 1248 (6756) the principality of Moscow was destroyed, as well as many monasteries in other cities, and that of the city of Great Kitezh. 'At least, this is how it was seen.'

(These additional details about the legend of the hidden city of Kitezh were added to the three versions.)

When someone takes a decision to go to Kitezh and starts by praying, fasting, and shedding many tears; when that person also decides to starve rather than ever leave the city, he will certainly arrive there. He will not even leave the city if he has to suffer many insults, for God will save him by ordering the angels to protect him, and record his life in the Book of Life. With this honest decision, a seeker follows the path of salvation as described in the Holy Books about the lives of hermits.

According to one of these books, there was once a devout man who perpetrated the sin of fornication with a girl. The girl went with him to a monastery and died by the entrance. She was saved. In the same way, another girl travelled through the desert with him and died on the way. The angels took her soul and raised it up the ladder of heaven. In this way, every man will be judged as he turns to God at his last hour.

Just as, according to this Holy Book, the girls are liberated from the dark and inhuman Babylonian world, every 'converted' man will be saved from it. In his Book of Revelations, St John Bogoslov described that judgment at the end of the days. He saw how, naked and without shame, the woman World rode a seven-headed dragon. In her hand she holds a dish full of evil; she reaches this stinking dish to people burning with passion. The first to receive it are the patriarchs and kings, princes and generals, and all those who have great power and desire power. However, if someone wishes to be saved, he must renounce the world and its treasures.

Thus John, inspired by the Holy Ghost, describes how the woman and the dragon followed him in his isolation in order to lead him away from the path of righteousness, though he wished to live a humble life of spiritual contemplation.

The dragon of damnation teaches people to take the easiest path. He leads

19

them astray from the right path onto the path of evil, preventing them from following the right path. He tempts them to lead an immoral and dissolute life and taunts those who are on the right path.

When the Lord wishes and aims to save someone who has been misled in this way, he convinces that person and helps him even more with his divine blessing to lead him onto the path of a perfect and humble life.

No one has ever been abandoned by God anywhere. I called to him and he heard me; does he not hear the prayers of those who call for help? Does he not reveal himself to those who seek him? The Lord joyfully accepts all those who come to him and call on him.

Generally even the powers of heaven do not see the face of God. But when a sinner is converted on earth, all these powers suddenly see the face of Christ in his divine glow. All the saints in heaven are filled with great joy for every single sinful soul that is converted.

The heavenly powers, angels and archangels, cherubim and seraphim are the beginning and end of all power, dominion and holiness. The prophets, apostles, saints, the just and the martyrs are among them. They all feel joyful about every single sinner who is converted. However, when someone does not wish to be saved, and does not desire salvation, the Lord does not impose it upon him. Yet when someone unceasingly and wholeheartedly desires this salvation, and unhesitatingly pursues this without harbouring any evil thoughts, the Lord will do everything possible for that person. The Lord reveals Himself to such a person, and will lead him to a sheltered place. Our Father strives day and night to hear their prayers. A prayer from their mouth is redolent of frankincense. Such people also pray for 'everyone else' who wholeheartedly seeks salvation, without making any false promises 'just as they do'.

When someone turns to them because he wishes to be led to that protected place, 'just like them', and does not harbour any sly or treacherous thoughts, or have any ulterior motives, they will gladly accept him 'in their ranks'. However, he must guard against dangerous and evil thoughts, as well as against doubt, which will keep him away from the protected place. This person will be led along the path of freedom by the Lord, together with others. In the end he will receive a message from a hidden city or monastery.

In every monastery a chronicle is kept of the progress of those who are approaching.

I will return to the fact that a person who has been called will go astray, and start to doubt and boast. This means the path will remain hidden to him, and it will seem like a forest or a void. He will achieve nothing, and all his efforts will be in vain. Because he has wandered off the path, he reaps resentment and taunts. God allows this to happen to him, and condemns him to the darkness of hell for eternity, because he has desecrated the holy place.

However, at the end of eternity a miracle takes place. The hidden city becomes visible to him again, just as in the past this happened with one of the many hidden monasteries described in the biographies of those saints who travelled far and wide.

The city of Great Kitezh was also hidden and protected by God's hands. 'But now that we look at her from the future, we declare: She was worth the endless search and the shedding of many tears. The Lord also covered this city with his hands, and it was no longer visible.'

However, in the case of this city it was despite the prayers and supplications of those who justifiably despaired. (They were right to despair, as shown by the fact that even before they suffered the pain and troubles of the Antichrist, they were sorrowing for the world day and night.)

Our fathers informed us that their fathers told us that our people had to withdraw from the principality of Moscow because of the tyranny of the Antichrist, his impure and unclean commandments, and the destruction of the city of Kitezh. 'Others say that Kitezh was submerged in the Svetli-Jarr.'

After the disappearance of the city and a hundred years after the rule of the godless and dishonourable Khan Batu, who laid waste to the whole region of Uzol, burning settlements and villages, that region was overgrown with forests, and Kitezh and its monastery could no longer be seen.

This chronicle was written in the year 1251 (6759). It was sealed by holding a council and submitted to the Holy Church of God.

(*First conclusion*)

This Holy Scripture is for the confirmation of all true Christians who wish to hear it or read it, and do not wish to make it into a scandal. However, when someone mocks us or takes us lightly because we have given him this Scripture, he should be aware that he is not blaspheming against us but against God and his Holy Mother, Our Lady, the Virgin Mary. In the Scripture her great name, Mother of God, is praised and exalted, for her name alone protects and saves.

She also covers the holy city of Kitezh with her hands, and prays to her Son for the people. 'Do not despise my request, dear Son, you who have shed your blood for the whole world. Protect and save those who call on my name with unwavering faith and a pure heart.'

For this reason, protect the city of Kitezh with your hand O Lord, for we have written about this city, made the Scripture into an article of faith and submitted it to your Church. Nothing can be added nor taken away from this, our article of faith. Not a comma nor a full stop may be changed in it.

(*Second conclusion*)

Anyone who adds anything to this or changes it will be damned, according to the traditions of the saints who sealed and passed down this Scripture.

(Third conclusion)

However, if someone does not believe this, he should consult the biographies of the saints who lived in those days, and then he will find for himself how many similar events took place then.

Praise be to God and his Holy Trinity, and to his absolute immaculate mother who safeguards the city of Kitezh and protects all the saints. Amen.

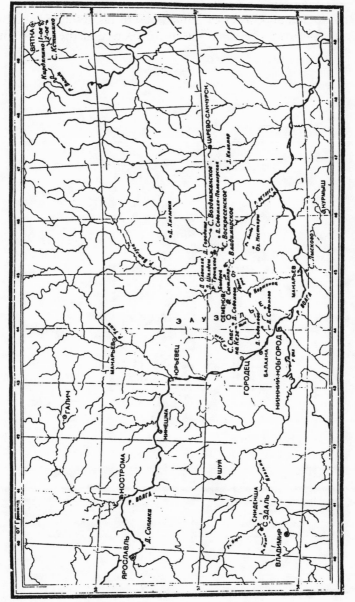

The region around Great and Little Kitezh.

23

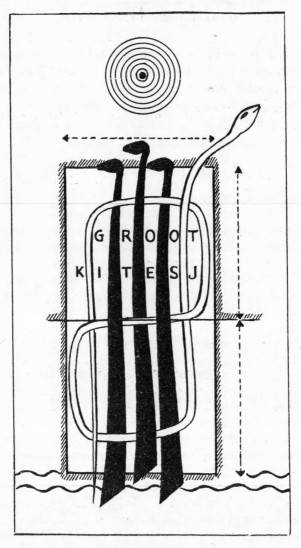

The plan of Great Kitezh.

The Legend of Kitezh: Twentieth-Century Version by W. Belski (The Legend of the Invisible City of Kitezh and Lady Fevronia)

Written by W.J. Belski in 1905, commissioned by M. Rimski-Korsakov for an opera about the legend of Kitezh. Translated from the French and German versions of the text of the opera of Kitezh, as contained in the Russian, French and German piano arrangement of the opera, published by M.P. Belaieff, Leipzig, 1926.

Introduction by W.J. Belski

The following works served as a basis of the legend:

1) the so-called *Chronicle of Kitezh* by Meledin which was included by Bessonoff in his foreword to the fourth edition of the Songs of Kirejevski;
2) a number of traditional tales about the invisible city of Kitezh, some of which are also mentioned in Meledin's Chronicle, and an episode from the saga of Lady Fevronia from the city of Murom.

As anyone who is familiar with these texts will understand, the motifs which can be found among them are completely inadequate for a large, complex theatrical work. In order to create a complete theatrical work that adequately outlines the actions and views of the characters contained in it, and clearly describes the locations where these actions take place, the author of this work considered it a challenge to write numerous far-reaching additions to the many fragments and ideas in the available texts and to the oral traditions. These are based on the living philosophy of the soul of the Russian people. Nevertheless, there is hardly a single detail in the entire poem that is not derived from some Russian myth, saga or legend.

The attack by the Tartars on the Volga, and other events, are not rendered historically in the legend, but are described freely as they occur in the popular imagination.

Similarly, great care was taken regarding the use of language, which is not based on thirteenth-century Russian — the century in which the story takes place — but is based on the rather solemn and literary use of language and mode of expression of later centuries, during which the tale slowly developed in the Russian popular imagination. If any literary criticism is brought to bear on this modest libretto, it might start by pointing out the lack of dramatic action in most acts. In order to clearly reveal the spiritual aspects of this subject, the author chose to describe the organic interrelationship and logical change of moods of the heroes on the stage in very broad terms. Such a description does not lend itself to dramatic action, and this should be emphasized if such criticisms are made.

Perhaps it is appropriate to mention that the libretto was commissioned by Rimski-Korsakov, even before he composed his work 'Zar Saltan' in 1899, and that the final version of the libretto was completed after lengthy joint discussions both regarding the content of the story and the way in which it was elaborated. The text contains nothing which does not have the composer's agreement.

Introduction by Munin Nederlander

As W.J. Belski points out in his foreword to the libretto, he should be characterized as a writer who is a representative of Russian Symbolism, like the better known Alexander Blok.

Russian Symbolism was a (literary) movement at the end of the nineteeth century and the beginning of the twentieth century, and in a sense it can be considered as the final Christian offshoot of the Pan-Slav development of the middle of the nineteenth century. It was concerned with the interpretation of Pan-Slav ideas and sought to disseminate them by linking them with the symbolic content of Russian legends dating from before the Tartar invasion.

My verse translation — it could be sung to the music of Rimski-Korsakov with few changes — is fairly free in several places, but this also applies to the French and German translations on which it is based. These translations are very different and contain numerous clichés. I did not attempt to translate these French and German clichés in a literal way. When I allowed myself to be free with the translation, I made sure that I was never inconsistent with regard to the nature of W.J. Belski's symbolism. On the contrary, in the romantic passages I adopted a traditional style, and in the battle scenes I used a double meaning with reference to the victory over the Self which corresponds entirely to the ideas of W.J. Belski's work.

Basic verse Text
(A Libretto for an Opera in Four Acts)

Cast:
Prince Juri Vsevolodovich
Prince Vsevolod Jurivich
Lady Fevronia
The drunkard, Grisjka Kutjerma (Grisjenka)
Officer Fyodor Pojarok
A shepherd boy
Two rich citizens
A goesli player
The tamer
A guild leader of the beggars
Khan Bedjai
Khan Burundai
The bird of paradise, Alkonost(us)
The bird of paradise, Siren
The people (peasants and youths)

Act one: In the woods on the other side of the Volga
Act two: In Little Kitezh on the Volga
Act three, scene 1: In Great Kitezh
Act three, scene two: On the shores of Lake Svetli-Jarr
Act four, scene one: In the forest of Kersjenez
Interlude
Act four, scene two: In the invisible city

The action takes place in the year 6751 after the creation of the world.

Act 1

*In the forest on the other side of the Volga, not far from Little Kitezh, stands
a humble woodcutter's hut surrounded by a circle of oak, elm and pine trees.
A stream murmurs. It is afternoon in the middle of summer. As the birds
sing and the cuckoo calls, Fevronia gathers medicinal herbs and hangs them
in the sun to dry.*

Fevronia

O STRONG, GIANT OAK FOREST realm of yellow and green,
    I feel at home only in your leafy chambers.
You protected me more than my father's love,
You were quietly good to me, more than my loving mother.
Did you not sing words and songs of consolation
In my ear when I was young? Did you not tell me fairytales?
In the evening you lulled me to sleep with a breath of wind.
It is good my child — sleep sweetly!
In the daytime you brought playfellows on my path,
Birds, four-footed creatures to dance and play games with.
I happily ran along with everything that hopped around.
No, I never had time for the slightest cares.
Thank you, giant oak forest, for giving me so much.
Let time not cut you down unnoticed.
All your trees together formed a roof over my head,
And your grass was a mat where I could rest in peace.
The morning dew served for me to bathe in.
Silence contemplating a deeper silence quiets
The tumult of the day — there is never any guilt —
I hear your voice like a soft plaint,
I hear your voice, the voice of silence,
I hear the voice of the forest.

Dear friends, tell me where you are,
Birds, four-footed creatures, tell me.
Come out, appear before me,
Come out of the dense bushes.
I have all sorts of good things to eat,
Sweet seeds, nuts, a worm, a maggot.
Are you there?

*A crown of birds from the marsh and forest flies nearer, surrounding
Fevronia without a trace of shyness. She turns to the crane.*

28

Fevronia
Wise crane, are you sad?
Why do you walk around so despondently?
Did you find nothing to eat on the ground?
And you are such a strong crane.

*A young bear walks up; it rubs against Fevronia's knees and rolls round and
round to attract her attention. She gives him some bread.*

Fevronia
Little bear, what have I heard? It is sometimes said
That you crack open honeycombs and steal honey.
But for the moment I will believe
That you mean well; people like to gossip.
One day a tamer will show how musical you are
Travelling through the country and in towns,
How charmingly you can dance.
They will say: give me such a dancer.

*Fevronia moves to a distant corner of the forest where an elk shyly shows its
head crowned with antlers.*

Fevronia
Elk, do not be afraid. Please come.
The bear and the bird are not your enemies.
Oh! What is that? Are you hurt?
Did a hunter's dog bite you?

*Fevronia examines the wound on the elk's neck. The bear lies at her feet,
and the crane stands next to her. A flock of other birds patters around the
group.
Fevronia does not notice when Prince Vsevolod steps out of the foliage. He
looks pale. The animals scatter in all directions. The prince stands still in
utter amazement. Then Fevronia's eyes are on him.*

Fevronia
A singular young man
Wearing a coat of wolf's pelt.
It does not suit his handsome face,
Which is like that of a king.
Where are you from, my friend?

Prince Vsevolod
Is she an illusion or reality?

29

Am I dreaming or awake?
It is as though I have always known that face,
Completely unknown to me now.
Yes, I think her eyes are just
Like the sun and the moon
Shining in the firmament
At the painful moment
Of my very first childish sob.
Is she an angel? Only light,
Only for my happiness,
Like the stars seen at night?
Or is she a wicked witch,
Secretly lusting for sex?

Fevronia greets the stranger.

Fevronia
Be welcome friend. If you are tired,
Stay awhile. Take what I have:
Bread with golden jelly and copper syrup,
Honey from the lime tree and the wild rose.

*Prince Vsevolod leans against a tree, tired out. Fevronia passes him a wooden
plate with bread and honey, and a mug of water.*

Prince Vsevolod
It is dusk. The path homewards will soon disappear
In shadow. I should hurry.

Fevronia
I know the way in the forest everywhere, friend.
If you like, I will lead the way for you.
But you look as if you are hurt.
Your arm is covered in blood.
How did that happen?

Prince
As I was hunting, I was attacked by a bear.
I struck it down. It hit my arm.

Fevronia
Do not worry.
Let me tend your painful wound
Without delay,
I will wash away the dust and grime

30

with rainwater.
I will find herbs
In the green valley —
Blossoms and some leaves
To bind up your wound.
The bleeding will cease,
And the fever will drop.

*Prince Vsevolod eats some bread and honey and drinks some water. Fevronia
gets the herbs from the wood and goes back to Vsevolod. She turns back the
sleeve of his jacket and binds up his wound.*

Prince Vsevolod
How is it possible that it is precisely
Her face which makes such an impression on me?
Even when I explain it to myself,
It remains a mystery — a secret.
Where would she look best?
Not in the royal palace.
Her virginal purity
Belongs here in these unspoilt woods.

Fevronia
If this bandage works,
The fever will go down.
But I am trembling too much.
He is more charming
Than the woods, fields and lakes.
I suddenly lack courage
In the face of his penetrating gaze,
I retreat in fear.

Prince Vsevolod
Tell me who you are. Who are your parents?
Do you live alone in these woods?

Fevronia
I am Fevronia. I live in a tiny cottage,
Two leagues from here, with my brother.
He takes the honey from the beehives,
Deeper in the woods. We live
A simple and contented life.
The poverty does oppress us sometimes in winter,
But what does it matter?
With the rains of spring come,

And the flat fields flood,
The flowers and trees will soon be decked
For a splendid summer,
King Winter, who reigned too harshly,
Disappears. Princess Spring
Raises her head. Every year she weaves the soil
To make a flower-studded tapestry.
And she brings the whole wood
Back to life — life from which life
Emerges again. Ten thousand birds
Are mating and warble a thousand songs.
This daydream will never bore me.
You do not understand what a wonderful place this is.
I even wonder whether the light of the ground
Is not lighter than God's throne.

Prince Vsevolod
Oh, dear child, remember that ancient songs
Teach us a different wisdom. They say:
Dreams lie. You have to defend yourself
Against dreams. Hold on to physical reality.

Fevronia
Have patience with me; I don't know any better.
Nobody taught me in the past.
But tell me — does the wound still hurt?

Prince Vsevolod
Hardly at all. I feel no pain. It's like magic.
How can I thank you?
Do you know the powerful spell which,
When you say it, charms the animals
And cures illness?
Child, are there any churches here? I want
To thank Christ for my cure.

The shadows are growing longer, and the sun is big and red. The forest is like an enormous church.

Fevronia
No, there is no church in these parts.
But is not God present everywhere?
Do not think that the forest has been
Forgotten by God. This is God's temple
As much as all the churches in the cities,

32

North and South. Look with clear eyes.
Day and night this forest church is open
For you and me. And day and night it smells of sweet thyme.
The sunlight bathes us in God's essential glow.
When darkness falls, the firmament is on fire,
Like a candelabra on the altar.
Day and night a choir of many birds sings
In the bushes, in the grass, the marsh and the shore
Heavenly Father, we sound your chords.
Christ, praise be to you because you were crucified.
Holy Mother, for your love, our thanks.
Earth, echo their divine word, as we do.

Prince Vsevolod
Lady, I thank you! You spoke simply,
And with astonishing grace. Your words
Are certainly the peak of happiness. But
The wise teach us something quite different.
Their advice is: do not seek happiness on earth.
They consider that this world is a
Vale of sadness. Therefore I would most
Like to withdraw. Joy is in the blood of youth.
Youth has the courage for life.

Fevronia takes hold of Vsevolod's hand and gazes lovingly into his eyes.

Fevronia
My love, who can live without joy?
Do you want to live without happiness?
Look around you: everything that is alive lives
As happy as light.
See how full of joy is every creature.
Believe me, bitter tears are worth nothing
When they are shed for your own sadness.
It is only a tear of joy or pity that falls
As a dewdrop of love on the earth.
Even sin cannot really pull you down.
You know, a man who lives like a beast
Is the one who needs your love the most.
Christ lives in every human soul and
Suffers with one of his own free will.
I see the Lord in he who suffers,
And therefore I am drawn to that tortured soul.
If I do not think about a lost love,
The whole world literally shines like gold.

33

Joy showers down from the heavenly blue.
The miracle of growth and blossoming unfolds
A greater miracle, seen by no Argus's eye,
The temple of the world is built again.
Just as when Mary's son came into the world.
Choirs of angels come down to earth.
A bell rings like Easter Day,
And God's nature is aflame as at Pentecost.

Prince Vsevolod
What you say condenses into reality:
As though words of praise awake a whole world.
Strong, gigantic forest, in the depths of your greenery
A warm flower blossomed unperceived.
I almost forgot myself for that flower.
I am Vsevolod, a man from the town.
Be my wife in this earthly Jerusalem.

Fevronia
Dearest, but who am I? Will I be the wife
Of a hunter from the town?

*Hesitatingly, Fevronia stretches out her hands to Prince Vsevolod. The Prince
takes his ring and slides it onto Fevronia's finger.*

Prince Vsevolod
Do not refuse. Allow me to place my golden ring
On your finger. It fits. Keep it.
Take it as a seal of my trust.
Do not blush. Let the most beautiful flower of the forest
Be entrusted to the Lord of the city.

Fevronia
I am not bowed down by shame.
My blood rises up with pure joy!
Am I really meant for you?
In reality, rather than in a dream?
Yes, I realize that if this were a dream,
The sunlight would not be visible to me,
The glow in my heart would be a chill,
The song of the birds would be a silence.

Prince Vsevolod
Undaunted and soft as a dove
Is what you seem to me.

Oh! Perhaps happiness will not pass me by
Divine joy also suits me.
Place the happiness of your heart in me
For it is close to the joy of God.
Place the happiness of your heart in me.

Fevronia
I belong to you.
As you belong to me.
By your side, my friend,
I feel neither the pain, nor fear.
At your command,
I will lay down my life.
I have no fear of death.
I care more for you
Than for this fragrant wood.
But tell me, dearest,
How can I release you
From your sadness?

The sound of hunting horns is suddenly heard in the forest. The Prince takes the silver horn which hangs from his belt and answers the call.

Hunters' voices
Yes, today the hunt passes through the oak forest.
It has cost many hares their coats.
Hawk, falcon, crow, and raven flew up in alarm,
And the forest is more intensely silent than bare rock.

Prince Vsevolod
Ah, I hear my friends approaching.
I fear that I must go straightaway,
But I will come and fetch you very soon.
I thank you again, Fevronia!

Again the hunters' horns are heard. Fevronia and Prince Vsevolod bid each other farewell.

Hunters' voices
Our Prince had a fantastic idea.
He dressed himself in the pelt of a he-wolf.

Fevronia
Hunter, hunter, come back.

Prince Vsevolod, who has already begun to move away, turns back to her.

Prince Vsevolod
Dearest, what is the matter?

Fevronia
Nothing. I swing between fear and hope.
I would like best to be with you and with people,
But I also want the solitariness of this realm of dreams,
Of this green kingdom.

Prince Vsevolod
Do you think that you will miss the plants and animals
When you are in my kingdom of stone?
I promise you: we will stop hunting animals.
I will protect the forest.
But now I must really go. Duty calls.

The Prince leaves very quickly.
*He has barely left when the hunters appear, led by the Adjutant, Fyodor
Pojarok.*

The Hunters
He drives the game courageously: oxen, fox,
Boar, goose — they all run from him. The horns sound.
Everyone goes after their favourite prey. What luck.
But where is our hero, where is Vsevolod?

Fyodor Pojarok turns to Fevronia.

Fyodor Pojarok
Strange lady, where are you from?
Just now it seemed there was no one here.
Have you seen our master pass
Wearing a wolf's coat?

Fevronia
Certainly. You will easily catch him up.
He went that way. But tell me:
Where does he come from? Who is he?

Fyodor Pojarok
Strange. You really do not know who he is?
Our leader is Prince Vsevolod,
Son of Juri, our ruler and yours.
And he came, like we did, from the castle
In the middle of the city, the royal castle.

Act Two

*On the banks of the Volga, Little Kitezh shines in the morning sun.
There are many rows of stalls in the market of the town opposite the
inn. Everywhere groups of people are waiting for the wedding
procession in honour of Prince Vsevolod, the son of the ruler of the
city, Juri, and Lady Fevronia, a girl from the forest on the other side of
the river. Here and there, there are small groups of beggars (mendicant
monks, rather than tramps). Next to the inn a Tamer plays the flute,
while he makes his bear do tricks. The bear attracts the attention of
outsiders, peasants, and their wives and children.*

The Tamer
Master Bear! Watch out!
Show these crowds of people
How the fat parson,
Leaning on his stick,
Climbed up the clock tower,
But got stuck on the ladder.

*Leaning on a stool, the bear hops and shuffles about as the tamer plays the
flute.*

The Tamer
Master Bear, do it again.
Amuse the people and show them
How he has turned around,
And is coming down, step by step.
How, when he came home,
He complained to his wife:
'Wife, what hard work.'

*The little bear walks round, taking small steps. The tamer plays the flute
and people laugh. Then a stately, dignified old man appears: he is the goesli
player.*

Goesli player
Just be quiet, good people. Stop talking,
Little Bear, stop making that racket.

The People   [Peasants]
Sing to us about the City of Jerusalem   [Peasants' wives]
Let us hear what the Bard has to say.

Goesli player
Bulls with golden horns walked to the city

37

From the holy, radiant Svelti Jarr.
There were exactly twelve, no more, no less.
On the way a mother cow went to them
And she asked: Did you see anything strange on the way?

The People
Singer, this is about the lake and the city.
This is the start of the song of Kitezh's dirge.
This is how the song of Juri starts,
Our ruler, the song of Juri.

Goesli player
Our road, said the herd, went around God's city,
And we saw a lady who also walked
Around Great Kitezh. She was wondrously beautiful.
In her hand she had a magnificent book. She was reading.
But her cheek seemed to be wet with bitter tears.

The People
Certainly, this song is about sorrow.
Oh, we weep with our lady.
This song is about terrible pain.
This song is about the end of the world.

Goesli player
Silly children, complained the cow.
You twelve did not even recognize our celestial mother of heaven.
She shed her tears because she already knew
What despair was waiting in Kitezh; the end
Of the world for all eternity.

The People
Christ, spare us by the miracle of your great love.   [Peasants]
Have patience with our sins.   [Peasants' wives]
Why do we have to suffer?   [Young people]
We live peacefully in the areas
Which came to us from you. Ah! Nobody,
Nobody knows why we deserve to suffer.
Christ, spare us Kitezh. If necessary, spare it
Only for the sick who live there.

The Beggars
Kitezh is a refuge for the poor.
We, who have nothing and strive for peace,
May live in Little Kitezh,

This city represents the heavenly Jerusalem.
Here we found mercy.
Christ, if possible, spare this city of cities.

The People
Pain was suffered here for the people. [Young people]
The light of the city revives the exhausted.
No, no disaster must befall Kitezh: [Peasants' wives]
We do not want to live outside Kitezh.
God will protect our royal city. [Peasants]
He also protects our King Juri.
Has the wedding procession still not arrived? [All]
Hopefully, nothing has happened to the carriage.

The tamer leads his bear through the crowd.

Tamer
Master Bear, watch out again.
Show the frightened people
How the bride of our Prince
Is never tired, but is making herself up.
Look how she preens before the mirror
To see how beautiful she is.

The Tamer plays his flute. The Bear holds a small spade in his paws and pulls funny faces. The people laugh. The bear grabs hold of a woman and wants to dance with her. Some rich townspeople approach the ridiculous scene.

Rich townspeople
See how the simple folk enjoy themselves. [First citizen]
But look, there is some reason for it. [Second citizen]
Was it a good idea, this circus on the street?
Since the Prince has chosen a wife from the wood, [Third citizen]
The people feel related to the ruler.
And we, the merchants, are no longer worth anything.
This wedding is doing great harm to the land, [Fourth citizen]
And is bringing dishonour to our women.

The drunkard, Grisjka Kutjerma, stumbles out of the inn. He pulls himself together and walks into the market.

Rich townspeople
Well, well! Even Grisjka is here!
His joy knows no bounds.

Grisjka
Great heavens! We're merry souls.
I'm here now, and God knows where tonight.
My hand hasn't done a second's work.
I'm happy for today is today.
I'm grateful to anyone who will give me a penny.
I'll drink to anyone who'll feed me and buy me a drink.

Rich citizens
I won't give a penny to a beggar   [First citizen]
But I will spoil a drinker.
Off you go, back to the tavern   [Second citizen]
And drink your alcohol like tepid tea.
Be jolly in honour of the bride.   [Third citizen]
Give her greetings from the god of wine.

The rich townspeople throw Grisjka some coins. The beggars immediately
approach.

The Beggars
Fathers, give to us, the poor.
Have pity on us.
Be kind-hearted, help us, help us.
God will reward you.
Remember us all
By giving us a little something.
God will make you happy.
At the end of time.

Grisjka turns to the beggars, mocking them.

Grisjka
Good for nothings. If you greet me as a lord,
Perhaps I'll give you something, like a lord.

The Beggars
Drunkard! Look after yourself.   [Leader of the guild]
Who has neither friends nor relations?
Only a boozer.   [All]
Who gets nothing but mockery and shame?   [Leader of the guild]
Exactly. A drunkard.   [All]
Let him clink his glass, let him get drunk   [Leader of the guild]
Let him fall about, let him make a spectacle of himself.
Who forgets to serve the Lord?
It's the drunkard, only the drunkard.   [All]

40

Who has even forgotten how to pray?	[Leader of the guild]
Again it's the drunkard, the drunken drunkard	[All]
He cannot enter the house of God.	[Leader of the guild]
He shakes and shivers outside the church door.	
Drunkard, drunkard, drunkard, drunkard.	[All]
He will soon die in dire distress,	[Leader of the guild]
And will not receive God's forgiveness.	
Woe bedtide thee, drunkard.	[All]
He will soon die in dire distress,	[Leader of the guild]
And will not receive God's forgiveness.	
Woe bedtide thee, drunkard.	[All]

Grisjka
Come, come dear people, it is the way it is.
I'm used to suffering and privation.
Anyone who makes do with nothing from their earliest days
Is not easily deterred by worries and concerns.
Yes, I thank the spirit of hops and yeast
Which lightens my heavy burden of cares.
It has shown me what life is.
It has refreshed my thirst like rain on the field.
When I no longer have any banknotes,
I'll still have enough change for a tipple.
And I can sell my shirt or vest for a drink:
For shame and disgrace are paper thin.

Grisjka Kutjerma disappears back into the tavern. The tamer makes the bear — which is still holding the short spade in his paws — do some new dance steps. He accompanies the animal on the flute. The people crowd round them laughing. The beggars bow deeply before the passers-by.

The Beggars
Be generous and give to us pious beggars.
God will reward you.

The beggars are not given very much money, so they decide to leave for Great Kitezh.

The Beggars
Let us be on our way
To the city of Great Kitezh,
Where anyone who wants to eat can do so.

Grisjka Kutjerma comes out of the tavern. He is tipsy and dances and sings. The common people surround the chatterbox; the rich townspeople smile, but stand at a distance.

Grisjka
It is a feast today. Listen to the sound of bottles.
Hear the cooks working hard. Listen to their prattle.
Our bride from the fields, with no shoes or shirt
Has assumed airs for an elegant wedding.
Wearing a fur coat with a tail for a collar,
She rides around the land as proud as a peacock.

People start to thump Griskja and force him to be quiet.

The People
Get away, you rude dog.   [Several people]
Get out of here and shut up for good.
If necessary, beat the drunkard till he goes,   [Others]
Grab him by the hair or kick his backside.

*In the distance, bells can be heard pealing, and soft music is heard. The
people stop talking and listen. Some curious people take the trouble to move
to the front to see whether the wedding procession is approaching.
The ringing of bells and the music gets louder.*

The People
Listen to the merry music in the distance!   [Young people]
Listen, the wedding procession is coming round the corner slowly,
So that no coach loses a wheel.
The bride of King Vsevolod sits   [Peasants' wives]
On a seat of velvet and gold
In the wedding coach made of pure rosewood.
Listen the wedding procession is coming round the corner,
Hail Fevronia and Vsevolod!   [Peasants]

*Three coaches bedecked with red and gold come into sight. The first coach is
full of goesli and domra (Russian flute) players, the marriage brokers are in
the second coach, and Fevronia and her brother are in the third coach. The
coaches are accompanied by a knight on horseback, Fyodor Pojarok. The
coaches are followed by many other knights, including Prince Vsevolod, the
bridegroom. The people walk up to the wedding procession and bar the way
with ribbons like those which are used to decorate the coaches.*

The People
Come people, come quickly.   [All]
Close together so that the procession is halted.
Keep calling: Prince and Princess,   [Working people]
Pay the working people a toll. Do us a favour!
All call out: Prince and Princess,   [Peasants]
Pay the peasants a toll. Do us a favour!

The beggars
Kusjma Djemian,
A fire and lightning smith
Forges a ring for Vsevolod and his Queen.
For in the church,
It will bind them more closely
Than the heavens
Surround the land and sea.

[Peasants]
Who wants to pass?
Do not let them through.
Strangers, halt.
Let no one pass.
First say who you are   [Young people]
Otherwise: turn back.

Who wants to pass?
Do not let them through.
Strangers, halt.
Let no one pass.
First say who you are   [Young people]
Otherwise: turn back.

Fyodor Pojarok
Juri has said:
Take the young bride
Quickly to Great Kitezh
Take her to the House of God.

The People
Hail, O Light   [Peasants]
Hail, Lady of Light
You are holy, Light.
Hail, Fevronia Vasilievna.

Hail, O Light   [Peasants' wives]
Hail, Lady of Light
You are holy, Light.
Hail, Fevronia Vasilievna.

The Rich Townspeople
Oh, how simple the bride looks.   [A few]
Is she to be our mistress?
Yes, she is. She belongs here.   [Others]
She is surrounded by an angelic orange glow.

43

The coach with Fevronia and her brothers stands still.

The People
Holy art thou, Light! [Young people]
Holy art thou; Lady of Light!
Holy, holy are thou, Lady of Light!
Holy, holy art thou, Lady of Light!

You were equal to us in the green kingdom. [Peasants]
Once you were poor and miserable like us.
Now you have been raised up. The throne awaits you.
Hail, O Light, Hail, highest Queen.

You were equal to us in the green kingdom. [Peasants' wives]
Once you were poor and miserable like us.
Now you have been raised up. The throne awaits you.
Hail, O Light, Hail, highest Queen.

The semi-drunken Griska Kutjerma, who had been sent away, again tries to struggle to the front. The people try to prevent him from getting close, and beat him back.

The People
Go away! Clear off! Your loud talk and insults will spoil the wedding.

Fevronia is surprised by the hardness of the people to the notorious, semi-drunken rebel rouser. She takes his side.

Fevronia
Why do you hit him?
Why does he have to go?

The People
It is Grisjka, the bad-mouth drunkard. [One of them]

Fyodor Pojarok
Don't take any notice of the scoundrel.
Ignore what he has to say.

Fevronia takes pity on the outcast rascal.

Fevronia
Let nobody's heart harden.
Christ praised the teeth of a rotten dog.
Grisjenka, pass the guard of knights.

44

Grisjka
Welcome here, beloved mistress.
You are better than the very best,
But do not flash the gold you have acquired,
In fact, we are all made of the same wood.

The Guard try to push Grisjka away. Fevronia stops them; gently she turns
back to the drunkard.

Fevronia
Why should I be vain, or proud.
I am quite ordinary like everyone else.
It is because I have been raised up so high
That I deliberately greet the common people.

Fevronia bows deeply before everyone standing around.

Grisjka
Do not feel joy about anything.
Great joy is often accompanied by great sorrow.
If fate is too kind to you,
This gives rise to jealousy in the unlucky.
Let the wedding feast be what it is.
Throw away the glitter, as well as the poison.
Don't you feel the ghost of disaster yet?
Bow down before his grim face.
Give that demon what he wants.
Give it to him, and enjoy nothing, just like me.

Fyodor Pojarok
Don't take any notice of the scoundrel.
Ignore what the wretch has to say.

Fevronia
Pray to the Holy Basil.
Ask the protector of drunkards
To help you to be yourself.
Pray, Grisjka, with all your soul.
Allow him to destroy the God of Wine.

Grisjka Kutjerma feels criticized and very insulted.

Grisjka
Rubbish! Do not pretend to be so holy.
Where do you get the right to do that, peasant?

45

I predict that today or tomorrow
You will be a poor beggar girl once again.
And although you hardly deserve it,
I offer myself as a dear friend.

*The Knights grab Grisjka by the collar and drag him away. The crowd
pressed forward, wanting to beat him.*

The People
Shut your trap, scoundrel!
Wash your mouth out with salt.   [Some]
Tie him up and take him to the forest.   [Others]

Fyodor Pojarok
Clear the way! The music is almost here.
Men and women. Sing and have fun.

The women start singing, accompanied by goesli and domra.

The People
With bells ringing like a stormy hunt,   [Women]
Three fast sleighs speed to the Royal City
Over snow-white wooden bridges,
Over roads where the red carpet has been rolled out.
Let everyone sing   [All]
And dance and jump for joy.
Music drifts towards us from the first sleigh   [Peasants]
The friends of the bridal couple are in the second sleigh,
But the third sleigh is carrying our Virgin of Light,
Lady Fevronia Vasilievna.
Music drifts towards us from the first sleigh   [Peasant women]
The friends of the bridal couple are in the second sleigh,
But the third sleigh is carrying our Virgin of Light,
Lady Fevronia Vasilievna.
Let everyone sing and dance and jump for joy,   [Peasants]
Eat bread and drink wine in their honour.
With the bridal couple in our thoughts the meal tastes delicious,
And feeds the heart and soul more than the stomach.
Let everyone sing and dance and jump for joy,   [Peasant women]
Eat bread and drink wine in their honour.
With the bridal couple in our thoughts the meal tastes delicious,
And feeds the heart and soul more than the stomach.

*The horns sound in the distance. The wedding procession goes on and the
people follow behind the coaches and knights. However, some who are
listening attentively hear the trumpeting in the distance.*

46

[Some attentive listeners]
Quiet! It is as though trumpets are sounding . . .

The people disperse in several intermingling crowds.

The first crowd
They are horses — and coaches   [Peasant women]
Which are rattling wildly
The clouds seem to
Get darker in the distance.
What terrible disaster
Is about to befall us sinners?
Misery threatens all of us.
Unthinkable torture,
And immeasurable dangers.
Like an army of locusts
The Tartars are coming upon us!
Like an army of locusts
The Tartars are coming upon us!
At the commands of God's angels
The glaciers disappear from the mountains
The hellish fanatics
With devilish powers
Escape from the chasms!

It is as though   [Peasants]
Women and children are already crying
That there is no mercy.
Misery threatens all of us
Unthinkable torture
Like an army of locusts
The Tartars are coming upon us!
At the commands of God's angels
The glaciers disappear from the mountains
The hellish fanatics
With devilish powers
Escape from the chasms!

A second crowd appears, despairing and complaining.

The second crowd
What terrible disaster   [Peasant women]
Is about to befall us sinners?
Misery threatens all of us.
They are devils, not people.

47

Bloodless demons,
Betraying Christ the Lord,
With no shame for his altar.
Yes, with spears and swords,
They are on the way to the Holy Cities —
Little and Great Kitezh,
Raping our women,
Ignoring our children,
And trampling on them.

Oh there is no mercy.   [Peasants]
Misery threatens all of us.
They are devils, not people.
Bloodless demons,
Betraying Christ the Lord,
With no shame for his altar.
Yes, with spears and swords,
They are on the way to the Holy Cities —
Little and Great Kitezh,
Raping our women,
Ignoring our children,
And trampling on them.

A third crowd presses forward in despair.

The third crowd   [Peasant women]
What terrible disaster
Is about to befall us sinners?
Oh, there is no mercy.
Misery threatens all of us.
Can anyone escape?
Can anyone find a hiding place?
Night, and darkness, conceal us.
Mighty glacier, hide us.
Even as we make haste,
Like a raging wind,
There is no escape.
The enemy is ready.
There is no escape.
The enemy is ready.
Help, oh God, help!

Misery threatens all of us.
Can anyone escape?
Can anyone find a hiding place?

48

Night, and darkness, conceal us.
Mighty glacier, hide us.
Even as we make haste,
Like a raging wind,
There is no escape.
The enemy is ready.
There is no escape.
The enemy is ready.
Help, oh God, help!

A seemingly endless army of colourfully clad Tartars comes into sight. The people desperately flee in every direction; everyone tries to hide. A large group of Tartars herd the people back together with scimitars and clubs. It is virtually impossible to escape; only Prince Vsevolod manages to flee. Apart from him, nearly everyone is slaughtered — peasants, the remaining beggars, townspeople, knights.
Some of the Tartars have grabbed Fevronia and drag her to their leaders; they have spared her because of her beauty.

Some Tartars
Hey there! Hey there. Hey, hey, hey, there!

Two Tartar leaders on horseback, Khans Bedjai and Burundai, ride up to the soldiers who captured Fevronia. They jump down from their horses and have Fevronia clubbed. One of the Khans is immediately overwhelmed by her beauty.

Khan Burundai
What beautiful legs this bride has.
I've never seen such a lovely bitch.
I can have some fun with her.

Khan Bedjai
Beat everyone until they're dead. Let no one live.
She is Russian. She won't show us the way.
We won't get to the Royal City like this.

Khan Burundai
This is true. No one will tell us the way.
We won't get to the Royal City like this.

Khans Burundai and Bedjai
Great Kitezh is astonishingly rich,
Both in its treasures and its churches.
The streets are paved with gold and silver
And the gravel has been replaced by pearls.

A few Tartars drag another figure behind Fevronia. It is Grisjka Kutjerma.
The sly fox managed to hide longer than anyone. Now they have grabbed
him and he cries in terror.

A few Tartars
Well, well! We forgot one of them. Well, well!

Grisjka
Ah, have mercy, Lords.
Let me live. Brave leaders,
How can I, unworthy as I am, serve you?
Have pity on me. Have mercy.

Khans Burundai and Bedjai
Right! Your miserable life will be spared.
We will make you a Tartar soldier.
But one service is worth another.
Lead us straightaway to the Holy City of Kitezh.
The road through the forest must be the fastest.
Lead us by the secret path
To your incomparable royal city.

Fevronia
Oh, do not betray us Grisjenka.

Khan Bedjai
You, my beauty, keep your mouth shut.
Be quiet!

Grisjka Kutjerma is desperate. He cannot stand still.

Grisjka
Oh, you blackmailer. You serpent.
You offer me a sly reward.
Yes, you know how poor I am. How poor.
If I show you the way to Kitezh,
I will be a Judas to my people.
My conscience may not be clear,
But I do not wish to be a traitor.

Khans Burundai and Bedjai
Think hard and choose wisely, wretch.
If you make the wrong choice . . . we will tickle you
We will bang out your teeth,
Cut away your loins,

50

Shoot an arrow in your eye,
And roast you on a fire.
Then, if you like, you can go . . .!

With his soul in total confusion, Grisjka mumbles to himself.

Grisjka
God, damnation. What now? What should I do?

Burundai and Bedjai call out commands to their subordinates.

Khans Burundai and Bedjai
He won't show us the path,
Grab hold of the good-for-nothing.

Some Tartars throw themselves on Grisjka Kutjerma.

Tartars
Hey there! Hey!

*Grisjka is like a rat caught in a trap; he has lost the last trace of ingenuity
and feels forced to betray his people.*

Grisjka
No! Betrayers of God, I fear the pain.
Oh, the pain. I will obey.
You have forced me to do a deed
Which will make heaven weep.
My name will be Judas in future.
I will be damned to eternity.

Grisjka joins the Khans at the head of the Tartar hordes.

Khan Burundai
To Kitezh. Ha, ha, ha!

Khan Bedjai
To Kitezh.
We will destroy the whole of Rurik's land.
The Royal City of Russia will be burned down,
Russia's churches will be razed to the ground.
Our spears will spare neither children, women nor men.
The Russian armies are completely disarmed.

Most of the Tartars mount their horses and ride off, but a handful of
Mongols stay behind to prepare a carriage to follow the army with Fevronia.

Fevronia
God, protect the city against disaster and downfall.
Help its people and make them invisible.

Fevronia is dragged off to the carriage.

Act 3, scene 1.

*It is midnight in Great Kitezh. All the people, young and old, have
assembled in front of the Cathedral of Our Lady of the Assumption. Every
citizen is armed with the helmet of hope, the shield of faith, and the sword
of love. King Juri and Prince Vsevolod and their followers are standing under
an awning on a platform in front of the cathedral. The people surround the
adjutant, Fyodor Pojarok, who has just arrived. He leans heavily on a young
man, his head bent down.*

Fyodor Pojarok
Greetings, citizens of Great Kitezh.

The People
Many things have gone well for you, Pojarok!

Fyodor Pojarok
Where is our king? Answer me!
Did Vsevolod get here?

The People
Look, Fyodor. There they are in front of you.

Fyodor Pojarok
Ah! the day is like night.
I can hardly see anything.

*Prince Vsevolod goes up to his adjutant, who is clearly almost blind, and
gazes into his face.*

Prince Vsevolod
Fyodor, are you blind, my friend?

Fyodor Pojarok
Yes, I am blind. Blind!

Prince Vsevolod and the People
God, be merciful to him!
How did this happen?
Fyodor, Fyodor, how did this happen?
Fyodor, Fyodor, how terrible.
Oh, tell us, Fyodor, how did this happen?

Fyodor Pojarok
Listen to me. In the name of Christ, listen.
No one can suspect the danger in store.

53

The People
Speak, friend. Do not leave us in uncertainty.

Fyodor Pojarok
God the father has allowed the Devil to try us,
The people of Job, for a thousand years.

The People
Speak. Tell us what is inevitable.

Fyodor Pojarok
Mother Earth has given birth to hell.
Hordes of ghosts crawled from her innards,
Praying mantises of human proportions.
They are devouring our whole kingdom.
And they are seeing an even fatter prey:
Kitezh, the city of man fit for angels.

Prince Vsevolod and the People
Fyodor, Blind Fyodor! How terrible.
Do not hesitate. Try to tell us exactly
How many robbers are marching on Great Kitezh.

Fyodor Pojarok
I do not know the exact number,
But with the stamping of horses and men,
The squealing of wheels and cracking of wood,
Nothing else can be heard for miles around.
The breath exhaled by that great army
Has made the bright midday sun fade.

Prince Vsevolod and the People
Good, Holy Mother Earth,
What have we done wrong that you have
Saddled us with these devilish beings?
Fyodor, blind Fyodor. How terrible!
How was our outpost overpowered?
How badly did the people suffer?

Fyodor Pojarok
Little Kitezh was raped by the Tartars
Like a virgin. However, the inhuman hordes
Were mainly concerned with Great Kitezh.
The inhabitants of the outpost
Preferred injury to betraying us.

The People
Lord God, protect Great Kitezh.

Fyodor Pojarok
Yes! But one of us could not endure until death
The pain inflicted by the Tartar hordes.
One of them betrayed the way here.

The People
May God punish him.
His name will be Judas,
Judas of Little Kitezh.

Prince Vsevolod
Fyodor, my friend, you are blind now,
But tell me, did you catch a glimpse of my beloved?

Fyodor Pojarok
Yes, she is alive . . . would she were dead.

Prince Vsevolod
Has she been taken?

Fyodor Pojarok
God punish her . . . Ah! . . .
God forgive her her great weakness,
She and she alone betrayed you and us.
In the end she could not endure the pain.

Prince Vsevolod
What? She? The best part of me? Impossible.

Fyodor Pojarok
I was overwhelmed by those devils from the East.
They beat me about the head but spared me,
And said: 'Tell your king we are coming
The Rurik land is ours!
Our spear spares no one, neither woman nor man,
Only some virgins go to our khans —
You can guess what happens to them.
Your churches will be destroyed.
We will set fire to the whole of Great Kitezh.
We will banish your Christ,
No matter where his flock runs or turns.
The God of the Khans will soon be worshipped here.

We will teach the slave people to obey
And your armies will be overpowered.
Shame on you! Shame and disgrace!'

The people raise their hands up to God.

King Juri
The People
Christ, old and young are awaiting the grave.
Sow the seeds of courage in every heart.

King Juri
Fame and wealth are all vanity.
How mad, how blind we are always.
Our life is like the life of a mayfly.
In the evening it is time to die.
The soul, which is not a fly but a butterfly,
Rises up to the Throne of Justice.
The body becomes a worthless corpse.
It was dust and returns to dust after a while.
Fame and wealth are all vanity.
Great Kitezh, a jewel and a royal city,
Great Kitezh, a wonderful city of Tzars,
Did I design you so great and mighty
Merely to be destroyed by the Tartars?
Great Kitezh, I built you as a town
For seekers of true human dignity.
I dedicated you to Mary and Christ.
Their one holy heart beats in you.
Kitezh, Kitezh, die now like a fly.
Kitezh, now rise up like a fire.

Shepherd boy! Do not look so shy!
Climb up the tall clock tower.
Look ahead to see if you can see
Christ's dove of peace, north, south, east or west.

The boy quickly climbs the clocktower and peers in every direction. King Juri, Prince Vsevolod, Fyodor Pojarok and the people say prayers to Mary, the Mother of God.

King Juri, Prince Vsevolod, Fyodor Pojarok and the People
Heavenly Mother! Hear our weeping people.
Have mercy on us, take pity on us.
Pray for us, sad sinners.

The shepherd's boy
The dust rises up; it is swirling up in clouds.
The midday sun and evening moon are shrouded.
The Tartar army hastens to the desired city of Kitezh
Like an overgrown praying mantis.

The people gather in the street and in the square.
Many people are pointing and gesticulating.
Some are silent, inwardly exhausted,
As though this disaster is an ancient taboo.

The dust swirls up; a forest of swords
Stands out at right angles to the forest of the city,
To kill the peasants.
The crows are gathering, waiting for the prey,
And drink their fill of blood.

King Juri
Fate presses on us like a dead weight.
It is clear: Kitezh is the victim.
Brothers and sisters, our death is certain.
Let us turn again to the Virgin of Light
Let us pray for her to protect the city.

King Juri, Prince Vsevolod, Fyodor Pojarok and the People
Holy Mother of Heaven, look at us and have mercy.
Not on us personally, but on us as your community.
Hide Great Kitezh in your cloak of clouds.

The shepherd boy
Kitezh is in danger of complete annihilation.
The locust man walks through its streets.
The enemy flags hang everywhere.
The citadel shivers down to its last stone.
The markets and squares are empty.
Caravans of plundered jewels are moving through the city.
Where are they going?

King Juri
We fall into the enemy hand, still alive.
The disgrace is more cruel than death.
Kitezh, as you await slavery,
Let us turn to the Virgin Mother
A third time and say:
Please at least spare Great Kitezh.

King Juri, Prince Vsevolod, Fyodor Pojarok and the People
Holy Mother of Heaven, look down on us, and have mercy.
Hear us, oh hear us, oh hear us.
As the people of the calm and peace-loving City of Tsars,
We beg you: wrap us in your cloak,
And send your angel guards to the City of God.

The shepherd's boy
How the great lake of Svetli Jarr
Lies without a ripple and full of hope.
The mists glow in confusion
Like the lace veil around the head
Of a bride awaiting her groom.
The firmament reveals our faith!

King Juri
Even if your city is overrun
Your will be done, Lord, not ours.

*Prince Vsevolod steps forward and speaks to his druzina (personal
bodyguards)*

Prince Vsevolod
Loyal friends, I emphatically request you
To follow me from this threatened Jerusalem.
Take your goesli and your domra
And march towards the enemy with me.
Friends, we have the strength and the courage
To wear the helmet of hope.
To don the shield of faith and take up
The sword of the heavenly spirit.
Father, let us go, for the glory of Christ.

Prince Vsevolod's Guards
Yes, we will follow you. Be our leader!

King Juri gives his son and the guard God's blessing.

King Juri
Christ! Bless their sacrifice.
Let their blood be the seed for your church.

*Prince Vsevolod and the members of his guard bid farewell to their families
and go through Great Kitezh; they go to meet the Tartar hordes.*

58

Prince Vsevolod and his guard
Life or death, joy or grief.
It's all the same. we are on our way.
God be with us; Your rod, your staff
Consoled us. Weigh our dreadful fate.
Give us divine strength in the battle
So that he who conquers himself
Is stronger than those who threaten the city.
Those who stay behind, do not be sad.
Brothers in God, do not weep. Remember,
Death is only victory to us.
We go to heaven as a group.
We go to God.

Prince Vsevolod and his men pass through the gates of Great Kitezh and move on. A golden mist sinks down from the dark sky, becoming even denser. The bells in the city begin to peal.

Prince Vsevolod and his guard
Sisters, come. Gather courage, the end is nigh . . .
Do you wish to die without greeting us?
Come, so that your tears may mingle with ours.
Let them be tears of joy.
Hark! A rare and miraculous sound. Our bells are singing.
As though heavenly bellringers are striking the copper.
Yes, we see the angels guard Great Kitezh.

The shepherd boy
My gaze is clouded, clouded by the mist.

King Juri
An unknown fragrance of heaven is blowing towards us.
The mist covers the land and the city like a blanket.
Let us dissolve in it. The city glows anew in it.
We becomes ourselves in our body, spirit and soul.

The shepherd boy
What a fiery mist! Unbelievable, it cannot be!
The Svetli Jarr shines radiantly and we hide
In its cave of clouds. Or are we travelling away from the earth?
A living death: this is how we will resist the Tartars.

King Juri
Kitezh is sinking into the Svetli Jarr; it is sailing heavenward.
God the Lord has taken the city away from the Tartars!

It is glowing in the mother-of-pearl of fire and water,
The heavenly Jerusalem, the last Kitezh.

The shepherd boy
Cheer loudly, heaven. Cheer as though it were Easter.
Kitezh will be the head and the heart of the earth.

Fyodor Pojarok
Kitesh will be the heart and head of the earth.
The city and the country are shrouded in a thick golden mist.
The Tartars are slaughtering Prince Vsevolod and his guard in
   Kershenez.

Act 3, scene 2

The oak forest on the banks of the Svetli Jarr is shrouded in impenetrable darkness. A thick mist hangs over Great Kitezh on the opposite shore of the lake. Grisjka Kutjerma shows the Tartar army the way to the City of Christ. The traitor, closely followed by the Khans, Burundai, and Bedjai, makes his way through the thick undergrowth and comes to a small field which leads to the Svetli Jarr.

Grisjka
Look, there lies the Svetli Jarr,
Shining in the ochre gold of dawn.
On its banks, the royal city,
Great Kitezh, which even I love.

The Tartars try to penetrate the mist with their gaze.

Khan Burundai
Dirty lies! On that shore there are trees
And thick undergrowth.

Grisjka
Can't you hear the bronze bells tolling?
They are tolling, tolling, like tyrants,
The sound of thunder. The earth shakes.
The thudding sounds sicken my thumping heart.

Khan Bedjai
I could swear there's nothing to see.

Gradually all the Tartars reach the field by the water. They pull or push along the carts full of stolen goods.

The Tartars
Rotten country, half covered in woods,   [Some]
Half in pools of water.
A land of forests and endless marshes.
Our horses break their necks and legs
In this undergrowth full of rocks.
Icy damp which settles on the lungs,
Rises up slowly and then sinks down again.
Is there any point in our victory?
If our army cannot find a way through?
Our hordes have narrowly escaped   [Others]
Being lost in these waters which attract us like a magnet.

61

Icy damp which settles on the lungs,
Rises up slowly and then sinks down again.
Is there any point in our victory?
If our army cannot find a way through?

The Tartars surround Grisjka Kutjerma and push him about, while they shout insults and threats. Grisjka throws himself on his knees in front of the Khans.

The Tartars
Drunkard! It's your fault that we're lost.
You showed us the wrong way . . . deliberately.

Grisjka
My lords! Have mercy. Be patient!

Burundai and Bedjai prevent their subordinates from lynching the drunkard.

Khan Bedjai
Calm down. For the time being we will tie you to an oak tree,
Like a small boy who has been caught telling lies.
Start thinking about tomorrow.

Khan Burundai
If, by any chance, we unexpectedly find Great Kitezh
On the shores of that shining lake,
We will break your neck, my friend.
You are the fledgling who betrayed the nest.

The cart with Fevronia, which followed the Tartar army, also reaches the meadow on the shore of the Svetli Jarr.

Khan Burundai
But if you have betrayed us and there is
No royal city on the steaming water,
We will break your nose and jaws.

Grisjka Kutjerma is tied to an oak tree by a few Tartar soldiers.

Grisjka
Murderers!

The Tartars sit down on the ground. Some of them light a camp fire, others gather together their booty and set it out by the fire.

Khans Burundai and Bedjai
What bad luck that the Prince died!
Forty wounds and he didn't say a word.
No, he didn't lift a finger to show the way.
If he were here, I would tie him to a bed,
I would put my knee on his chest
And force him to speak.

*The Tartars break open barrels of wine and drink from silver goblets.
Burundai and Bedjai settle down in the grass with their men. They start
drinking seriously. Some of the Tartars divide up the booty.*

Khans Burundai and Bedjai
It is not the Russian who has had his fill of wine.
Who's drinking the firewater now? Cheers, mate!

The Tartars
The camp is blown about and the battlefield is silent.   [Some]
A flock of crows flies over one corpse after another.
The night brings a chill on the front.
The victor laughs, the pillaged land sparks.   [Others]
The proud Khans boast about their deeds.   [All]
They throw lots for Vsevolod's
Majestic helmet made of solid gold.
Hopefully it will fit one of them.
They throw lots for Vsevolod's shield
Unbelievably strong and old.
They throw lots for Vsevolod's sword,
Which looks like a Christian cross.
They do not yet throw for Vsevolod's bride.
See, she is silent and fasts and weeps.

Khan Burundai
Khan Bedjai, soldiers, I declare that
I want nothing of all this treasure.
I do not want any of these spoils of war
Except that lady there, so still and chaste.

Khan Bedjai
Unbelievable, how unselfish!
You get only what fate decides.
I am also attracted by her star-white face.
That princess seems made for me.

63

Khan Burundai
Nonsense! She hasn't looked at you for a second.
She wants me! I'm the one for her.
Ask her plainly what she thinks of you.
Just ask her which Khan she would like.

Khan Bedjai
Slavs make love when their lord wishes.

Burundai turns to Fevronia.

Khan Burundai
Do not cry, beautiful Russian girl.
Very soon we will return to the
Middle Kingdom. You will be my wife.
We'll make love every night dear, so you'll be faithful.

Bedjai laughs hatefully and imitates Burundai.

Khan Bedjai
Do not cry my beautiful Slav girl.
Very soon we will return to the
Middle Kingdom. You will be my wife.
The lashes of a whip will keep you faithful, my dear.

Khan Burundai
You won't let me have her . . . I'll hit you.
Give her to me. I saw her first.

Khan Bedjai
No, no, no!

Khan Burundai
Here, take this!

*Burundai hits Bedjai on the head with an axe. Bedjai falls down dead.
There is a moment's silence among the Tartar soldiers; then they go about
their business as though nothing has happened. Many of them are drunk,
and gradually fall asleep with their share of the booty.*

The Tartars
The camp is blown about and the battlefield is silent.   [Some]
The night brings a chill on the front.   [Others]
The victor laughs, the pillaged land sparks.

64

Khan Burundai pulls Fevronia onto his lap and kisses her.

Khan Burundai
Don't be afraid, my dear child.
Our belief is as simple as my little finger.
No incense is necessary, no prayers, no cross.
Only order reigns in my house.
Be more forthcoming, my child.
I can certainly do more than a Russian.

Then Burundai falls fast asleep. Fevronia moves away from him. During the
battle she caught a glimpse of her slain bridegroom and she mourns for him.

Fevronia
I pity only you, my love, not myself!
So alone, so dishonoured and so naked
You lie there, unmourned, unburied,
Not much more than carrion for the crows.
If only it were possible to go to you
I would warm you and kiss you. I would
Blow breath into your mouth. My sighs
Would make you breathe again.
My love, you would live
As intensely as I feel my heart tremble
So little can I move here.
You are bleeding and I cannot come to you
To give you half of my blood.

Fevronia weeps softly. Grisjka Kutjerma raises himself up and speaks to her.

Grisjka
Lady, listen — listen to me.
Move closer to me, very quietly.
Have pity.

Fevronia sits up with a shock and recognizes the drunkard.

Fevronia
Grisjka, Grisjka, you betrayed us.

Grisjka Kutjerma is utterly dejected.

Grisjka
Oh stop! Don't talk about it.
You don't know how afraid I am.

You don't know how my conscience torments me.
Why is one bell tolling after another?
Christ hasn't risen, has he?
Terrible! What a thundering noise.
The din will drive me mad.

Fevronia makes an effort to hear it.

Fevronia
What bells?

Grisjka
Lady, help me.
Have pity on me, have pity.
Please cover my ears with my cap.
I cannot endure each thundering stroke.
It will awaken the next day.

*Fevronia goes to the oak tree to which Grisjka has been tied and pulls the
cap over his ears.*

Grisjka
God! The cap doesn't help at all. The banging goes on.
It's clear that I can't escape it.

Grisjka furiously shakes his head and throws the cap back.

Grisjka
Lady, I have a plan. Untie me quickly.
Undo these dreadful ropes.
Then I'll hasten to the wood
And disappear behind the hill.
Once I'm free, I will certainly be converted.
I will go to a travelling holy man
To purify my soul from evil,
And I will stop drinking and do my duty.

Fevronia
What sort of life awaits you, Grisjka?
Wherever you go, you will be recognized immediately.

Grisjka
No, I won't. Your people are dead.
Of all the nobility, at most one boy.
Has escaped being hanged,
If they were not decapitated on the front lines.

Fevronia shivers. She is surprised that anyone can be like this.

Fevronia
Time will tell. The forest has ears.
Anyone you meet is certain to murder you.

Grisjka
Don't exaggerate. I'll tell everyone
The bride showed the Khans the way to Kitezh.

Fevronia steps back in horror.

Fevronia
Grisjka! As though I would betray my own people.

Grisjka
Well, after all!

Fevronia covers her face with her hands.

Fevronia
Oh, this is terrible.
Tell me, are you the Antichrist?

Grisjka
Stupid woman!
If only I were, I would not be here.
I'm a drinker, sick with drinking.
But as a drinker, I'm not unique.
In all the glasses and goblets of wine
I was only offered the world's tears.

Fevronia
You have too much self-pity.
In all suffering there is a seed of pleasure.
Don't you know that being blessed depends
On the joy of another person's happiness,
Regardless of your own sorrow?

Grisjka
You are like an angel: free of hate.
But jealousy and envy will not leave me alone.
When I see how well others do,
I feel that God has sold me short.
I can't stand people who are lucky

Because they leave only bad luck for me.
Why do I always live an empty life?
I feel hungry and sick and naked.

Fevronia expresses pity for Grisjka.

Fevronia
Yes, in this way you always see the worst.
If only you could be really happy just for one moment.

Grisjka Kutjerma's self-pity and egotism know no bounds.

Grisjka
I have never experienced true joy.
I have never learned what happiness is.
I have only every had bad luck.
And now these ropes are hurting me.
Untie them, Princess!

Fevronia
All right, I'll help you. Is it difficult?
If I succeed, you'll certainly go free.
I'll gladly accept death and torture.
Blame me for the treason.
When my time comes and I die,
I'll ask God for your release and that of the Easterners.
Grisjka, pray to Jesus.
He forgives every sinner his sins.   [*pause*]
I cannot manage to untie these bonds.

Grisjka
Take a sword to help you from the belt
Of the one over there with the beard.

Fevronia creeps up to Khan Burundai and takes the short sword from him.
He tries to embrace her, but is unsuccessful and falls asleep again. It is
daybreak.

Khan Burundai
Darling! Lie down with me at last!

Fevronia cuts through Grisjka's bonds with Khan Burundai's short sword.

Grisjka
Hurray, hurray! I'm free at last.
May God himself be my protector.

However, Grisjka is once more overwhelmed by the pealing of the bells.

Grisjka
Well, damn it all! I can hear those bells again.
They're clanging even louder than before.
The din will make me go truly mad.
Satan is ringing them. I can smell the brimstone.
God, I cannot walk, everything is reeling.
Heaven help me. The earth is running amok.

*Grisjka tries to run away, but he stumbles and falls on his face in the mud,
and lies motionless for a minute. Then he tries to move again.*

Grisjka
Is there no God who can change my dreary fate?
I want this misery to cease.
I would sooner make an end to it all.
Satan will laugh loudly if I really
Start boozing in the golden lake.

*Grisjka Kutjerma stumbles towards the Svetli Jarr as fast as he can. On the
shore of the lake he suddenly stops. The first rays of the rising sun light up
the surface of the water, reflecting the royal city of Great Kitezh.
The bells of the city ring louder and louder, a festive triumphant pealing.*

Grisjka
Where I heard Satan, now I hear God.
And where God was then, there is a cloud!
Lady, who has swallowed Satan?
What a laugh! Run, darling. Come on.
God ordered me: Go to Kitezh.

*Grisjka laughs like a madman and pulls Fevronia along the shore. His
shouting wakes up the Tartars.*

The Tartars
Who woke us up with all that shouting?
Who has suddenly got such a loud mouth?
Has the enemy occupied the camp?
Is it time for another battle?

*Then the Tartars see the vision of the sunken city of Kitezh in the Svetli
Jarr. Some of them get up.*

The Tartars
Hey, Tartar brothers, just see

What a miracle was wrought in the dark of the night.
Stand up! This has never been seen before.
Is this the secret of Russia's soul?
There is neither a house nor a bush on the Svetli Jarr,
And yet the strange royal city of this land
Is reflected in the glassy surface of the water.
Bells which are rung by nobody
Are pealing like a raging avalanche.

The Tartars are overcome by a boundless terror.

The Tartars
Run! No more delay. Let us leave this place.
It's as though heaven has attacked us.
Terrible! What an awful fate has befallen us.
Run away from here. Straight through the wood.
As though heaven has attacked us.
Terrible! Russia's God is the true God.

The Tartars flee into the forest, scattering in all directions.

Act 4, scene 1

The mist blots out the early sunlight. Uprooted pine trees and oak trees are scattered among the wild undergrowth at the start of the Kerschenez forest. A little further on, deeper into the wood, there is an open, marshy area, covered in moss. Grisjka and Fevronia slowly battle their way there through the bushes. Grisjka drags Fevronia along. Their clothes are torn to shreds. Grisjka seems to have lost his mind and Fevronia is totally exhausted. She sits down on one of the uprooted tree trunks.

Fevronia
Grisjka, let me go! I can't go on.
I'll fall down, I'm so exhausted.
Let's rest on this trunk.

Grisjka
We don't really have time to rest.
Has your life of leisure weakened you so much?
Sit down then. I'll sit here, you on the tree.
I'll go in the antheap, you can go next to it.

You have become proud, my dear.
At the royal court you forgot
Our shared, simple origins.
Didn't you once walk round with a begging bowl,
Calling: 'Dear people, give me something.
It doesn't have to be much, but nothing
Does not even fill a hollow tooth.'
Once you too, were always taking.

Fevronia
No! I picked berries . . . which you ate too.

Grisjka
Darling, with your manners I could also
Make a success with a trade in berries.
The dear Prince took them from you
As though he had never eaten! No more hardship.
In his thoughts he already saw you naked.
Your body attracted him more than any fruit,
But for me it is completely locked away.

Fevronia
Hold your tongue! Remember what you did.
Kitezh was lost through your treachery.

71

Grisjka
It's the same old song. but I see it differently.
I'm not a traitor, but rather I take the place
Of the dear Lord.
I did not murder anyone.
I merely fulfilled God's will for those who fell
And brought them before Christ's throne.

Fevronia
Grisjka, be silent and be converted. Pray!
Pray to Jesus Christ for forgiveness.

For the millionth time in his life Grisjka Kutjerma utters a very deep sigh,
pointing to himself.

Grisjka
It is very difficult for me,
Someone who — unlike me — sees
Hypocrisy as cleverness knows how to
Save himself from evil.
He thinks: Well friend, if you suffer tomorrow,
Be diplomatically silent.
Say your prayers at the evening meal.
Give the beggar as much as he wants.
Ask scoundrels how they are every day.
In this way you can reserve a place in heaven.

Fevronia
God, have pity on this man.
Give him just enough faith
To awaken some love in his heart.

Fevronia looks serious. Grisjka thinks she is angry and becomes as obedient
as a child.

Grisjka
Now even you seem bitter. Even you!
All right then, lady, let us pray together.
But not to Christ. I do not want to look up to Christ.
Christ's light blinds me.
I prefer to bow down before Mother Earth.
Lady, teach me this. Yes, please teach me.

Fevronia
Yes, I would like to teach you to pray, my friend.

Repeat after me, word by word.
Holy earth, mother of mercy and pity.

*Grisjka Kutjerma goes down on his knees and tries to repeat the words of
Fevronia's prayer.*

Grisjka
. . . Mother of mercy!

Fevronia
Yes, you feed us, good people and rejected sinners . . .

Grisjka
. . . And rejected sinners.

Fevronia
Mother, absolve him of his sins, poor Grisjenka!

Grisjka
. . . Poor Grisjenka!

Fevronia
His guilt is endless. It is immeasurable!

Grisjka
. . . endless, incredible, immeasurable!

Fevronia
Mother Earth, we have all sinned against you.
You have been sullied more often than a bed.
Let your tears flow, friend that is all that remains.

Grisjka
. . . friend, that is all that remains.

Fevronia
The tears of man are the salt that disinfects the earth.

Grisjka
. . . that disinfects the earth.

Fevronia
The tears of man will make her pure once again.

Grisjka
. . . once again.

Fevronia
We wish to sow the seed of the truly devout prayer
In the holy earth, perfected by tears:
Our meekness unfolds as a flowering crown,
Roses planted in the earth around the cross.

*Grisjka Kutjerma is silent. A shadow passes across his face; he seems to see
something terrible.*

Grisjka
What is that demon lurking behind you?
It looks like Satan himself. One eye is
Cold and blue, the other burns more fiercely than lye.
Grey smoke pours from his mouth. He will take our
Lives with his claws, and grant us death.

Grisjka springs up and starts to whistle and jump like a madman.

Grisjka
Satan, shall I sing?
Or shall I dance like a goat?
I will go on just as long as you want me to.
Just tell me what you want. And what else —
Oops-a-daisy, all of a sudden
Oops-a-daisy, pride reigns in us.
Father dragon, full of thorns.
With horns on ten heads.
Oops-a-daisy, on his lap.
Oops-a-daisy, she is naked,
The female dragon, more shameless
Than the apes.
Oops-a-daisy, give me one.
When I have been drinking,
Oopsa, Lord, I will sell you my soul.

*Grisjka whistles and screams in utter terror at something only he can see.
Then he buries his face in Fevronia's bosom.*

Grisjka
Darling! Please hide me.
Help me! Let me rest on your bosom.
Unceasingly — as though through glass — I see someone
In the middle of your heart.
Tell me truly, who is it?
Let it be! I know, it is the Lord of the City!

74

It is Satan with a burning wheel on his head.
He throws flames at my dark heart.
It is horrible, he has me in his power.
He burns me like a dead branch.
There is nowhere to go. Hold me.

Again, Grisjka pulls away from Fevronia and runs away screaming.

Fevronia
Grisjka! There is no one here. He is gone.

Fevronia stretches out in the cool, soft grass.

Fevronia
How delicious it is in the grass.
The pain and tiredness ebb away like water.
Our holy earth trembles softly.
She rocks me like a mother, strengthens me like a father.
To sleep in the grass! I want to sleep in the grass.
Father-mother earth, let me sleep.
Let me sleep in the grass.

As if by magic, candles are burning here and there in the branches of the trees. Suddenly paradise flowers of unimaginable beauty spring up out of the ground and on the branches: golden cruciform flowers, silver and red roses, lilies and many other flowers. Immediately next to Fevronia small flowers are glittering; a little way away they are larger, and further away still, they are even larger. However, the path to the marsh is still passable.

Fevronia
What unexpected beauty, what beautiful flowers!
What a wealth of colour all around me. How did they grow unnoticed?
It is as though today is a new day of creation.
I have suddenly remembered
The legend of the birds of paradise,
Alkonost and Siren
Heavenly messengers of birth and death.
On his giant wings of pure red,
One brought down the soft seed of heaven to earth,
Which the other had already dug up as a black field.
Just before eastern Eurebs' youngest day —
As many minstrels later prophesied —
Alkonost and Siren would cast
The seeds of death and life on Great Kitezh.
This city would then be a reflection in the Svetli Jarr.

I have never seen such beautiful flowers.
My worst despair is leaving me.

*Fevronia is silent for a while and contemplates the surroundings a little
longer. Then she continues her song.*

Fevronia
Flowers fold your leaves around me in a crown.
Protect my new lust for life.
Now that the royal city shimmers to nothing,
I will be very pleased to be your queen.
Oh, how festively you surround me!
Ready for a flowery dance of sun and light.
The light falls like a spear in your calyxes,
And a pink flame glows around your leaves.
A sudden spring enters the winter.
You show me a kingdom,
Which brings joy to a virgin who has suddenly lost her home.

*The birds of spring hum in the background. The legendary bird of paradise,
Alkonost, becomes a reality and speaks to Fevronia. However, he remains
invisible.*

Fevronia
Yes, the spring has returned.
To this meadow by the lake in the middle of the woods.
It is warm, but not really hot.
Everything that moves is active.
The birches drop their veils of lace.
What bride is waiting for her Lord?

The voice of Alkonost
Hope and pray. Do not lose heart.
Have faith. Do not doubt.
Your suffering will disappear completely.
Time heals all wounds.
Wait patiently, dear virgin.
The dawn of peace is breaking now.

Fevronia
Who do you belong to, lofty voice?
Are you human or the voice of a bird?

The voice of Alkonost
I am a voice in the red breast

Of the bird Alkonost.
Death will come to anyone
Who hears my song.

Fevronia picks the paradise flowers and plaits a crown.

Fevronia
Do you think I am afraid of death?
No, dying will no longer be difficult.
This spring I will see Christ.
He has robbed death of its sting.
Again and again my eyes are filled with wonder.
I am picking you, flowers of the sun,
Foliage of the moon and thistles of the earth.
Let me make you into a medallion.
Make an eternal crown on my forehead and on my hair,
As though I were a bride before God's altar.
On the threshold of death,
I prepare myself — small caterpillar of the soul —
To become a butterfly,
Seeking its home in the light of the sun.
Fairytale bird, show me paradise.
Bring me to my bridegroom at last!

The light over the flowers on the path to the marsh becomes denser. Prince Vsevolod appears in the light; he is made of gold. He walks in a golden mandala, his feet barely touching the earth. Fevronia arises and rushes towards him.

Fevronia
Vsevolod! Is it you? Your face
Is like a flame, your body glows like fire.
Are you an apparition or reality?
Am I living in reality myself,
Or am I caught in reflections?
Tell me, are you truly Vsevolod?

Prince Vsevolod
I am Vsevolod. Rejoice faithful bride,
Here I am, your bridegroom.

Fevronia
You seem to be more than alive, dead friend!
Yet show me your wounds.
All your forty wounds — since you fell.

I will restore them to health with my tears!
I will heal them with my kisses.

Prince Vsevolod
It is true that I was wounded forty times.
And I fell.
But that was before. I have changed.
Christ gave me a new body.

Prince Vsevolod and Fevronia
If this appearance is reality,
We will commit ourselves to each other.
We will conquer the power of the grave with love:
In time we will become one
In God's kingdom.

Fevronia
Turn your gaze to me!
Friend! I am Fevronia, it is I!

Prince Vsevolod
Yes, you are Fevronia!
As light as the wind,
As unafraid as the sea,
Like untrodden land:
An untouched virgin.

Fevronia
Yes, your eyes and nose and mouth
Are like the stars
Which determined my fate.
These bind us together
Like a Christian name and a surname.
Now you breathe out
The air of eternal life
And blow it into me.
And your word stands before me
Like the chalice of wine at Holy Communion.

Prince Vsevolod
In the wide blue of heaven
Your tears are more like pearls
Than the morning dew on earth.

After the first bird of paradise, Alkonost, the bird of death, Fevronia is now
addressed by the second bird of paradise, Siren, the bird of life. He is not
visible.

The voice of Siren
See! Your bridegroom! Why do you hesitate?
Prepare yourself for the wedding feast.

Fevronia
Who do you belong to, lofty voice?
Are you human or the voice of a bird?

The voice of Siren
Virgin, call me Siren, I am devoted to you.
Anyone who hears my song has eternal life.

Prince Vsevolod
Listen, bride, to what the bird says.
He knows how men live in peace here.
May the Lord Christ be merciful to us.
May his fiery glow shine on us.
Our eyes, which have finally finished weeping,
Are shown here as two stars.
They saw so much pain
That they were healed in heaven.
Our eyes, which have finally finished weeping,
Reflect God's Holy Ghost.

Fevronia
May the Lord Christ be merciful to us.
May his fiery glow shine on us.
Our eyes, which have finally finished weeping,
Reflect God's Holy Ghost.

Prince Vsevolod takes a piece of bread from his garment and gives it to
Fevronia.

Prince Vsevolod
Take and eat this bread to fortify you,
For the road is long: the road of pain and the road of joy.
Anyone who receives the fortifying bread of heaven
Will taste victory over death.

Fevronia accepts and eats the bread that Vsevolod gives to her.

Fevronia
It is good. I am replete. I will scatter
The last crumbs on the wings of the wind,
For the earthly birds of the meadow.

> *Fevronia scatters the last crumbs of the bread she has been given.*

Fevronia
Jesus, be merciful to me.
Take me into the heavenly city of Kitezh.

> *Prince Vsevolod and Fevronia slowly move away, hand in hand, in the direction of the Svetli Jarr. Their feet barely touch the ground. They disappear from earthly sight.*

Interlude

> *The bells of the Cathedral of Our Lady of the Assumption are still pealing of their own accord. Their song expresses the pilgrimage of Prince Vsevolod and Fevronia to the drowned city of Great Kitesh, the city that has ascended to heaven, so that in a certain sense it has become a celestial Kitezh. The birds of paradise, still invisible, speak.*

The voice of Siren
And Christ spoke
To the seekers.
You will soon inherit
The new kingdom of life,
Where there is no sun,
Where the moon does not rise.
This heavenly city
Lights up with its own strength;
Everything is light.
Nothing there has weight.
There is no conflict:
It is a realm of peace.
I am its heart,
I am its blood.

The voice of Alkonost
The Lord has promised
Man who suffered
The New Kingdom.
He guarded it
For those who worshipped him.

The word of Man
Has creative force
As the word of God.
Mankind finds consolation here
For the pain and distress
Which it has suffered.
Christ's consolation here
Is the last medicine.

Act Four, scene two

The cloud cover breaks apart; the clouds disperse, and in the distance the city of Great Kitezh glows, constantly changing, and increasing in its pomp and splendour.
Between the numerous houses and bridges, the enormous tower of the cathedral of Our Lady of the Assumption and the splendid castle of the King rises up in the West.
Fires are burning on the city walls.
All the facades and doors, and obviously all the city gates, are made of white stone and costly wood, decorated with jewels and pearls. Everything is adorned with paintings. In places, these cover the white of the walls with delicate hues of blue, grey and violet. The city is lit up from within; there are no shadows. On the square in front of the king's castle, a lion and a unicorn with a silver coat guard the entrance.
The birds of paradise, Alkonost and Siren, can now be seen singing jubilantly from the tall tower of the cathedral; their faces are those of women of astonishing beauty. The citizens of Great Kitezh are dressed in white garments. They hold lighted candles in their hands.
Among them walks Fyodor Pojarok, who has regained his sight; next to him walks the shepherd boy.

The voice of Siren
The secret door!
All time is present: timeless.

The voice of Alkonost
You may enter now!
Be one, now and always!

All the white clad citizens of Great Kitezh greet Prince Vsevolod entering the city through the main gate, and Fevronia, who is also dressed magnificently.

The People
We wish you great happiness and joy, lady!
We wish you great happiness and joy, lady!

Prince Vsevolod leads his bride up the stairs to the royal castle. She is beside herself with astonishment and claps her hands together.

Lady Fevronia
Kitezh is now really heaven!
I see that the doors, rooves, windows and statues
Are made of pure gems.

See! A unicorn with a silver horn!
Hark! The divine choir of birds
Is singing a song with human words!

*The people surround the couple on the steps of the castle and start singing a
wedding song.
Many accompany this on a goesli or schalmei.
Others scatter roses and lilies over Prince Vsevolod and Lady Fevronia as
they sing.
King Juri, Fyodor Pojarok and the shepherd boy look on from the raised
steps.*

King Juri, Fyodor Pojarok, the shepherd boy and the people
Just as the greyish white cloud of drizzle glides over the fields of flowers
    on earth,
Just as weightless and without colliding
The bride glides to her lord in spirit.
Let us sing, let us make music.
Let us honour this couple.

*Fevronia looks and listens to the praises, and meanwhile takes the hand of
Prince Vsevolod to hear his declaration.*

Lady Fevronia
This sounds like a wedding song.
I wonder who it is for.

Prince Vsevolod
Our wedding! It is ours!

King Juri, Fyodor Pojarok, the shepherd boy and the people
Lady, the gold and blue of paradise
Will be your garment of light, your aura.
And the crown which God promised
Every martyr, crowns your hair.
Let us sing, let us make music.
Let us honour the couple.

Lady Fevronia
I heard some of this song.
This is the marriage speech of Kitezh.

King Juri, Fyodor Pojarok, the shepherd boy and the people
Let us today
Sing for the royal couple,

Honour them with gold, frankincense and myrrh,
As their misery
Changed to joy.
Prepare the water of life straightaway.

King Juri comes down the steps.

Prince Vsevolod
See! My father comes towards us!

King Juri, Fyodor Pojarok, the shepherd boy and the people
The mercy of the Lord be with you!

King Juri
The mercy of God be with your, daughter.

Lady Fevronia
Greetings, community of Great Kitezh.
Oh, exalted father, greetings!
Forgive my humble origins.
Do not hold it against me that I am an orphan.
Take me into this holy group,
Which endeavours to become even holier.
Did I not see this already
In my past life on earth?

King Juri
What you dreamed in space and time
Is an eternal reality in your father's house.

Fevronia turns to the citizens.

Lady Fevronia
Brothers, sisters, one more thing.
It was dark when I entered the wood.
It was twilight in the meadow by the lake,
And at dusk I let Grisjka go free.
Then a light lit up in the city and in the land,
Turning stone white, adorning flowers
With a colour thawed from earlier colours.
Now the sun shines in all the sky.
Tell me, whence comes that brilliance?

King Juri and Prince Vsevolod
It is the prayers of mankind

Which make the light so strong and all-pervasive.
Like a fiery pillar from the slow age,
Belief in God rises up to eternity.

King Juri, Prince Vsevolod, and the voices of Siren and Alkonost
Yes, the light of the sun
Is not important here.
God's fire of mercy,
Strong and pure,
Flames up within us.

Fevronia is still not satisfied regarding the hows and wherefores of the way in
which the heavenly light works, and she asks more questions.

Lady Fevronia
Every garment is lit up from within
Like a haystack which is smouldering.
And the fire burns and bites like ice.
How can the garment be so razor-sharp?

King Juri, Prince Vsevolod, Fyodor Pojarok and the shepherd boy
Our cloaks glow like sharp ice
Because of our suffering in the past.
Because of the torture of the bygone century
They burn like the hay which smoulders.

King Juri, Prince Vsevolod, Fyodor Pojarok, the shepherd boy and the voices
of Siren and Alkonost
Such a garment of lightning has also been prepard for you.
It sparkles whiter than the whitest chalk.
It is your wedding dress, a new skin
Around the secret of your identity.

The People
Welcome into the city of the pure.
All suffering has disappeared here.
May Christ fill you with joy.
You will share our happiness.
We will be united by our joy.
Joy, joy . . .!

Lady Fevronia
Why am I praised thus?
Am I worthy of living in the light?
I certainly have many faults.
I was merely fond of everyone.

King Juri, Prince Vsevolod, and the voices of Siren and Alkonost
God feels the greatest joy
In the following three virtues:
Humility, love, and the courage
To bear witness to the truth
In a world of lies.

The People
Welcome into the city of the pure.
All suffering has disappeared here.
May Christ fill you with joy.
You will share our happiness.
We will be united by our joy.
Joy, joy . . .!

Prince Vsevolod
Bride, your virtues do not weigh lightly.
Let us marry before Holy God
In the temple of light.

Lady Fevronia
Bridegroom, one last question.
Grisjenka is wandering in the forest.
He is sick in his body, spirit, and soul.
He is really as weak as a child.
Can he not be brought here to be healed?

King Juri
Grisjenka is not ready for the City.
He does not desire life without time.

*Fevronia thinks of a possible way in which she can serve Grisjenka
Kutjerma, the drunkard and sower of confusion.*

Lady Fevronia
Then I will send the poor man a letter.
Grisjenka has nothing.
And perhaps a letter will serve as a heart
Under his belt.

King Juri agrees to Fevronia's plan.

King Juri
Good! Friend Fyodor will write the letter,
And the shepherd boy will bring it to him.

Hopefully all Russians
Will turn to Christ because of this deed.

At a sign from the king Fyodor Pojarok fetches a writing table, a roll of
parchment and some writing materials. He prepares everything to write the
letter. Fevronia stands next to Fyodor with King Juri and Prince Vsevolod,
and she turns to the officer to dictate the letter.

Lady Fevronia
Well, friend, write! If I express myself badly,
The Prince will correct me.
Grisjenka, I send you my warmest greetings,
Here is a short note from me —
Tell me, have you got that?

Fylodor Pojarok
Yes, I've got that down.

Lady Fevronia
Do not think that we are dead.
No, we live.
Kitezh was saved by Jesus Christ.
Everything here is full of light and shining,
The city, the people . . .
Everything here is timeless and spaceless.
That is why the spirit is joyful.
Kitezh is more intimate than a dream.
The silence has deepened here to a single note —

Fevronia turns to King Juri.

Lady Fevronia
Who is worthy to enter Kitezh?

King Juri
Those who have risen from the grave with Christ
And spread his word to all mankind!

Fevronia turns back to Fyodor Pojarok.

Lady Fevronia
Well, all the best. There is no one here
Who does not love you dearly. Pray for penitence.
Look at heaven at night: pure love sparkles
In the star-spangled, blue-black sky.

Look at the sun by day: it is not a golden star!
No, it is the fire of the faith of those who serve God —
Did I say the right thing?

The People
Certainly, Lady. Yes, that is how it is.

> *Fevronia continues to dictate.*

Lady Fevronia
Bow your head down to earth. Press your ears
To the ground. You will hear the bells of Kitezh
Down in the depths, making the earth tremble.
It will no longer disturb you —
Did you write that down, Pojarok?

Fyodor Pojarok
Yes, here it is.

> *Fyodor Pojarok gives the letter to the shepherd boy, who takes his leave.*
> *Fevronia turns to her bridegroom.*

Lady Fevronia
Let us enter the temple!

> *Prince Vsevolod and Lady Fevronia walk towards the Cathedral of Our*
> *Lady of the Assumption, the Temple of Light.*

The People
Living in the city of the pure in heart,
Joy will remain with us.
Joy, joy, joy, joy!

> *The gates of the Cathedral open up. An awesome light streams out of the*
> *temple. It completely swallows up Prince Vsevolod and Lady Fevronia.*

Our Lady.
A mosaic on one of the walls of the Sophia Cathedral in Kiev.
(Taken from: 'Russian Heroic Sagas and Legends' by Boris Raptschinsky.)

2.

Introduction to the Kitezh Legend

by Valentin Tomberg

Valentin Tomberg was born in 1900 in Leningrad, Russia; died in Mallorca in 1973. At a very young age he was the chairman of the Estonian branch of the Anthroposophical Association. Later he fled to Rotterdam from the Russian Revolution. After some time he disagreed with D. van Bemmelen and Zeijlmans van Emmerickhoven about certain questions regarding reincarnation. He left the Anthroposophical Association, became a Catholic, and settled in London. His most important works are: *Commentary on the Old Testament*, *Commentary on the New Testament*, *Commentary on the Apocalypse* (unfinished), *On Our Father*. All these works are in the form of mimeographs. His later works are less significant from the point of view of spiritual science.

The following article was first published in *Anthroposofie, Wochenschrift für freies Geislesleben*, 13th year, no. 12, 22 March 1931.

WHEN CONSIDERING THE CULTURE of a nation is it a matter of distinguishing the *Hüllen-Ich* (the lower or outer Self) of the nation from its true higher Self.[1] The individuality (the higher Self) of a nation is surrounded by a cloud of influences that emanate from other nations, influences which can be so profound that they appear to be essential characteristics of the people concerned. For example, in Russian a German is represented as the 'original philistine', a mean and small-minded character, a petty official. The image of a German is that of someone concerned with precision, pedantry, and triviality. In Russian eyes the stereotype of this German is a figure who gains his doctorate by 'publishing' an 'attempt at an introduction for an outline of a survey of the history of Luxembourg' (paperback edition, 7 volumes, octavo format). Obviously this stereotype is incorrect, for although German cultural life does contain a great deal of 'philistinism' and bourgeois mentality, the essence of the German soul is concerned not with bourgeois values but precisely with *combatting* them. The German essence is actually the force within Western culture that *conquers* bourgeois ideas. Anyone who does not see this victory, but merely the problem preceding it, can form only an incorrect image of

Germans. The bourgeois element in German spiritual life is not part of its essence, but belongs to the lower Self, the outer Self of that life. It is derived from Roman cultural life, which is incorporated in German spiritual life from outside.

Thus, in order to understand the German character, it should be seen not as a continuation of Roman cultural life, but as a victory over it. It is not the figure of Wagner (from Goethe's *Faust*) who is representative of the German character, but the figure of Faust. For although Faust was enveloped by the Wagner element — which is evident from the fact that he was a doctor and held doctorates in four subjects — he eventually conquered the Wagner element. Philistinism — the bourgeois mentality — is to the German character what Wagner is to Faust in the Faustian drama. To understand the typical characteristics of the German national character, it is far better to study the Faustian drama than to examine the German universities. The Faustian drama, which is based on a popular saga, reveals in Faust the forces that drive the destiny of the Central European soul.

The Doctor Faust saga is a 'truth dream' of the soul of Central Europe, a dream that expresses the most profound forces of the soul. A similar truth dream, this time of the East European soul, a dream that reveals different and most profound spiritual forces, is the so-called Kitezh legend (in the form of a poem written by W. Belski, and an opera by Rimski-Korsakov). This drama embodies the essential or primordial element of the Russian popular soul. It does so for everything which is now identified as 'Russian culture', and which for the most part forms the lower Self, the outer Self, of the Slav character. Russia's true essence lies concealed behind this enveloping cloud of influences from the Byzantine, Norwegian, Finnish, and Roman cultures. Inside this cloud Russia itself is still asleep. But while it sleeps, it is dreaming. The saga of the invisible city of Kitezh, which originates from the thirteenth century, is one of the dreams of the sleeping Russian popular soul.

In broad terms, this saga runs as follows. The old prince, Juri Vsevolodovich built two cities in the forest of Murom — one on the edge, which was also situated on the Volga; 'Little Kitezh', and one city in the heart of the forest, 'Great Kitezh'. The inhabitants of Great Kitezh were characterized by their hospitality. They gladly accepted everything that was strange and that came to them. They had a great capacity for assimilating things, but one day a force arrived that they were not able to assimilate: the Tartar hordes. These hordes overran Little Kitezh, and it was destroyed. The Tartars did not know the way to the inner city, Great Kitezh.

Among the inhabitants of outer Kitezh there was a man, Grisjka Kutjerma (which means: 'he who sows confusion') who betrayed the way to inner Kitezh. He blamed his treachery on the innocent and childlike Lady Fevronia, the bride of the successor to the throne, young Prince Vsevolod, son of King Juri. However, when the Tartars arrived at the city (situated on the lake in the forest, Svetli Jarr), a miracle occurred. The prayer of the people to the Mother of God for Salvation, accompanied by bloody tears, was miraculously answered. The city, with its entire population, became invisible. It rose up to celestial heights, or — according to another version — was submerged in the depths of the Svetli Jarr (the bright shining lake). The Tartars fled, frightened out of their wits. The traitor went insane. Lady Fevronia was taken into the invisible city as the future sovereign after being raised to this honour following her undeserved suffering (imprisonment, calumny, and starvation in the wood).

What does this saga reveal? In the depths of the popular Russian soul there is an image of a city, i.e. a community: not the image of a single hero who embodies the essence of the popular soul's ideal, but the image of a social community, which was worth recording. The saga describes the progress of the city and its destiny, the path and the destiny of a community worth recording, which was threatened by its counterpart, the intolerant Mongol 'Orda'. In this saga it is not the path and the destiny of any individual seeker that are central, but the question and the purpose of a collective tolerance of evil.

Lady Fevronia does not have an individual path or goal to aim at. She is not important in the saga for what she does but for what happens to her. Her *destiny* is the most important thing. Her destiny is not a personal destiny; it is suffering in the general interest, for the city. This suffering is undeserved from the point of view of her own individual destiny; she did not cause it herself. It has no causes in the past. It is a suffering for the future, in the future common interest. This reveals a profound and essential aspect of the true Russian soul. It is this attitude to suffering aimed at the future common interest that is so distinct from the European attitude. In Europe there is a tendency to deny suffering — to view it as something caused by our mistakes. In Russia suffering is experienced as something that is a preparation for future glory. Suffering is not interpreted merely as a payment of debts, but also, and above all, as a divine choice.

Suffering is honoured; there is an empathy with suffering at the most profound level of the soul. Everyone who suffers, even if the suffering is deserved and is experienced as punishment, is still honoured in the same way. Even the deserved suffering of punishment undeniably contains an element of the undeserved. In a sense, every punishment contains an element that is undeserved. This undeserved suffering is for all mankind, for the future general well-being. Therefore all undeserved suffering is a preparation for the future of all mankind. Just as Christ prepared for the future of the world through his undeserved suffering, even the most humble individual can achieve a similar goal when he suffers.

The view of suffering rooted in the Russian soul is therefore not primarily concerned with the significance of the individual Self. Let me repeat it: the view of suffering as a result of an error or wandering by the Self, suffering as a lesson and as retribution, is not the Russian view. According to the Russian view, every form of suffering contains a collective power that transcends the Self. This Self-transcending power gives suffering a quality of general humanity. The cause of suffering cannot be found only in the individual Self but also in the effect of mercy which brings suffering and which comes from above. Thus suffering is not only the *law*, but also *mercy*. It is not only the expression of the acts of the individual Self, but also the expression of the effect of the supra-individual Manas in man, the Spiritual Self, which is the Spirit that Man shares with the rest of mankind. The image of the ascension of the city of Kitezh thus reveals the consequences of undeserved suffering of all men for all men. It is *this* image of suffering (as collective mercy and a collective predestination) that burns in the popular Russian soul by means of the interpersonal quality of Manas, and determines that soul.

In the Faustian saga the problem of suffering is treated very differently. It is seen as the struggle of the Self of a single individual who is at the centre of the saga. This individuality suffers and is redeemed as a result of error and guilt. Thus Faust is following a very lonely path. Everything is there for him — things are significant only insofar as they are significant for *him*. Faust is ambitious. He is always striving to achieve a particular goal that he wants to reach for himself and by himself. Gretchen, Helena, and the land reclaimed from the sea are his goals, and he will go to any lengths to attain them. They are merely steps in the development of his Self.

Faust's attitude is very antisocial. The only community that accepts this lonely figure with mercy is the community of the heavenly powers, but this happens only after his death on earth. It is only after his death that Faust becomes a member of a community; throughout his lifetime he walks alone. What really matters to him finally? What is the positive element that he expresses in symbolic terms? A most important aspect of Faust is not moral purity or correct conduct, but his inner strength to resist the common power of the world of phenomena without being erased. The heavenly band describe the positive element in Faust: 'Wer immer strebend sick bemüht den können wir erlösen' ('We can delivery anyone who struggles'). Faust has the strength not to drown in the ocean of the world with his consciousness; his Self always remains upright, and the heavenly band value this in the same way as moral saintliness — full of childlike innocence and penance. This is why Faust's ability to keep his Self upright makes it possible for him to enter the same realm as childlike innocents, 'midnight's children', and the deserving penitents.

In the saga of the holy city of Kitezh the heavenly powers should really have said: 'We can deliver anyone who does not *fight against* suffering.' It is not the individual but society that is delivered. For the question on which the Kitezh saga is based is: 'How can *we* be delivered?', while the Faust saga gives the answer to the question of the individual's delivery. Goethe's *Faust* is not concerned with justification of egotism, but with depicting the path of the human Self, which achieves unification with the spiritual world by means of a strong inner struggle (egoism), and this despite the egotism involved.

Similarly, the Kitezh legend is in no way concerned with justifying passivity or the group spirit or herd instinct. Just as the Self force of the Faustian figure is hallowed by heaven, the capacity for the deliverance of Kitezh is hallowed by heaven. There is an egoism which is justified in heaven; in the same way, there is a universality which is justified in heaven. Just as Faust's actions open the door of heaven for him, the passivity of Lady Fevronia, who represents Kitezh, opens the door to the invisible and celestial city of Kitezh. There is activity that is justified, but it must be directed downwards, and then higher activity tends towards mercy; there is also a passivity which is justified, but it may only be developed to higher regions. This justified activity develops the spirit of the German people, while its Self develops. The Russian soul develops passivity, so that in future it will receive the spiritual Self, Manas, from above. The Faustian saga and the Kitezh saga reflect two significant movements on earth: the drive of the Self and the drive of the spiritual Self, which are manifestations of the essential forces of the German and Russian souls respectively.

Valentin Tomberg

Some of the most important questions relating to Kitezh as the future Slav cultural legend are: What people actually inhabited Little Kitezh, and in particular, Great Kitezh? What is their common karmic background? It is not difficult to answer these questions in a general sense in the light of Western European spiritual science, and to state that the population of Kitezh consisted of people who followed Christ and the effects of his mercy. Before everything, they received the blessings granted by the mysteries of the Eucharist, the Holy Grail, Holy Communion, or whatever term is used.

The people of Kitezh are in the first place people who take Christian communion — in other words, who live by the laws of Christian communism. Once again it was Valentin Tomberg who gave indications on the basis of his own spiritual scientific investigation, making it possible to answer the above questions in detail in a very concrete way. His work, *Anthroposifische Betrachtungen über das Alte Testament*, (pp. 86 ff, manuscript edition) describes the following preparations (particularly of the Jewish people) for the future development of Manas (particularly in the Russian people):

> About the isolation of man wandering in the desert, about the world as a desert, and about Christ who precedes man, formerly as a Jew, today as a Christian . . .
>
> This is the greatest danger of isolation, the hypertrophy of the will at the expense of thoughts and feelings. With this hypertrophy all the passions are inflamed in a sort of feverish activity, and therefore the senses are hidden by a mist of drives. The healing, cool objectivity of the thought processes and the purity of the feelings of the heart are clouded by this feverish activity. When man is lonely, he feels

feverish, hungry and thirsty — as though travelling through a desert . . .

Because the Jewish people were predestined to produce Christ, who strengthens the unique but is so inclined towards the isolation of the human self, the Jewish people also made preparations for what would develop in the future as a Manas culture (from slavery), in order to combat isolation. A Manas culture is a culture in which man and his conscience, i.e. the higher aspect of the self, transforms the astral body (with the lower, self-seeking Self) into Manas, an essential component which unites people.

This preparation also mean that the Jewish people were removed for a time from external influences in order to be able to receive something new. For some time the people had to live in isolation. This essential lack of influence brought the people into a spiritual desert of hunger, thirst and heat.

Suffering is the only way in which man, after the Fall, can change his essence in a spiritual, heavenly direction. Joy strengthens man to work at a material level, but pain opens him to divine intervention and changes in his essence. Pain opens man's spiritual eye.

On the journey through the desert, led by Moses, true happiness preceded the Jewish people in the form of the pillar of fire and cloud: Christ in nature. This pillar of fire enabled the people to make the painful journey through the desert. True suffering, which was not based on guilt, was experienced by the Jewish people in the form of hunger, thirst, and heat, in the form of the hypertrophy of the will at the expense of thoughts and feelings resulting from the isolation caused by the desert. These experiences were expressed in the constant so-called 'murmuring' of the Jews. For this True Suffering the Jewish people as a whole — not the individual Jew — was compensated by a particular sort of sleep, to the extent to which it had done without shade and food and drink in the daytime (and repressed its murmuring).

This compensation was the so-called rain of manna (from the night-time pillar of cloud, Christ in nature). Clearly the rain of manna is none other than the first awakening of the Manas seed in the astral world of sleep and unconsciousness. In the morning the Jewish people felt revived by the manna. Just as the dusty horizon of the day signified only an unintelligible, monotonous, and winding road for the Jewish people towards an unknown destination at an unknown time, the night spoke to the people of the secrets of a future kingdom of Manas.

At night the people realized that the impoverished life in the horizontal plane — of which it was part, through no guilt of its own; to some extent, though it was guilty of murmuring and idolatry — was a condition for the promised kingdom in the vertical plane which would bring happiness. The souls who experienced the communal manifestation of Manas in the desert at night, together with Moses, form the karmic community of Manas people in the subsequent millennia.

The impressions of that time survive in those souls. However, the inner individual possession of Manas will mature only in the sixth or Slav cultural period. These people form the karmic nucleus of the Manas community of Philadelphia.'

Valentin Tomberg

Philadelphia means 'city of exceptional brotherly love'. Rudolf Steiner's lectures on the Apocalypse, given in Nuremburg in 1908, make the following point:

96

St John the Evangelist who wrote the Apocalypse refers to Philadelphia as the sixth of seven Christian communities in Asia Minor. The seven communities represent the seven Aryan cultural periods in which mankind has expressed himself in the post-Atlantean era. We are now living in the fifth cultural period. The sixth will be the Slav cultural period.

It is therefore self-evident that the brotherly Slav Kitezh (as a city of the future) is identical with the brotherly Slav Philadelphia (as a city or culture of the future).

Each of the seven Christian communities — Aryan cultures — received a letter from St John, the author of the Apocalypse. This described how the community concerned could prosper or degenerate with regard to Christ's intentions for mankind, what threats there were and what delights are in store.

To begin this interpretation of the Kitezh legend, we will continue with a short outline of the seven Aryan cultures, more or less based on the letters of St John, in order to provide a better understanding of the identification of Kitezh as Philadelphia and of the entire cultural framework surrounding it.

The first Aryan cultural period, the Ancient Indian period, lasted from 7227 to 5067 B.C., when the sun was in Cancer. It is represented in the Apocalypse by the community of Ephesus. 'Ephesus' means border town. In time, it bordered on the Garden of Eden of Lemuria, which had been destroyed by fire, and on Atlantis, which had been submerged in water. In the Indian culture, man revealed his (twofold) Self in the ethereal body.

The second Aryan cultural period, the Ancient Persian era, lasted from 5067 to 2907 B.C., when the sun was in Gemini. In the Apocalypse, it is reprsented by the community of Smyrna. 'Smyrna' means cup of sorrow. In the Persian culture man revealed himself in his astral body. Just as man was easily able to find the world of the spirit in the border country of Ephesus through his memories of Atlantis (by practising yoga), but found it difficult to work the natural earth — because of the same memories — in Smyrna, man was able to keep faith with the earth through his heavy toil. It was this, as well as the hostility that it evokes in lazy people, and the threat of being tied to the world and enslaved by matter, that made the Ancient Persian culture a Smyrna, or cup of sorrow.

Ephesus was threatened by the salvation of the renunciation of the world, a salvation that made the developing Self shine with a light in the ethereal body. This blessed renunciation of the world is derived from Lucifer, the leader of the first type of evil forces. Smyrna was threatened by the suffering caused by being tied to the world, a suffering that was as a burden for the development of the Self in the astral body. This suffering of being tied to the world is derived from Ahriman, the leader of the second type of evil forces.

The third Aryan cultural period was the Egyptian Chaldean era, which lasted from 2907 to 747 B.C., when the sun was in Taurus. In the Apocalypse it is represented by the community of Pergamon. 'Pergamon' means city of the snake. In the Egyptian Chaldean culture, man revealed his Self in the soul, especially in the soul of perception. The soul is a system of snakes. The image of the snake refers both to the sacred twofold snake of Hermes and Aphrodite, the basis of the soul of androgynous, immortal man, and to the unholy single (halved) Aeschylus snake, the basis of the soul of sexual mortal man, who requires healing and health.

Pergamon — or Egypt-Chaldea — was the city (culture) in which, apart from the evil of Lucifer and Ahriman, there was a third type of evil, the evil of black magic and the destruction of the world. This evil was derived from the so-called Asurian forces led by Soradt. On the other hand, it led to modern white magic, the magic which served as the first preparation for the development of man to return to an androgynous, immortal creature, and therefore also prepared the way for Christ, the king of the soul. This corresponds with the words: 'I have called my son from Egypt'. The Jews started their above-mentioned journey through the desert at the end of the third cultural period, and laid the basis for the development of Manas in the sixth Slav cultural period. In this respect they continued the preparations that were made in the Ancient Persian culture.

In fact, the last three cultures repeat the first three and spiritualize them (around the focal point of the fourth culture). The fifth culture does this for the third, the sixth for the second, and the seventh for the first. In other words, the first three cultures prepare the way for the last three. The fact that during the third cultural period the Jews continued the preparations of the second cultural period for the sixth, thus deviating from the scheme, is because the development of Manas in the sixth or Slav culture is so important. Mankind will be transfigured into a new root race (the sixth Slav root race which will succeed the present fifth Aryan root race), through the development of Manas. In this root race the consequences of sin — death and sexuality — will be overcome. The fact that the Jews were capable of continuing these preparations is because their leader Moses (with Hermes) was the spiritual heir of the Ancient Persian leader, Zarathrustra.

The fourth Aryan cultural period, the Graeco-Judaic-Roman medieval period, lasted from 747 B.C., to A.D. 1413, when the sun was in Aries. In the Apocalypse it is represented by the community of Thyatira. 'Thyatira' means the city of the indomitable. The indomitable refers to Christ, the healer of the soul, the Saviour of the Self, and the Redeemer of the world. Christ paralysed — and still paralyses — the three types of forces of evil, and opened the way for mankind, leading to the so-called 'Alchemical Wedding', the wedding of the soul and the spirit, which will eventually mean that man will once again be an androgynous and immortal being.

For this purpose Christ established on earth the mystery of the Eucharist, the mystery of the Holy Grail. The body and blood of Christ — bread and wine — is the food with which man can transcend his incompleteness and mortality. In a sense the Eucharist is a twofold communion, for it concerns two mysteries. The first mystery of the Eucharist is of a ceremonial nature and was instigated on Maundy Thursday; this could be called the ceremonial mystery of the Eucharist. The second mystery of the Eucharist is of a practical nature, and was formed by Christ's road to Calvary, the Crucifixion and Entombment on Good Friday, and his Resurrection on Easter Sunday. This could be called the mystery of the Eucharist in Deed and Truth. In the first mystery the cup of the Eucharist, or Grail, is a (symbolic) chalice; in the second mystery it is the earth. In the second mystery the earth contains the body and blood of Christ. The first mystery of the Eucharist was brought to Western Europe by Joseph of Arimathea and to the Caucasus by St Andrew. The second mystery of the Eucharist was taken to Eastern Europe by the rhythms of the earth.

Corresponding with these traditions, the Grail legends of the Western European kings, Arthur and Parsifal, present the Grail as a chalice, while the Grail is not explicitly mentioned in the legends of the East European King Vladimir. In these legends it is simply the earth. In the East European legends, there is no reference to a quest for the Grail, but of the way in which it is developed. The heroes of the Grail in these legends are peasants. They work and till the earth, like the body of Christ (Gospel According to St John).

A description of the way in which the food from the Grail can lead to an androgynous and immortal state can be found in Johan Valentin Andreas's book, *The Alchemical Wedding of Christian Rosenkreuz*. This Christian Rosenkreuz will be the ultimate Grail king of mankind. He is no other than John, Christ's favourite disciple, who was a central participant in both mysteries of the Eucharist.

The possible development for eternal life contained in the mysteries of the Grail was granted to man on the basis of the development of the Self in the so-called soul of the intellect and the emotions, a development which is parallel to the character of the fourth cultural period. In the soul of the intellect and emotions, the Self becomes so mature that it can participate in the mysteries of the Grail without being erased, and without reverting to a sort of paradise situation. (Another situation with eternal characteristics, but without any development of the Self.)

The continued preparations on behalf of the future Slav Manas culture were taken in the fourth cultural period by the prophet Mani, who founded the Manicheans. This was a movement in which every man who experiences the world like a desert, as the Jews once did, can transform the tendencies provoked by this experience into brotherly love by murmuring. This brotherly love is the magic force that will persuade people without brotherly love to feel it, so that evil can be combatted in a Christian way. Within Manicheism there are possibilities for the development of the mysteries of the Grail to 'fight this fight'.

Manicheism led to a great deal of envy because of its pretensions and importance. Finally it was eradicated altogether. However, small groups survived and founded new Manichean movements. Some examples include the Bogomil Church, the Cathar Church, and above all, the historical Kitezh, as we shall see.

The fifth Aryan cultural period is the Roman–Germanic–Anglo-Saxon era, which lasts from A.D. 1413 to 3573, now that the sun is in Pisces. It is represented in the Apocalypse by the community of Sardes. This is the present cultural period. 'Sardes' means place of danger. This meaning refers to the freedom of choice of man's Self, which was saved by Christ and achieved independence in the fourth cultural period. It also refers to the related danger of making the wrong choice, a choice for evil.

In Sardes, the Self develops in the so-called conscious soul. This means that because of a growing (self)-awareness and consciousness, it has a choice of remaining at the self-seeking lower aspect of its being (the lower Self), or of developing the higher aspect of its being (the higher Self, the conscience) at the expense of the former. The higher Self is sometimes described as 'the inner Christ'. It is 'the seed of Jesus', a spark of the cosmic Christ in the human heart.

However, with the growth of knowledge it is not only man's freedom of choice that grows, but also man's loneliness, the extent of his experience of the desert and the murmuring. Anyone whose knowledge increases also increases his pain, whether the knowledge is used for selfish ends, or even — and especially — if it is used to transcend selfishness.

In order that man will not be destroyed by loneliness in the fifth culture, the cosmic Christ has manifested himself since the beginning of the twentieth century in a new way as the Indomitable Son of God, and is reviving the mysteries of the Grail in a new way. Just as he revealed himself in the third cultural period and led the Jews on their journey through the desert in the form of a pillar of fire and cloud, as the true Joy to strengthen them on their arduous daily journey through the sand, he is revealing himself today in the fifth cultural period, which is a repetition of the third, as a spiritual pillar of fire and cloud in the ethereal world. He offers himself from that world and in that guise at Holy Communion in the form of bread and wine, ceremonially both in deed and in truth.

In this way, modern man can follow two paths if he wishes: a) the primary Rosicrucian path which leads to the Alchemical Wedding; b) the same path to serve the endeavours of the Manicheans.

In general, at the beginning of the fifth cultural period, Western Europe chose the first path, based on the mystery of the Grail as an up-and-coming cultural area of consciousness and the soul, while Eastern Europe — Kiev Rus — as the future cultural area of Manas, chose the second path, based on the second mystery of the Grail. In this way, Kiev Rus continued the preparation for the coming Manas culture, which was started by the Ancient Persians, the Jews and the Manicheans, in the area where it will prevail in the future.

The twin cities of Kitezh, described in the legend(s) as a historical place, and the deeds of the Round Table of King Vladimir of Kiev, form the undisputed high point of this preparation, as we shall see.

The Jews' journey through the desert culminated in the historical city of Kitesh, particularly their central experience of being led to the Promised Land by the pillar of fire and cloud, in the assimilation of Kitezh in heaven, or its descent into the fiery mists of the Svetli Jarr. The practice of Mani's gospel of brotherly love culminated, in particular, in the historical city of Kitezh, in its citizens' acceptance of their fate, which was described above. The preparation for the future Manas culture was manifest in the best and fullest way in this twofold culmination.

To return to the two paths mentioned above, a subtle nuance can be distinguished. Apart from the primary path of the Rosicrucians, the Manichean path of Eastern Europe was also followed in Western Europe. (In a sense this was the same path, though it served and was coloured by Mani's objectives.) This took place in medieval France in the Cathar Church, and is carried on today in the Netherlands in the ecclesiastic community 'Lectorum Rosicrucianum'. In relation to groups that primarily follow the Rosicrucian path — in the Middle Ages, these were the Aristo- telian and Platonic scholastic philosophers; today, the Anthroposophists — these churches have a spiritual role of 'female calling and bearing', as opposed to male fertilisation and leadership. In fact, a similar relationship also once existed between the Platonic and Aristotelian scholastic philosophers themselves. On the other hand, those who followed the primary Rosicrucian path inspired the preparatory work for the Manas culture in early Russia.

The considerable influence of the Varangians in Kiev Rus, without which King Vladimir's Round Table and Kitezh could not have existed, must be explained and understood in terms of this inspiration, as must part of the subsequent acts of Dimitri Ivanovich. In this context there is even an official Slav Call for leadership addressed to Western Europe, and a Varangian- Germanic Answer to this Call. This will be dealt with in detail in the outline of early Russian history.

There is another aspect of Sardes as the place of danger. The three opposing forces — but particularly Soradt and Ahriman — are concerned in our present fifth cultural period, which brings freedom, with inducing man to be evil and destructive as a self-conscious being. In order to achieve this, Soradt founded an academy in Gondishapur in the seventh century, which aimed to destroy the future Manas culture as well as all the pre- paration for that culture. The destruction of Manas was the basic aim of this academy. It wished to train people without Manas and without a higher Self. These people were known as 'Tartaros' people, or people from the abyss. In the Kitezh legend they are represented by the Tartars. They were the only people who could not be taken into Kitezh. They have no spirit; they live only once; they could not and cannot be assimilated in the pillar of fire and cloud of the Svetli Jarr. It was merely their (temporary) fate to ensure that Kitezh was assimilated by it. In order to lead man into evil — and bind him to the world — Ahriman is due to incarnate in the West in the next century, and will found a spiritual school which will cause the present culture of consciousness and the soul to degenerate into a culture that is bound to the earth.

In principle, Ahriman will fail because of the effect emanating from Christ's ceremonial mystery of the Eucharist (although the culture of consciousness and the soul will be materialized). In principle, Soradt also failed and will continue to fail because of the effect emanating from Christ's mystery of the Eucharist in Deed and Truth (although there will be large hordes of Tartaros people).

The sixth Aryan cultural period, the Slav period, will last from A.D. 3573 to 5733, when the sun will be in Aquarius. This is represented in the Apocalypse by the community of Philadelphia. It will succeed our own cultural period. As mentioned above, Philadelphia means 'city of exceptional brotherly love'. It is Kitezh in a future, non-historical sense. The group(s) of people which travelled through the desert with Moses and transformed the murmuring into a sense of brotherly love, together with Mani, will be of vital importance in the Slav culture. An enormous Manas culture encompassing the whole world will spread from the Slav countries: a global Christian communism based on the union of the Slav manifestion of Manas and the Germanic force of the higher Self, based on the Slav Call for that force (in order to give structure to the Manas culture) and the Germanic Answer to it, will take over from present communism, which is based on an unasked for union of the lower West European force of the Self and the brotherly love based on blood ties that prevails in Asia. In this replacement the mosaic Manichean preparation for Manas will be transformed into a manifestation of Manas, as outlined particularly in the Kitezh legend(s). In these, the Ancient Persian culture is repeated and spiritualized. The inhabitants of Philadelphia-Kitezh in future will for the second time take up the yoke of True Suffering.

Just as this suffering was caused by the physical journey through the desert in the time of Moses, it will be experienced in a new way (from the fifth cultural period) in the sense of a social journey through the desert. The people of Manas will voluntarily undertake this social journey through the desert, in the first place because they will voluntarily share with brotherly love the ever-decreasing resources of the earth with the exploiters of the earth. Secondly, they will voluntarily do justice in a heavenly way to those who descrate the laws of earth, by showing them the other cheek without looking at them when they are struck first. Thirdly, it is because they will voluntarily allow those who deny spiritual freedom, the actual freedom to choose whether or not to persist in evil, even when they are the victims of it. In the culture of Philadelphia the social journey through the desert will have the character of breaking down barriers.

Just as the physical journey through the desert was compensated by a rain of manna, the social journey through the desert will result in the compensation of inner fertility, particularly because of its characteristic breaking down of barriers. The higher Self will arouse the Manas in the astral body, and the two will unite, forming a double system of snakes, and laying the basis for a new, androgynous and immortal existence. This unification will obviously also involve the two mysteries of the Grail that make this process possible: the ceremonial mystery of the Grail for the Self and the conscious soul, and the 'practical' mystery of the Grail for the Manas.

The way in which these two mysteries are united is in a sense identical to the phenomenon of the Slav Call for Self force in the Manas and the Germanic Answer to it. In this way the Alchemical Wedding of the spirit and the soul, the intermingling of the two mysteries of the Grail and the simultaneity of the above-mentioned Call and Answer are all interrelated. In the future city of Kitezh — at the same time, the citadel of the Alchemical Wedding, the citadel of the Grail, and the citadel of the culture linking East and West — every person who has a spirit is allowed to enter if he wishes, no matter how evil his character, even if it is as evil as Grisjka Kutjerma.

In the earlier mysteries one was only allowed to enter by being chosen; in the present mysteries one is allowed to enter, provided that one has a suitable philosophy; in the future one can enter Kitezh if one wishes to. If one is not able to adopt a suitable lifestyle and philosophy oneself, others can do this for one.

There will certainly be an end to the future Kitezh as well. People of evil intentions, very often Tartaros people, will bring about the so-called war of 'All against All' on the earth. This will also destroy the future city of Kitezh. However, it will do so in a very special way, as was the case for the historical Kitezh. By that time the whole astral world will be condensed into a single radiant lake of light, a single, radiant, final Svetli Jarr, a single last pillar of fire and cloud encompassing the cosmos, which can be identified with the cosmic Christ, who will no longer be manifest in the ethereal world but in the astral world. The ultimate city of Kitezh will go up or be submerged in this last pillar of fire and cloud as Christ's ultimate Ecclesia (Church). It will be assimilated in this to be transformed into a new root race, the sixth Slav root race, which will conquer evil and become androgynous and immortal through its own creativity.

The root race will no longer leave the last pillar of fire and cloud, or the last Svetli Jarr. On the other hand, the last pillar of fire and cloud and the last Svetli Jarr will encompass the whole earth and all those who have remained evil will literally become animals. This will occur without the loss of any particular absolute separateness.

The capacity for magic in mankind when it has become divine will increase to such an extent that in the post-Kitezh mysteries they will no longer have to repel even people without a spirit, people who are half-animal, Tartaros people. Even they will be assimilated in these last mysteries.

By means that are still completely unknown today, in certain eugenic ways — the so-called 'cross-births' in which a divine person and an animal person share a single spiritual system, a single microcosm — in the social setting of an unbelievably intense Christian communism, they — the divine people, or last Manicheans — will be able to unite those people who have no spirit with the spirit and lead them along the path of evolution towards becoming a true person and god.

The seventh and last Aryan cultural period, the Brazilian–American period, will last from A.D. 5733 to 7893, when the sun will be in Capricorn. In the Apocalypse it is represented by the community of Laodicea. It should be noted that in this cultural period, time will develop in such a way that these distance years will not follow each other consecutively, but in a sense pass at the same time as earlier years. Therefore the dates given for the years are fictional, for the last Aryan cultural period will coincide with the sixth.

'Laodicia' means the place where what is concealed is revealed. This refers to the statement in the Apocalyptic tract that when the Self develops in the Buddhi, when the ethereal body is transformed into the Buddhi — and that is the cultural mission of Laodicia, the cultural mission in which the Indian culture becomes spiritualized — the success and failure of this mission become visible in man's appearance. The Manas people of the Slav cultural period will fulfil the mission of the seventh cultural era, and this will be manifest in their appearance. Because of the transforming character of the destruction of the world, and because of the formation of a new root race from an old one, they will have a divine appearance.

The people who do not wish to develop Manas in the Slav cultural period will often find it difficult to make up the retarded development. They will abandon the Buddhi development and acquire an animal-like appearance. They will be true Tartaros people and form a group that will become a seventh root race. When time and space are different from ours, the people of Kitezh will endeavour to use magic to convert the evil aspect of mankind to good, first in a cultural context, as mentioned above, and later in a root race context. All this is summarized with regard to the city of Kitezh: Kitezh is the city of exceptional brotherly love, true Christian communism, the city of the Manichean brothers — the city that alternately manifests itself in the pillar of fire and cloud that is Christ, the radiant lake of Christus Astralis, the Svetli Jarr — or is assimilated by them.

Notes

For an understanding of his article on Kitezh, Valentin Tomberg assumes that his readers have a knowledge of Anthroposophy, for many of them subscribe to the Anthroposophical Journal in which the article was published. Therefore Tomberg did not explain all the concepts he used; furthermore, he was not in the habit of using references. In general, he referred to Anthroposophy as a whole. Therefore we must assume a knowledge of some of the concepts used here (and in the following chapters). However, some of the least well known concepts will be explained either in these notes or in a subsequent list of notes, or in most cases a reference to the relevant literature will be given.

3.

Early Russian History up to 1236–40

When Kitesh and Kiev Rus Fell, as the History of the Slav–Rurik Call and the Answer to it.

The Legend of Nikola the Holy

ONCE UPON A TIME, Nikola, the Russian popular saint, had a very strange vision. (Nikola means: 'He who leads the people to victory', and also 'I conquer, in the sense of the self that conquers'.) An angel of the Lord appeared before him; the angel was on horseback and held sickles in his hands.

He called: 'Wake up, Nikola! Get up and go to your country. The time has come for the harvest!'

Nikola woke up, seized with fear. He made a deep bow before the grave of Christ where he had prayed tirelessly for all the Christians on earth, and walked to the holy land of Russia, crossing over sea and land. Nikola did not recognize his own country. Russia lay like a desert before him, laid waste, burned and trampled by the enemy, and only the wind blew over the deserted steppe. There was no trace of justice to be found in all the land. This greatly saddened the saint. He raised his staff, and always wishing to help, he started his journey through Russia. He walked from the Volga to the Moskva, from the Dnieper to the icy White Sea.

He punished unjust rulers, he chastised the wasters and exploiters of the mother country. He liberated innocent prisoners, stopped executions. He raised two lads from the dead after they had been cut into pieces. He gave toys to poor children. He turned the winter wheat to the sun, made the grass grow, gave sun and rain at the right time. He put the cattle out to grass in summer, and brought them into the barns in winter. He advised the peasants, and freed their carts when they were stuck in the mud.

Without Nikola, every peasant would be helpless. Nikola is the only one who really sees who is in need. Ask him, and he will always help. He will tell the Redeemer everything, and can even mollify Elia (Elijah) so that the rye is not flattened by the hail. Nikola the Good walked through the land of Russia throughout the year until the day of St. Nicholas in winter. He heard vespers in the cave monastery in Kiev. When the bell there pealed for the second time, he was already in the Cathedral of St Sophia in Novgorod. When it pealed for the third time, he was already on his way to the Kazan Cathedral in Petersburg, and before the end of the Holy Mass he was already in the Cathedral of Our Lady of the Assumption in Moscow.

At Nikola's command, all the winds brought great frosts. Then the saint scattered silver over all of Russia from north to south and from west to east, and blessed the land — his hungry, thirsty suffering Russia, which was in great need. He blessed it so that it would be able to establish a wise order and not commit the sins of curiosity, self-interest, and stupidity; so that it would not be mocked by the world for its foolish behaviour; so that it would not be accused of laziness. Three times he blessed Russia, and then walked calmly over the clouds to heaven to celebrate the day of St Nicholas there.

The saints of Russia and throughout Christendom had looked out for him that day. When Nikola finally arrived in heaven, Elia asked him why he had not arrived a bit earlier.

Nikola answered: 'All that time I have been busy with my Russians, and it has made me dog-tired. There is no hope for them: they are thieves and murderers, robbers and arsonists. Fathers fight their sons, and sons their fathers. They are devouring each other.'

'All right then, I will let my thunder and lightning loose on them. I will destroy everything and even make the Russian soil burn!' called Elia the Thunderer in indignation.

'And I will not give them any more dew!' added St George.

'And I will send a plague to Russia!' decided the hot-headed St Cassian. (He once set fire to the moustache of St John Chrysostomus in a fit of pique.)

'The angel of the Lord ordered me to eradicate all the Russian people,' said Nikola the Merciful, 'but I pitied them and let them live. They're having such a hard time.'

Then Nikola stood up, raised the chalice of wine which had been poured for him in honour of his birthday. He raised it to the glory of God who created heaven and earth. It almost immediately fell from his hand, and he fell asleep. Elia called him, but Nikola did not hear him; Elia called him a second time, but Nikola did not hear him. Then Elia shouted out so that he would wake up, and Nikola woke up. The saints asked him what had happened and Nikola told them.

'In the bitter, icy sea sailed a ship with grain, with three hundred monks from the Solovetski monastery on board. They wished to celebrate the feast of St Nicholas in Myra in Lycea. Suddenly the ship was beset by a terrible storm sent by the heathen goddess Welesha. The monks called for my help to save them from the foamy grip of Welesha. Then I was filled with the Holy Ghost and saved them. That is why I fell asleep here and the chalice of wine slipped from my hands. But look, the glass has not broken and not a drop has spilt.'

Then all the saints feasted and they asked Nikola: 'Help us too, when we are in difficulties.'

(End of extract: abbreviated version from: *Nikola the Good* by A. Remisov, Zeist 1986.)

In order to indicate the link between the content of the Kitezh legend(s) and the content of the bylini (at least, most of them), or more precisely, in order to indicate that Kitezh can be interpreted as the social or Christian communist conclusion of the prior development of the Grail in Kiev, it is necessary to relate Kitezh to Kiev in a historical sense. This is only possible by considering Russia's early history as an organic whole. Therefore this history, which was first written down in about 1190 by Nestor, a monk, in the so-called 'Nestor Chronicle', will be outlined here with a commentary, so that the links will become clear.

It is not the case that there is a one-to-one correspondence between all the (Russian) heroes from the bylini and the Kitezh legends, and the heroes from early Russian history. In fact, the reverse is the case, as will become clear. However, this does apply with regard to the founder of the Round Table of Kiev, and that of the Christian Communist city of Kitezh (and several legendary heroes).

The bylini of the Round Table of Kiev identify the legendary founder of that Round Table, King Vladimir, the Red Sun of Kiev, with the historical King Vladimir the Holy of Kiev. The beginning of the Slav Church version of the Kitezh legend identifies the legendary founder of Kitezh, King Juri, as a historical great-grandsom of Vladimir the Holy, Georgi Vsevolodovich, the ruler of Pskov. The way in which these characters are rooted in historical genealogy, as outlined here, adequately indicates that the legendary heroes concerned really lived as the historical characters referred to.

In the special context of early Russian history as an organic whole, which will reveal the so-called Slavonic Rurik Call and the Varangian Answer to it, one historical figure (corresponding to the Kitezh legend) is shown to be linked by genealogy with the other character (corresponding to the Round Table of Kiev). Similarly, Kitezh and that Round Table are also interrelated. This objective relationship applies in addition to the development of the Grail, as in the Grail of Kiev, which cannot really result in any other form of society than a communist society such as that of Kitezh. Kitezh fulfils Kiev.

J. and R. Engelen's book, *Rudolf Steiner über Rusland (Rudolf Steiner on Russia)* tells how Rudolf Steiner's spiritual–scientific research relating to Russia resulted in his viewing early Russian history as a preliminary, mythological outline of its future history. A similar interpretation applies to an even greater extent to the 'mythological reverse' of that history, i.e. to the Kitezh legend and in relation to the bylini.

This matter should be viewed in relation to the ideas described in Chapter 2, 'Introduction to the Kitezh legend' about the seven cultural Aryan periods, particularly the fourth, fifth and sixth cultural periods. In the fourth and fifth cultural periods Manichean preparations were referred to for the sixth cultural period, and the sixth root race era, in which Manas (the Manas of mankind) will be developed in a cultural sense or in a racial sense (obviously on the basis of individual Manas development), and in which an attempt will be made to render those people who are no longer capable of that development suitable for it.

These preparations finally culminated in the future area of the Manas cuture. The twin cities of Kitezh, described in the Kitezh legend(s) as a historical place, and the preceding deeds of the Round Table of King Vladimir, as historical events, form the unquestioned climax of these preparations. Therefore Russia's early history and all the parallel mythological events anticipate Russia's future history in the form of a working plan for the future cultural and racial development of Manas. Generally and specifically, everything concerning this history and its mythological reverse side (the bylini, the Kitezh legends) as a process of the Call and the Answer, as the link between Kitezh and Kiev, is therefore also related to Russia's future and to Russia as a future Manichean cultural area and racial area.

The idea outlined above does not only apply in terms of spiritual science. The mythological reverse side of early Russian history is itself aware of this, and mentions it. Therefore this is also a historical reality. This is revealed in the Kitezh legend which states that Great Kitezh, submerged in the Svetli Jarr, will one day rise up. One of the bylini (the bylina 'How the Bogatyri of Holy Russia meet their death') reveals that the dead Russian heroes of the Grail will one day return to save Russia — this time for good. Furthermore, the Novgorod bards kept this and all the other bylini alive by means of their magical powers of recitation, in the belief that this would help to bring back to life the Russian heroes.

The author, Zamjatin, described how this early Russian history, in the form of songs, concluded in the present: 'Russia has no other future than her Russian past (not her Soviet past)' (Quoted by Kyrill Gradov in 'The Way Back', an article in the NRC Handelsblad on 22 November 1986).

This retrospective theme can be formulated in a more general way: Russia's early history is an historical icon of Russia's future which is lost in time. The account of this history — the written history, the bylini and the Kitezh legends — constitute a permanent literary icon of this, or simply 'The Ikon'. It should be remembered that an icon must be interpreted as a depiction, an anticipatory image in the form of a basic incarnation for and of an essential aspect that will come. This underlines the fact that Russia is aware of and bears witness to the literary icon, the icon of its future, just as this future was anticipated in the historical icon. As such, the whole of Russian iconography is not much more than the logical result of this basic pattern of icons in Russian history and historical writings. This theme will be explored in greater detail in Chapter 5.

The realization of the Apocalyptic character of early Russian history serves to heighten that character. This is a third point that should be remembered in relating this history.

The Russian people form a branch of the great Slav race, the race that is descended from the Persians and Scythians, and is related in particular to the Finns and the Varangians (Germanic races). In the mists of antiquity these people gradually moved to the west. In the centuries before Christ they lived in present-day southern Poland, Rumania and west Russia. Three groups of Slavs can be distinguished: western Slavs, southern Slavs and eastern Slavs. The western Slavs were the predecessors of the Czechs, Slovaks and Poles. The southern Slavs were the predecessors of the Yugoslavs (Serbs, Croats, Bosnians, Montenegrans, etcetera) and of the Bulgarians.

The eastern Slavs were the predecessors of the Russians. They were subdivided into several tribes or *rods* with which we are concerned here. The two leading *rods* were the Poljanje and the Slavjanje. The names of these tribes are terms derived from Ancient Persian. Poljanje (from Polvene) means the workers and tillers of the earth as the sacred body of the planetary spirit. If it is assumed that today Christ is the planetary spirit of the earth, the sacred significance of Poljanje is therefore: the tillers, ploughmen, or labourers of the body of Christ. Freely translated, 'Poljanje' means peasants.

The Slavjanje (from Slovene) were the carriers or bearers of the Holy Word. Freely translated, 'Slavjanje' means singers. The whole of the eastern Slav race excelled in its agriculture and singing. The Poljanje excelled particularly in the former, and the Slavje (later on) in the latter. Coming from the west, the Poljanje settled in southern Russia and founded the city of Kiev on the Dnieper, and further to the north, Chernigov and Rostov. Coming from the west, the Slavjanje settled in northern Russia near Lake Ilmen, where they founded Novgorod on the Volchov, and Pskov to the west. (Later on, the Poljanje, coming from the land of Slavjanje founded the city of Kitezh to the east of Moscow in Central Russia.)

With regard to the meaning of the names of the main eastern Slav tribes, it is interesting to remember the following details. It was particularly the Poljanje, the peasants of Kiev, who founded the culture of the Grail related to the farming community, as mentioned in the introduction to the Kitezh legend. The discussion of the dual character of the Christian mystery of the Eucharist revealed that in Kiev the earth was viewed as the Holy Grail, and that King Vladimir's knights of the Grail were not seeking a chalice, but were workers of the Earth Grail, in other words, peasants. In the discussion of the bylini, particularly those about Mikoela Seljaninovich and Ilja Muromjetz, who were both peasants, this theme is also prominent.

It was particularly the Slavjanje, or singers in Novgorod (during and after

111

the collapse of Kiev Rus), who sang about the great deeds of the Poljanje in the south of Russia. The Slavjanje minstrels were known as the Skazitjeli. Throughout the centuries there has been great speculation regarding the question of why it was only in Novgorod that the Slavjanje sang and kept alive these Kiev bylini, which had been disseminated everywhere by the Poljanje as they fled from the Tartars during and after the Tartar invasions of Genghis Khan and Batu Khan in Southern Russia. No satisfactory answer has ever been found to this question. However, if we remember that the Slavjanje (word-bearers) were predestined to sing these songs because of their name, this explains why the bylini were only sung by them.

In the discussion of the bylini, particularly those on the two Novgorod heroes, Vaseli Buslajev and Sadko, it will be pointed out that they form an aspect of the so-called function of a herald like St John, which Novgorod fulfilled for Kiev. In the functioning of Novgorod as St John, Russia's knowledge of its own future, i.e. what is called the Icon, becomes a magnet which attracts that future.

Let us return to the eastern Slav tribes. In addition to the Poljanje and the Slavjanje, there were also the Sewerjanje (the northerners) and the Drewljanje (the forest-dwellers). We will not dwell on the sacred aspect of these names, referring to a spiritual relation with ice (tundra) and forest respectively. The Sewerjanje and Drewljanje were at a much lower level of cultural development than the Poljanje and Slavjanje. The latter's civilization was as advanced as that of the Germanic tribes.

The Germanic tribes had the unconscious skill to organize themselves in a social, political, and military sense. They had this skill as a result of the unconscious inspiration of certain spiritual forces. In this way they prepared themselves for some time during the fourth Aryan cultural period — separately from the contemporary intellectual and emotional soul culture of the Greeks, Romans, Jews, Arabs and Romanians — so that they would have the skill in a conscious sense (in the Self) during the fifth cultural period.

The eastern Slavs (Poljanje and Slavjanje) had the unconscious intention of allowing each other spiritual freedom, giving each other equal rights, and sharing the fruits of the earth amongst each other with brotherly love. Unconsciously they started fulfilling Christ's law of love: 'Love God above all others, and your neighbour as yourself.' This intention was again inspired in an unconscious way by certain spiritual forces. In this way they prepared themselves during the fourth Aryan cultural period — separately from the cultural development of the time — so that in the sixth cultural period and in the sixth root race era, they would have this intention in an entirely conscious way, as a characteristic of Manas (to serve Manicheism). As the development of Manas requires external force of the Self, even when it is operating unconsciously — for the development of Manas in itself requires the death of some internal Self force — the eastern Slavs endeavoured to unite with the Germanic tribes (at that time known as the

112

Varangians). As a result of the unconscious inspiration of the spirit of these peoples, the following developments took place.

There was a temporary domination by the Swedish Varangians of the eastern Slavs who lived in unconscious Christian brotherly love. The unconscious impulse to prepare the development of the conscious soul was present in the former's architecture — *wanderlust* and social structure — and took place in the light of Christianity. However, this domination resulted in the eastern Slavs appealing to the Swedish Varangians for social leadership.

The Varangians sent three princes from their Rus tribe to the eastern Slavs. Only the oldest of the three, Rurik, lived a long life, and in the year 862 he settled in Novgorod to rule over all the eastern Slavs up to 879. He reorganized the eastern Slav nation both socially and militarily as a republic. As mentioned above, this request from the Slavs and the Varangian compliance with it have been called the Slav Rurik Call and the Varangian Answer to it. It will become clear that this 'Answer' started with Rurik's reorganization.

Most historians assume that the eastern Slav nation acquired the name of Russia because it was named after Rurik's tribe Rus. On the other hand, Rudolf Steiner believed that the name Russia was of Finnish origin, derived from the Finnish word 'Ruotsi'. This word means: the people that breathe in the Word or Logos, anchoring its essence. In fact, Ruotsi means the same as Slavjanje: the Bearers of the Word.

Rurik of Rus made his social and military arrangements by granting large tracts of land to the generals in his army. They settled on the land as a military nobility. These military noblemen extended their territories, often at the expense of the Slav peasants.

This Varangian Answer of social and military help brings us straightaway to a paradox. It immediately reveals that while early Russian history expressed the process of the Call and (persistent) Answer, i.e. the process of the unification of the Varangian Self and the Slav Manas, strictly in cultural and historical terms for the future, light is shed particularly on the negative side of unconscious inspiration, on non-Manas aspects. Unconsciously inspired man (culture) often remains bound to former laws of evolution, such as the survival of the fittest, an eye for an eye and a tooth for a tooth, quite outside this unconscious inspiration, even if this inspiration is concerned with the preparation of the Self and the development of Manas, which in themselves require conscious inspiration. This is apparent in a cultural and historical context.

It is only when this early Russian history expresses and idealizes the process of the Call and Answer in a mythological sense, i.e. particularly in the bylini and the Kitezh legends but also in many historical legends, that its Manas icon aspect is revealed in the first place, as we have seen and will show again in the following chapters.

This means that Russian history depicts Rurik and his followers as Manas

113

people in terms of the Self to a much lesser extent than the heroes of the bylini and the Kitezh legend. Rurik and his followers are preparing a future Manas culture, but apart from their moments of enlightenment, they often are and remain unconscious groups. The Bogatyri of the bylini and the rulers of Kitezh do the same, but in the context of the stories in which they play a role they are to some extent Manas people with a Self — they are Self and Manas icon people. These ideas serve to define the first and second point of view, from which Russian history is written, and are also an expression of its first and second essential characteristics.

Let us examine Rurik's followers. During Rurik's reign, Kiev, the capital of Poljanje, paid tribute to the Chazars, a people of the steppes, of a Jewish religious persuasion. Two of Rurik's generals, Askoljd and Dier, defeated that nation and established a new principality in Kiev, though it was not incorporated in the Republic of Novgorod.

Rurik died in 879. His son Igor was still only a child. The government of northern Russia was taken over by Oleg, a regent and a member of the child's family. In 882 he conquered Kiev for Igor, killed Askoljd and Dier, and elevated this city in Poljanje which had been conquered, to become the capital of Russia. Novgorod receded further and further into the background.

It could be said that Novgorod had first expressed a strictly cultural and historical aspect of the herald function, for which it was predestined with regard to Kiev, so that later (after the downfall of Kiev) it could be taken up again and serve as a basis to fulfil a more artistic and mythological aspect of that function, i.e. to collect and spread the bylini. In this the bylini would be used to refer back to the mythological aspect of Russia's former Manas culture and anticipate that of Russia's future. This corresponds with what was said about the function of Novgorod as a herald and, as mentioned above, it will be discussed in more detail in the next chapter in the commentary on the bylini about Vaseli Buslajev and Sadko.

Oleg made an unforgettable impression on his Slav subjects, as though he were a magician with power over nature. After his death in 912 the people of Kiev identified him as the so-called Older Bogatyr Volga Sviatoslavovich. There is one bylina that describes how he used magic to subdue Russia's rich but initially wild nature. The identification of Oleg with Volga is the first example of a one-to-one correspondence of a historical figure with a mythological hero. The following legend about Oleg underlines that he was unconsciously inspired by Volga, i.e. that he was a Self and Manas icon person with a large element of the brute in him.

Oleg was told that it was his fate to be killed by his horse, a symbol for the physical–personal aspect of his being. Therefore he killed and buried the animal, and consequently, to compensate for his weak Self force, he became ascetic. Many years later he repented of his act and dug up the animal. (Asceticism and the accompanying unconscious inspiration cannot permanently replace the Self and the Manas, and the accompanying

114

conscious inspiration.) A snake in the horse's skull bit and killed him. He was overcome by the essential force of the personal element, the so-called serpent fire of the soul as an impure force. This will be explained in more detail below.

Nevertheless, Oleg created order in Russia's nature, just as Rurik had created order in a social and military sense. Therefore Oleg continued to provide the (historical) Varangian Answer to the Slav Call for order. Thus the Varangian Answer is an answer with a genealogy, a genealogy which is parallel to that of Rurik's dynasty.

The legend of Oleg's death reveals once again that Oleg's creation of order bore within it the seeds of transience, and therefore had a temporary character — it could not be more than a temporary expression, an icon, of the eternal future. This transience characterizes the entire genealogy of the Varangian Answer, as will be indicated repeatedly. Kiev Rus, the Round Table of Kiev, and the holy city of Kitezh achieve a certain stage of development, but were destroyed because they were not created by man fully enough to survive.

When the Varangian Answer culminated in the Christian communist order of Kitezh, an evil but necessary fate entered into force: foreign powers overran Russia. All this contained in the Kitezh legends, and will be explained in more detail.

Oleg died in 912. After his death Rurik's son Igor ruled over Russia from 912 to 945. He did not create order in the land, but acquired new territory where order could be created. In 915 he conquered the south-eastern coast of Persia, and in 944 assured the tribute of Constantinople. Many different cultural influences vied for supremacy in southern Russia at the beginning of the tenth century: the influence of Islam from Persia, the Christian influence from Constantinople, and the Jewish influence from the conquered Chazar people. On the one hand, the state of Poljanje expanded on its own initiative; on the other hand, diverse spiritual influences from all the occupied territories in Russia vied to establish a monopoly. It was during Igor's reign that the basis was laid in Kiev for the famous religious choice of King Vladimir the Holy of Kiev later on.

Igor was captured in 945 during a campaign against the savage Drewljanja. Their leader tied Igor's legs to two treetops that had been forced together, so that the body of the king was torn apart when the treetops were released.

Igor was married to Olga, a Slavjanje woman from Pskov. After the death of her husband she governed the greatly expanded Russian kingdom from 945 to 957 as regentess for her young son Sviatoslav. According to legend, she avenged herself on the Drewljanje in the following way. She proposed marriage to their leader. However, when the leader sent delegates to arrange the ceremony, she killed all the members of the delegation. She went to the capital of Drewljanje, Korosten, which was almost impossible to enter, besieged it and informed the leader that she would make peace for the price of two doves per household. Olga tied burning torches onto the tails of the doves she had been granted, and then let them go. They flew back to their houses and Korosten burned down. Previously Olga had made peace with the Greeks in Constantinople, and had been converted to Christianity.

The legend of her victory over the Drewljanje shows how after her conversion it became her mission to introduce a new religious order in Russia — initially in an external sense. Thus her mission became her contribution to the Varangian Answer for order.

The legend can justifiably be interpreted as false treachery by a vengeful widow (Olga as a brute child of her time), as well as a Christian activity of an inspired Christian, a Self and Manas icon person (without a consciousness of Self). In the latter interpretation the doves are the symbol of the Holy Ghost. In combination with the fire of Olga's faith, they consume the heathen world of Korosten, and in this way succeed in converting the Drewljanja. History has shown that the Russians found it difficult to accept her order, probably because of the difference between her intentions as an inspired person and as a private person, though these differences are concealed in the legend. The order decayed and that decay can be viewed as a vague foreshadowing of the subsequent decay of Kiev Rus and Kitezh as a result of similar causes.

Olga died in 969. She was later canonized by the Russian Church.

In 957 Olga's son Sviatoslav took over the government of Russia from his mother at the age of 15. Despite his Slav name, he was more of a Varangian than a Slav. He was a military man through and through, and was totally uninterested in his mother's religion. The conversion of Russia to Christianity did not continue during his reign (957-72).

After subduing all the savage Slav and many Mongol tribes in the east, the Greeks asked him to go to war against the Bulgarians, who were troublesome in Constantinople in the west. He defeated them and annexed their territory to Russia. This was not in accordance with the agreement he had made with the Greeks. Therefore he entered into war with his former allies who had paid tribute to him. Despite his courage and against his own expectations, he was in danger of losing the war. However, after a long and useless seige of the city of Drista, the Greek King John Cimisches offered him an honourable peace, which Sviatoslav accepted. Returning to Kiev from Drista in 972, he was unexpectedly attacked and murdered by members of the subdued Pjetsjenjeg tribe.

Sviatoslav did not create a new order in the life of Russia, but he intensified and consolidated the social, political and military order instigated by his ancestor Rurik. With Sviatoslav the genealogy of the historial Varangian-Rurik Answer to the Slav-Rurik Call was consolidated. The eastern Slav culture during the time of Sviatoslav was holding its breath as it were, for the imminent enormous leap forward in the Varangian creation of order.

Sviatoslav had three sons: Jaropolk, Oleg and Vladimir. Before his campaign against the Bulgarians he appointed Jaropolk stadtholder of Kiev, Oleg stadtholder of Rostov, and Vladimir stadtholder of Novgorod.

When Sviatoslav was killed in 972, Jaropolk was no longer content with the territory alloted to him and began a struggle to gain power over all of Russia. This struggle lasted until 980. In that year Vladimir defeated Jaropolk's army with Varangian reinforcements and had Jaropolk killed. Oleg had already been killed by Jaropolk.

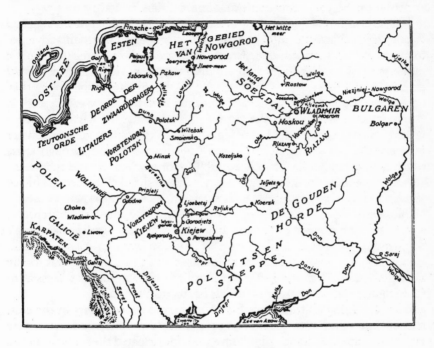

Russia in the 11th, 12th and 13th centuries.
(Taken from 'The History of the Russian People, Part 1'
by Boris Raptschinsky, W.J. Thieme, Zutphen 1927.)

Vladimir settled in Kiev in 980 to become Russia's sole ruler. He reigned from 980 to 1015. Initially he worshipped the ancient Russian Gods. Peroén the Thunderer, Volos the Singer, Jaroviet the Warrior, Lado the Lover. However, they did not have a permanent effect on him. According to the legend of his conversion, in about 988 he summoned representatives from the Jewish, Muslim, and Greek Christian religions to Kiev, so that on the basis of their religious arguments he could choose which religion he and his people would follow in the future. Vladimir saw a great deal of good in every religion, but he considered that the Jewish god Yahweh was too much a god of vengeance, while the god of Islam, Allah, was too much a god of commands and prohibitions. For him, Yahweh and Allah's promise of a heavenly life to replace the earthly vale of tears was subject to conditions which were too strict and only applied after death.

In the end Vladimir chose Christianity, because Christ seemed to him to be the god of brotherly love, and because this god announced that the kingdom of God, which was generally thought to exist only in heaven, could be revealed on earth through brotherly love and love of one's neighbours. To confirm his choice, he married the Greek princess Anna, the sister of the Christian emperor Basilios II of Constantinople.

The historical account of Vladimir's conversion is rather different. According to that version, King Vladimir only chose Christianity in order to be able to marry Princess Anna. She had been granted to him by Emperor Basilios II as a reward for defeating the Bulgarians who had threatened Constantinople, though only on condition that he would become a Christian and make Kiev a Christian state.

The same story is told of the great Kaghan ruler of the Khazars, who is believed to have summoned representatives of the three major religions to debate the merits of their beliefs. (See *Dictionary of the Khazars*, by Milorad Pavić, London: Hamish Hamilton, 1989).

According to both legend and history, Vladimir had all the images of the heathen gods burnt, and the large statue of the heathen god Peroén, which he himself had ordered to be erected on a hill in Kiev when he was a young man, was tied to the tail of a horse, dragged through the streets of Kiev, and thrown into the Dnieper.

Shortly after his conversion Vladimir commissioned the first stone cathedral in Russia: the Cathedral of Our Lady of One Tenth in Kiev. (The ruler contributed a tenth of his total income towards the building of this cathedral — hence its name.) In addition he built many monasteries, schools and almshouses. Vladimir accepted the Bible and the Christian sacraments, but he did not adopt Church Latin. He had the Christian texts translated into Ancient Slav, which was to be one factor in the emancipation of Russian and Greek orthodox Christianity, in relation to the Roman Catholic Church. Later he was canonized by the Church, and was given the name Ravnoapostolny ('like an apostle').

The historical King Vladimir, known as 'the Holy', is identified, as indicated above, with the legendary King Vladimir, known as the 'Red Sun', who is the subject of most so-called heroic bylini. This identification is the clearest example of the one-to-one correspondence between a historical and a mythical hero.

As there are a number of references to the historical King Vladimir, and his genealogy can be verified, it can be assumed that he really was a historical figure, and can serve as a framework for the outlined pattern of correspondence in which Kiev can be related to Kitezh.

Because of his above-mentioned deeds, the historical King Vladimir is also viewed as the founder of the Christian Russian single state of Kiev Rus (988). In this sense he is a sort of Russian Charlemagne. Like him, and like his ancestors, he occasionally serves as an unconscious inspiration, which led to the esoteric Christian aspect of the state, as well — usually — as an uncontrolled person. This led to the survival of many aggressive and heathen elements in that state, and to a wild personal life.

The legendary King Vladimir of the heroic bylini was the founder of the Round Table, a Slav fellowship of the Grail, which was aimed at liberating Russia from all sorts of unhealthy forces, symbolized by dragons. As such, he is the Russian King Arthur, virtually always unconsciously inspired, virtually entirely a 'Self and Manas icon person'.

Just as Sviatoslav had consolidated Rurik's military and social order, King Vladimir, as a historical hero, consolidated Olga's religious order. In this consolidation — which was no more than the foundation of Kiev Rus — once again he included all the orders of his ancestors aimed at the outside world, i.e. Russia's exoteric order. As a mythological hero he also started to work on Russia's inner moral order, i.e. its esoteric order. As the 'Red Sun' — the symbol of the Grail sun, clarified in the following chapter — Vladimir gave Russia its own Grail Christianity, the basis for the later historical communist Christianity of Kitesh. With his Round Table he laid the foundation for the subsequent foundation of Kitezh, the Christian communist state of the twelfth and thirteenth centuries.

Summarizing these matters in non-historic terms for the sake of clarity, it could be said that the social and military expansionism of the Varangians in space and time, which unconsciously led to Christianity, and the moral drive towards brotherly love amongst the eastern Slavs, which also unconsciously led to Christianity, intermingled by means of a genealogical process of Call and Answer in the Slav and Varangian kings' development of order. This led to the establishment of a temporary eastern Slav culture anticipating the future culture.

This culture culminated in the foundation of the Christian state of Kiev Rus, particularly as a result of the conversion to Christianity of Olga and Vladimir. Olga brought Russia an exoteric Graeco-Slav Christianity based on the Christian culture of Constantinople, leading it away from Varangian Slavdom. Vladimir, as a mythological hero, brought Russian an esoteric Slav Christianity, the Christianity of the Grail described in the bylini. These two forms of Christianity, particularly the latter, formed the basis for the communist state of Kitezh.

In 1015 Vladimir died a peaceful death. He had seven sons. Like his father Sviatoslav, he divided his land among his sons before his death. His oldest son, Sviatopolk, a savage, inherited Kiev. After his father's death, he immediately had his pious brothers Boris (of Rostov) and Gljeb (of Muerom), who were later canonized, treacherously killed. This evil deed is referred to at the beginning of the Slav Church version of the Kitezh legend. Not long after this double murder Sviatopolk killed another brother (Sviatoslav), and then marched against the brother who had inherited Novgorod, the intelligent Jaroslav. After four years' fighting, and with the help of his father-in-law, King Boleslav Chobry of Poland, the ruler of Novgorod defeated and killed the aggressive Sviatopolk, later nicknamed Okajannys, the Damned.

His acts show the extent to which the swing from manifestations of lust for power to the establishment of an order based on unconscious divine inspiration applied within the genealogy of the Varangian Rurik Answer every bit as much as it applied in the life of a single Russian ruler. Apart from Jaroslav, Vladimir's son Mstislav had also survived. According to the Slav Church version of the Kitezh legend, he was the father of the founder of Kitezh.

From 1019 to 1054, Jaroslav was the sole ruler of Kiev Rus. In accordance with the tradition of his ancestors he established a particular order among the eastern Slavs. Jaroslav provided Kiev Rus with an official political and legal order. He had the first Russian law book drawn up, the *Ruskaya Pravda*, (the Russian Truth). In the so-called regulation of the Senoriat he formally provided that the eldest son of a Prince of Kiev should take over his father's throne, and that the younger sons would become city rulers. Jaroslav's legal order, in complete contrast with the orders of his predecessors, was to a large extent the work of man, and was hardly influenced by unconscious spiritual inspiration.

This is clear, for example, from the lack of legends about Jaroslav and the development of his order, since legends always indicate a spiritual influence. As the work of man, his order was not yet characterized by human Manichean perfection, based on conscious spiritual inspiration, to enable it to take root, though it did have a characteristic of 'iconless' personal skill and integrity.

Jaroslav is identified as the most influential ruler to reign over Kiev Rus, even though the orders of Oleg, and particularly of Vladimir, were much more fundamental and profound. However, these were not really the work of man. Jaroslav already had a strong Self, like the later Varangians and the west European people of a conscious soul culture. He was ahead of his time, and was therefore known as Jaroslav the Wise.

The wisest aspect of his legal order was the fact that he adopted a legal form for what was most important to the eastern Slavs of his time: the respect for man's spiritual freedom, equal rights for everyone, and the manifestation of brotherly love in sharing the fruits of the earth. The weakness in his approach was that he did not sufficiently understand that freedom only applies in spiritual life (outside this, for example in sharing the fruits of the earth, it only leads to freedom in the sense of being un-restrained); that equal rights apply only in a legal sense (outside this framework, again for example in sharing the fruits of the earth, it leads to equal portions of food for a baby and a builder, and in spiritual life, to equal conditions of employment for a civil servant and an inventor); that the manifestation of brotherly love applies only to the sharing of food, clothing, warmth, and so on (outside this context, for example in the legal world, it gives rise to nepotism and class-related justice).

Because of the wisdom of Jaroslav's legal order, the kingdom of Kiev reached its economic and social zenith under Jaroslav. It had a triple political framework, a curious juxtaposition of autocratic, aristocratic and democratic elements. Obviously the autocratic element was the ruler himself. The aristocratic element was formed by the ruler's council of advisors, the Duma, which mainly comprised military leaders and boyars (land owners). The democratic element was formed by so-called 'vetsches' or municipal councils of towns in which any free person could participate. The decisions of the vetsche, who could arbitrate in all sorts of unimportant matters such as quarrels between neighbours, as well as important matters such as appointing or deposing the city ruler (see the beginning of the Slav Church version of the legend of Kitezh), had to be approved unanimously. In Novgorod, the cradle of Kiev Rus, the vetsche was more influential than in other cities.

Jaroslav's legal order, or state, was unable to survive because of its inherent weaknesses, and broke down after his death. For example, the requirement of unanimity in the decisions of the vetches was unjustified. This requirement is an incorrect combination of freedom of expression (an aspect of spiritual life) and equal treatment (an aspect of legal life), and the result was that the cities became ungovernable. Furthermore, his sons were quite unable to make peace with the senoriat. This arrangement merely replaced a great ancient inequality (disinheriting all the sons of a ruler, apart from the eldest), by a lesser inequality.

During Jaroslav's reign the hermit Ilarion built Kiev's famous 'Cave monastery', Kiejevo-Pieterskaya Lavra. The Russian Church believes that the mortal remains of the saints buried there (and in other cave monasteries) are everlasting and are awaiting resurrection. This means that they are waiting for the resurrection of the Russia of the future, so that when this has arrived, they can carry this kingdom spiritually as new saints. This 'waiting' of the saints is parallel, and to some extent the same, as the waiting of the bogatyri, for the time when that Russia of the future can be activated, as described in the next chapter. This spiritual waiting of the saints started at the time of Jaroslav's legal state, which was itself founded on the force of Self. It is also paralleled by the sleeping king legends of Arthur and his twelve knights.

After Jaroslav's death in 1054 the struggle between his sons and grandsons for the succession was so long and intensive that it was not until 1113 that one of Jaroslav's grandsons, Vladimir Monomach, the ruler of Chernigov, was able to restore unity to Russia and take over the throne in Kiev. He put an end to the Polovtsen, who had exploited the quarrel for the succession between Jaroslav's followers and increased the chaos of half a century of discord. He then successfully marched against Constantinople, which was becoming increasingly independent of Kiev.

He won such a convincing victory over the Greeks that they recognized him as their emperor (according to legend), and presented him with a crown that later became the Russian crown of the Tsars and was known as 'the hat of Monomach'. Vladimir accepted the hat, but never wanted to wear it himself. (His successors wore it, and it was only in the reign of Peter the Great that the hat of Monomach was replaced.)

Vladimir Monomach was a chivalrous, courageous and God-fearing man. His testament to his sons ends with the words: 'Children, fear neither the battle nor the wild beast. Be a man. Nothing can hurt you if it is not the will of God. God protects better than man.'

Vladimir Monomach died in 1125. He had not brought order to Russia in any new field, but as a private person, and unconsciously inspired as a Self and Manas icon person, he had brought together and harmonized the orders of his ancestors, insofar as these concerned the external aspects of life. In his time, the (historical) Answer of the Varangian Order to external aspects of life was expressed in a harmonious way at least as long as he lived. After his death this expression became an unharmonious cacophony. The inner esoteric order of Kiev Rus, which had been introduced by Vladimir, the Red Sun of Kiev, with the Round Table of Kiev, survived for some time. It was the dissolution of the external order of Kiev Rus that led to the greatest development of its inner order, culminating in the foundation of the Christian communist city of Great Kitezh in 1168.

The sons and grandsons of Vladimir Monomach feared neither battle nor wild animal. But against the wishes of their dead father, and like so many earlier pretenders to the throne, they fought among themselves to be the sole ruler of Russia. As a result most of Kiev Rus's principalities were weakened and they were no longer able to successfully defend themselves against the incursions of neighbouring territories. The chaos throughout the land was even greater than it had been between the end of the reign of Jaroslav in 1054 and the beginning of the government of Vladimir Monomach in 1113. Only Novgorod, which was largely protected by marshes and woods against enemy incursions, achieved a fairly high standard of prosperity.

In 1157 Andrei Bogoljubski, the brave, skilled but despotic ruler of Vladimir-Suzdal, situated on the Oka and the Volga, succeeded in taking Kiev. He was a son of Juri Dolgoruki ('of the long arms') and a grandson of Vladimir Monomach, who had inherited Suzdal. After taking Kiev, Andrei Bogoljubski decided to remain in his provincial capital. This city was situated in an area where the Slavs were increasingly mixing with Finns, which led to the new tribe of the so-called Great Russians. Later on, Moscow became their capital. In 1174 Andrei Bogoljubski was murdered for his despotism by a group of rebellious boyars. With him there was an unharmonious end to the historical Answer the the Varangian Order for the external aspects of life — the exoteric Varangian Order.

He was succeeded by his brother Vsevolod (III) Boljoje Gnjezdo (the Large Nest). He became the founder of a new generation of rulers, hence his nickname. However, these rulers only ruled in name, as a result of the Tartar domination. Vsevolod ruled from 1174 to 1212. He was not like his brother, and did not subdue his people with violence but served them with diplomacy and peace.

During the life of the two Suzdal brothers (while the former was ruling), which was the perfect expression of the answer of the Varangian Order to the external aspects of life, partly through violence and partly through peace, the son of a namesake of the latter founded Kitezh. He was the ruler of Pskov, Georgi (Juri) Vsevolodovich, a distant cousin of the two brothers. It was this distant cousin who was introduced as the great-grandson of Vladimir the Holy in the Slav Church version of the Kitezh legend.

Prince Vladimir Monomach
(After an old Russian Church banner. According to 'Antiquités de l'empire de Russie'.)

In this way, continuing the genealogical beginning of the Slav Church version of the Kitezh legend, the legendary founder of Kitezh can be identified as one of the many great-great-grandchildren descended from King Vladimir the Holy, or one of the many distant cousins related to Andrei Bogoljubski and Vsevolod Boljoje Gnjezdo.

As in the case of King Vladimir the Holy, Georgi Vsevolodovich was also sufficiently rooted in the Rurik dynasty that he may be assumed to have been a historical person. In relation to the legendary Juri, the founder of Kitezh, he can probably be identified as the figure who serves as the link

123

with King Vladimir, both the historical and the legendary king. In more precise terms, Georgi (Juri) Vsevolodovich, like King Vladimir the Holy, was both a significant legendary figure and a more or less historical figure, forming what was referred to above as a one-to-one correspondence.

It may be stated that Kitezh and the Round Table of Kiev are interrelated, because the legendary founder of Kitezh as a historical person appears to be related in a historical, genealogical sense to the legendary founder of the Round Table of Kiev as a historical person. Within the context of early Russian history as an organic whole, this relationship is revealed by the Slav Rurik Call and the Varangian Answer. More precisely, it can justifiably be stated that:

a)   this relationship expresses the esoteric aspect of the Varangian Answer, which culminates in Kitezh, just as the exoteric aspect of the Answer is expressed.
b)   Kitezh therefore serves as the social conclusion of a Grail Christianity initiative introduced in Kiev in the form of a Christian communist city state (as a utopia for the future).

The various Varangian Orders that have been reviewed did not all develop on the basis of conscious spiritual inspiration and the related development of the Self and of Manas; nor was this the case with regard to the Christian communist Order of Kitesh. Like all historical individual orders, it was merely a historical icon, anticipating a future order, and therefore it had to disappear. All that remains is the legend as a literary icon. Sixty-eight years after it was founded in 1236, Kitezh disappeared from the surface of the earth as a result of Tartar aggression.

This was during the reign of Vsevolod Boljoje Gnjezdo's son, Juri II. Under Vsevolod, Russia became a Mongol vassal state. In 1237 Batu Khan conquered the whole of Kiev Rus apart from Novgorod, where its ruler, Alexander Nevsky, with the help of Novgorod's favourable position between the woods and the marshes, succeeded in remaining free of the Mongol yoke and, moreover, the oppression of the Swedes, the Teutonic Knights and the Lithuanians, whom he defeated respectively in 1240, 1243 and 1246.

The bylina 'How the bogatyri of Holy Russia meet death' explains Russia's subjugation from a mythological viewpoint (together with the Kitezh legend). When Russia was overrun by Mongols, or Tartarism represented by a lack of Self, (i.e. when the Mongol Orda was introduced), some unasked for Answers start to sound to the Slav Rurik Call. The Mongol Orda is the order that implies the lack of spiritual freedom, which treats every person equally by treating him as though he has no Self. It uses a form of taxation rather than brotherly love in sharing out the fruits of the earth.

In the first place, there is the actual Mongol Answer, a Luciferian Answer. There is also an unasked for Varangian Answer (in addition to and after the asked for Answer), an Ahriman materialist answer given to Tsar Peter the Great by the Anglo-Saxons. (It should be noted that Slavdom certainly did not require this Answer, but Peter the Great asked for it as the representative of the Mongol influence in that Slav nation.) Finally there is the unasked for Answer of Soviet Communism, an Ahriman and Luciferian Answer, given by the Anglo-Saxons and the Mongols together. These two last Answers further emphasize the outline of the first Answer of the Mongol Orda.

In the commentary on the bylini about the bogatyr Ilya Muromets, the theme of these unasked for answers is raised again. It should be pointed out again that no matter how dramatic they are, they were and are necessary to transform the unconscious pre-Manichean Christianity of early Russia into the conscious Manichean Christianity of the Russia of the future, by means of a new 'Self-conscious' Answer of the Varangian Order.

To return to Alexander Nevsky of Novgorod, it should be noted that eventually he did pay tribute to the Mongols as a result of the pressure of his isolation, although he succeeded in saving his city from being taken. During his reign some of the Kiev Poljanje fled to Novgorod. As stated before, it was the Novgorod Slavjanje, and only they, who started to sing the bylini of the Poljanje as well as their own. Thus in a magic sense they became 'word bearers', and the witnesses to St John preparing the path for a future Kiev Rus. This was like a seed, dormant in the stories of the historical Kiev Rus, just as they had first been such witnesses for the historical Kiev Rus in a social and material sense at the time that their republic was founded during the reign of Rurik.

In other words, they received the literary icon of Russia's future, the icon as a tangible remnant of Russia's vanished early history (and the intangible historical icon of that future). As witnesses, they come to life to draw that future towards them by magnetism.

The genealogy of the (historical) Answer of the Varangian Order to the Slav–Rurik Call

Period		Event	Significance
Republic of Novgorod	862	Rurik comes to Novgorod from the land of the Varangians (Sweden) and founds the Varangian dynasty. In this way he answers the (historical) Slav–Rurik Call for order.	Social, military and political order of Russia.
	862–79	Reign of Rurik in Novgorod. Republic of Novgorod.	
Kingdom of Kiev	879–912	Reign of Oleg. Oleg transplants the democratic order of the Republic of Novgorod to Kiev and transmutes it into a kingdom.	Order in the savage nature of Russia.
	912–45	Reign of Igor	Russia expands so that order can be established in a larger territory.
	945–62	Reign of Olga	Religious order of Russia (exoteric).
	962–73	Reign of Sviatoslav	Consolidation of Rurik's social, political and military order.
	973–80	Jaropolk fights for the throne of Russia.	First period of disorder as a prelude to Russia being overrun by the Tartars.
	980–1015	Reign of Vladimir the Holy	Consolidation of Olga's exoteric religious order.
	988	Vladimir founds Kiev Russ. Foundation of the Round Table of Kiev.	Development of a Russian Grail Christianity as a basis for the later Christian communist city of Kitezh (esoteric).
Kiev Rus	1015–19	Fight between Vladimir's sons to become sole ruler over Kiev Rus.	Second period of disorder as a prelude to Russia being overrun by the Tartars.

1019–54	Reign of Jaroslav the Wise.	Legal order of Russia.
1054–1113	Fighting between the sons and grandsons of Jaroslav to become the sole ruler of Kiev Rus.	Third period of disorder as a prelude to Russia being overrun by the Tartars.
1113–25	Reign of Vladimir Monomach.	Summary and harmonization of all (exoteric) individual orders.
1125–57	Fighting amongst the sons and grandsons of Vladimir Monomach to become the sole ruler over Kiev Rus.	Fourth period of disorder as a prelude to Russia being overrun by the Tartars.
1157–74	This fight was won by Andrei Bogolyubski, the ruler of Vladimiar Suzdal. Vladimir-Suzdal becomes the capital of Kiev Rus.	The end of Russia's order in the external areas of life. The order in the inner areas of life in the land continues.
1174–1212	Reign of Vsevolod the Great Nest.	
1165–68	Building of Great Kitezh as a Christian communist city (state) by Juri Vsevolodovich, the ruler of Pskov, distance cousin of Vsevolod the Great Nest, and great-great-grandson of Vladimir the Holy.	Development and manifestation of the Christian communist city (state) of Kitezh as the social conclusion of King Vladimir, the Red Sun's Round Table quest for the Grail.
1168–1236	Growth of Kitezh. According to the Belski version of the legend of Kitezh, Juri Vsevolodovich and his son, Prince Vsevolod Jurivich ruled over the (double) city.	
1236–7	Destruction of Little Kitezh by a renewed attack of the Tartars led by Batu Khan. Great	

	Kitezh ascends or descends into the Svetli Jarr. Death of Juri Vsevolodovich and Vsevolod Jurivich.	End of Russia's order in the inner areas of life. End of Russia's esoteric religious order.
1237–40	Conquest of Russia by the Tartars under the leadership of Batu Khan. End of Kiev Rus. Only Novgorod stands up to the Tarts to some extent.	Russia in disorder because it is overrun by the Tartars.
1240–63	Alexander Nevsky, ruler of Novgorod, officially succeeds in opposing Tartar domination. However, in fact the city pays tribute to the Mongols.	The Novgorod Slavjanje singers start to sing of the heroic deeds of the Kiev Poljanje bogatyri.
1263–1380	Tartar domination. Moscow develops as Russia's most important principality.	Second inner function of Novgorod as a herald for Kiev.
1380	Dmitri Donskoi defeats the Mongols at the battle of Polje on the Don.	Brief repetition of Russia's order by the Varangians, as it had been.

Notes

The legend of Nikola the Holy is used here as a quotation preceding the outline of early Russian history. This quotation beautifully expresses the content of the story from 'a heavenly point of view'. It is not an epic poem as the earthly reverse side of this story. It is not a bylina and is therefore not included in any of the cycles of bylini.

The legend is the sort of story that relates Russia's destiny from the point of view of what must happen, and be prepared for this in and from the spiritual world — while the early history, the bylini, and some biographical legends like those about Oleg and Olga and the Kitezh legend relate this destiny (historically and mythologically respectively) from the viewpoint of what should happen and be prepared for this on earth. Legends such as those about Nikola the Holy, as well as Russian fairytales (which describe this preparation from the world of the soul), are not contained in this publication. The above-mentioned legend was quoted here to indicate that many stories other than the bylini and the Kitezh legend deal with matters with which the latter are concerned from a different point of view.

The Call and Answer aspect of Russian history, both past, present and future history, is expressed most basically in the last instance in the Call for technical and social help in building the temple of Jerusalem, and in King Solomon, who is lacking in Self but has great astral wisdom and the technically and socially skilled architect, Hiram Abif, who is strong in Self. The help that was asked for, and the Answer that was asked for, were both given, but ultimately fell on the wrong soil because of envy on the part of the asker of the achievements of the person who was asked.

The temple of Jerusalem (a symbol of an entirely new Manas world), just as the historical Kiev Rus or Kitezh is the image of a future Manas culture and a future Manas root race, was therefore not as perfect as it might have been.

For the basic pattern of Solomon's Call and Hiram Abif's Answer, see Rudolf Steiner, *The Temple Legend and the Golden Legend*. Furthermore, this Call of Solomon and Answer of Hiram Abif are also a reflection of an even more fundamental 'Call and Answer': of the multiple Call and Answer principle from the cosmology of Mani. This concerns the Call for assistance and liberation of primeval man, who has been sent down to the world of sin (where he was unable to redeem that world and became ensnared in it), addressed to the Father who sent him, and the latter's Answer (in the form of his son Jesus). For the basic pattern of this very first Call and very first Answer in the world, see Eugen Roll, *Mani, the Messenger of Light*.

The Call and Answer aspect of future Russian history in particular, viewed as a religious matter, can be identified in retrospect with the theorem of the Flioque. This theorem comprises:

1) The eastern Slavs traditionally believe that the Holy Ghost only

emanates from God the Father, and as such is merely a divine force of Self which comes to man outside his own Self, and provides him with unconscious inspiration.

2) The Germans believed, and still believe, that this Holy Ghost also emanates from God the Son (Christ), and as such is the Self of mankind (experienced in conscious inspiration).

3) The eastern Slavs must adopt the Germanic viewpoint by asking questions.

4
The Russian Bylini

Introduction

The epic Russian legends, which serve as the mythological counterpart to early Russian history (and several successive periods of history), take the form of the so-called bylina. The Kitezh legend and several biographical legends, such as those about Oleg and Olga, are exceptions to this. They take place on earth, not in the spiritual world.

The literary form of the bylina is very simple. The number of syllables per line is not prescribed (between approximately 7 and 16), and the emphasis is always on four syllables, which are not the last ones. The bylina is usually in verse form, and in some cases there is some indication of a division between verses. Generally there are 'parallel lines' in which the second line repeats the content of the first line in different words.

As stated above, the bylini were recited only in Novgorod and its surrounding areas — sometimes recited, sometimes sung — by *skomoroch*, or *skazitjeli* (minstrels). They were recited from memory, sometimes with additions. Several centuries later, the bylini were transcribed (by the great collector of folklore Kiriaveski, Rybnikov, and Hilferding). The heroes of the bylini are called *bogatyri*.

The bylini are divided into three groups. Firstly, there are the 'mythical bylini'. These refer back to Russia's distant past, and anticipate Russia's distant future (Russia during a sixth Manichean root race era). The bogatyri that play a role in these bylini are the ancient or primeval bogatyri. There are four of them: Sviatogor, Volkh Vseslavyevich, Volga Slavovslavjevich and Mikoela Seljaninovich. There is a mythical bylina about each of these bogatyri. The collection opens with these four mythical bylini.

Secondly, there are 'heroic bylini'. These are set during the time of Russia's early history (a less distant past) and anticipate Russia's near future (Russia during the sixth Manichean cultural era). The bogatyri who play a role in these bylini are the younger bogatyri. In addition, the bylini are about *kaliki*, who are ancient bogatyri converted to

Christianity, and who do not play a part in the mythical bylini.

The heroic bylini, of which there are very many, can be divided into cycles. Firstly, there is the Kiev cycle, the so-called cycle of the Round Table, or Christocentric cycle. The most important younger bogatyri who play a role in these are King Vladimir, Ilya Muromets, Dobrynya Nikitich, Alyosha Popovich, and the counterparts of the last three: Michailo Ivanovich Potyk, Stavior, Godinovich and Vasili Budimirovich. The most important kalika who plays a role in this bylini is Ivanich.

There are also several shorter cycles, each consisting of one bylina, such as the Song of Igor, and the bylina about Prince Roman Mstislavich. The most important young bogatyri who play a role in these are Prince Igor and Prince Roman Mstislavich respectively. Finally, there is the Novgorod cycle, or 'Cycle According to St John'. The most important young bogatyri who play a role in this are Vaseli Buslajev and Sadko.

The third group consists of 'historical bylini'. These are set in the time between early and future Russian history. To the extent that they are true bylini they are completely unimportant (and are not included in this work), and to the extent that they are important, they are not real bylini and the heroes who play a part in them are not true bogatyri. Two leading examples of the second category are the bylini about Dmiti Donskoi and Dmitri Ivanovich (the so-called pseudo Dmitri Ivanovich). These 'bylini' will not be included separately. They have so little mythological character that they can simply be viewed as part of history. Therefore this part of history concerning the two Dmitris will be described and interpreted in Chapter 5.

The present chapter will deal with the bylini in the first two categories, with commentaries. We begin with the four mythical bylini, of which the first is about the ancient bogatyr Sviatogor.

The Mythical Bylini

Sviatogor

The bogatyr (knight/hero) Sviatogor sat on the highest peak of the sheer Holy Mountains, as motionless as the rock itself. He meditated on his youth. He had always won every fight, but with his strength, his weight had also increased. Now the earth could no longer carry him, and he was sitting down.

After resting for centuries, the giant decided to risk once more sinking down into the soft earth, and he came down from the Carpathians on his steed. The steppe was empty as far as the eye could see, and he called out: 'Is there nowhere a knight who dares to fight me?' He threw his club, which weighed 300 poed, up into the air, and caught it as though it were a ball. The earth shook with the thunder of his voice, but there was no answer. Sviatogor went on: 'If I could find the gravity of the earth, I would attach a ring with a chain to heaven and pull heaven and earth together and link them with a bridge. That would be a wonderful way to test my strength, as no hero will come to me.' No sooner had he finished speaking than a figure appeared walking on the horizon. He was not in a hurry and carried a small sack on his back.

Sviatogor spurred on his horse, but miraculously he was unable to catch up with the walking figure. The giant called out: 'Hey there! Wait a moment!'

The walker stood still, took the sack from his back and placed it on the ground. Sviatogor greeted him and asked what was in the sack. The stranger answered: 'Illustrious Sviatogor! You are so strong that you can throw your club which weighs 300 *poed* into the air, and catch it as though it were a ball. Could you help me with my burden, and take this sack on your back?'

Sviatogor dismounted, and without thinking tried to pick up the sack. He was unable to do so, and no matter how much he strained, until he was sweating and bleeding, he could not manage to do it. Finally, he called out: 'What's in the sack, and who are you?' The walker answered: 'I am a peasant, Mikoela Seljaninovich. The gravity of the earth is in this bag. Sviatogor has found the gravity of the earth, but he is unable to lift up the earth in his turn.'

Commentary

Sviatogor is Russia's first ancient bogatyr. His name means 'holy mountain, mountain of initiation'. The increase in his strength and weight over the years — until he realizes his own name and becomes himself a 'holy mountain' — expresses how the ancient divine strength and will come to rest and are elaborated in the history of the world.

The holy mountain represents, *inter alia*, the heathen, non-Christian principle of initiation of the so-called Will or Father mysteries of the pre-Aryan root races with important offshoots into the fourth Aryan cultural period. Sviatogor is, *inter alia*, this principle, the essence of the Father mystery, and he is an initiate of it.[2]

Among the people of the north, who also include the Slavs, an initiate into the mysteries had to prove that he was worthy of his initiation into the mysteries by demonstrating his will and courage. The facts that Sviatogor had rested enough, and became active one again, and particularly his challenge to the peasant Mikoela Seljaninovich, the bearer of the gravity of the world, represent how the primeval divine strength and will are brought into motion on earth once again because of a realization of the divine limitations and rigidity, and the desire to do something about this.

The pre-Christian mysteries of the will, which provided knowledge and control for the entire pre-Christian world, seemed to be complete and perfect in themselves by the beginning of the Christian era. However this completeness was a sort of rigidity. It is true that the Ancient Mysteries wished to crown their previous work by connecting heaven and earth —

the aim of all mysteries, for heaven and earth need each other — but they are unable to do so because they cannot find the gravity of the world. The gravity of the world is the human Self, which is capable of loving freely. The earth, represented in the aspect of the lower Self, and heaven, represented in the aspect of the higher Self, are joined not outside that Self as the centre of gravity of the world, but within it.

The ancient pre-Christian mysteries were not familiar with the fusing, connecting power of love of the free human Self, and therefore they were unable to join heaven and earth by means of this Self. They merely used the spiritual forces of the physical Atman element, the forces of the will. They inspired man outside his Self through his unconscious will (physical being). Therefore they became much too great and too heavy, in the context of the will, as well as too important, and in the figure of Sviatogor they start to seek what they are lacking.

On his quest, Sviatogor spies Mikoela Seljaninovich, Nicholas the son of a peasant. At first he is unable to catch him up. It is only when Mikoela permits him to that he is able to approach him and greet him. Mikoela carries a small sack on his back. When the ancient and strong Sviatogor who has a powerful will is asked to pick up the sack, he is unable to lift it even one centimetre from the ground. According to Mikoela, the sack contains the gravity of the world, and he, Mikoela, is the only one who can carry this sack — without any difficulty.

Mikoela is a peasant, a Holy Peasant, which means that he works and ploughs the earth as the Holy Grail, the body of Christ, the Christ Self, which is Universal Love. This task makes him a Christopherus, or bearer of a Self, in contrast with Sviatogor. As a pre-historic (and post-historic) man, though not as a bourgeois man, he has an individual Self, a spark of Christ's Self, and therefore he is capable of loving freely, like Christ.[3] Through this task he is able to carry the heaviest power in the world — loving freely — which suffers everything and moves mountains without any difficulty. Obviously he carries this as something very small, his own Self, the centre of gravity of the world.

Initially Sviatogor does not bear a Self, he is unable to find the gravity of the world himself, and is therefore unable to carry love. He comes from the so-called world of the Father. He is taught and initiated by someone from the 'world of the Son' by Mikoela, the guardian and bearer of the human Self.[4]

The story of Sviatogor is the story of the earth and the destiny of the ancient divine strength and will. It reveals how the age-old principle of strength and the will in the pre-Christian world, the world of spiritual material principles, acquires a new meaning in the Christian principle of love. From the perspective of the future, the story of Sviatogor is the story of the future transformation of the physical body into Atman (during the Slav root race).

The interpretation of this first bylina requires even further clarification.

The mysteries cannot merely be classified as ancient pre-Aryan or pre-Christian and post-Christian mysteries, or, for example, as mysteries of the will and mysteries of love. It is also possible to classify them more in terms of their content. In this sense there are mysteries of measurement, number and weight. The mysteries of measurement should serve as a basis for the development of an occult technology to serve mankind — originating from America.

The mysteries of number are the basis for the development of an occult medical science serving mankind, originating in Western Europe. Those of weight are the basis of the development of an occult science of eugenics to serve mankind, originating in Eastern Europe. The interconnections between the last two mysteries and various aspects of life had a deleterious effect on mankind. For example, if the mysteries of weight are linked to the field of technology, this technology is led into black occult channels, such as those of nuclear physics (in which very heavy elements play a role). The mysteries of weight, as the mysteries of the human Self and love given freely, should be linked to the field of eugenics, the field in which sexual love is ennobled in such a way that two parents, two Self people, can use it to arrange conception so that they know in advance which third Self person they will incarnate and give a physical body with its proper seed of Atma.

Thus in a sense the mysteries of weight, the mysteries of Sviatogor, relate specifically to Eastern Europe. It is significant that the main body of bylini start with the bylina about Sviatogor, thus referring to the future aspect of Sviatogor (and that of Mikoela Seljaninovich), to Sviatogor as the first bogatyr in post-history, and as the ultimate Self-conscious Atman person of the sixth root race.

Volkh Vseslavyevich

In her palace in Kiev, Princess Maria Vseslavyevna gave birth to a son: Volkh Vseslavyevich, who was to become a magician and found Novgorod. The earth trembled at his first cry, and the moon swelled up in a curious way. His father had been one of the last and tempestuous descendants of the famous lineage of the Ureus Naga, the house of the sons of the Good Serpent, and when his son was born, his strength passed to his child.

When he was only an hour and a half old, the infant called in a stentorian voice: 'Mother dear, do not wrap me up in swaddling clothes, but give me a harness and a club weighing at least 300 poed.' When he was seven years old he had mastered all the usual arts, and by the time he weas ten he had mastered all the unusual arts. He could change himself into a falcon or a wolf without difficulty, as easily as writing a letter. Three years later he marched against the heathens with his own guard.

When a rumour spread in Kiev that Saltyk Stavrulyevich was planning to conquer Russia from India, King Volkh sent a reconnaissance party. He changed himself into a falcon, flew to India, perched on the window-sill of Saltyk's palace, and heard the Indian ruler say to his wife Azvyakovna: 'It is my royal will to march against Holy Russia. I will conquer nine cities there and give them to my sons, keeping Kiev for myself.' However, Queen Asvyakovna discouraged him: 'Dear husband, do not pursue this plan. Last night I dreamed that a white falcon flew from the west, and a black raven from the east. The birds met high up in the air and fought for life or death. The falcon won. I knew that it was none other than Volkh Vseslavyevich, and that you were the raven.' Furiously, Saltyk answerd that he would conquer Russia nevertheless.

Volkh now changed himself into a stoat, crept to the Indian arsenal and gnawed all the bows, arrows and lances in half. Then he once again assumed the form of a falcon and went back to pick up his guard. A few months later, Russian warriors overwhelmed India. For want of any serviceable weapons, Saltyk and his soldiers had no choice but to withdraw to their invincible capital.

Once again the Russian son of a serpent availed himself of magic. He changed not only himself, but also all his warriors, into ants, and they crawled through tiny holes into Saltyk's fortified residence. Volkh turned the ants back into soldiers, and apart from 7000 virgins to make love to, they slaughtered all the Indians, including King Saltyk. Amongst those who were spared was Queen Azvyakovna. She married Volkh Vseslavyevich of her own free will. He divided India's gold, silver, horses and cows amongst his warriors, and himself became king of the land on the Ganges.

Commentary

Volkh Vselavyevich was Russia's second ancient bogatyr. He was a magician and general, endowed with almost divine powers, just like Sviatogor. (At the time of the Slav root race he will be Russia's second post-historic bogatyr.)[5] His name means: Bearer of the world of the Volkhov. Volkh was the founder of Novgorod (new town), the capital of the Slavjanje (bearers of the word), which is situated on the Volkhov. The legend states that he owes his magic powers to his ancestry. His father was one of the last tempestuous descendants of the Ureus Naga, the order of 'the Masters of the Serpent' — those who had mastered the fire of the serpent, the power of the soul which activates the chakras.

This indicates that once again this bylina outlines Russia's future with the spiritual trappings of the past: Volkh's father was descended from the ancient white magicians of Egypt, who were preparing the future androgynous condition of man, as discussed earlier. Volkh had mastered all the usual and unusual arts by using the power of the fire of the serpent; he knew everything, and could do everything. Being omnipotent and omniscient, he could change himself into a raven, a falcon, a mouse, an ant, or any other animal as easily as writing a letter.

This means that he had completely mastered his astral body surrounding the fire of the serpent, the body that is composed by definition of the powers of the astral signs of the zodiac (Aries, Taurus, etc.) and other animal constellations (e.g. Falcon). These forces are most effective in the animal kingdom, so that a particular animal actually is what an ordinary person merely has as a characteristic. For example, Aries is the will, while an ordinary human only has this will as a characteristic.

As an extraordinary person, Volkh Vseslavyevich was able to make use of the astral forces in the same way as the animals, in other words so intensely that he actually became a particular astral quality. Without any difficulty he was able to transform the serpent's fiery strength, the serpent's central fire force, into the will of Aries, the perseverance of Taurus, the falcon's strength to pursue, the strength of the mouse which can transform fear of the world into courage, or the ant's finely attuned social strength to work. This capacity characterizes man who has spiritualized the astral body into the Manas.

The curious circumstance that Volkh has mastered the ability to change into an animal with as much ease as writing a letter, also indicates that this skill is inscribed or imprinted on his ethereal body, and that in this way he had spiritualized his body to the Buddhi. Therefore Volkh is a man who possesses Manas and Buddhi, just as Sviatogor is a man who also possesses Atma. Like Sviatogor, Volkh needs the help of Mikoela Seljaninovich, the representative of the human Self. This will become apparent in the fourth mythical bylina.

Although Volkh as a Buddhi man is described with the spiritual trappings of someone who is inspired only to be this from the spiritual world outside the Self — as was usual in the past — he also represents the prototype of the future Self-conscious Buddhi man (through Mikoela). As a self-conscious Buddhi man, he marches against India, the land of the masters of the ethereal body in a Luciferian sense in which the world is renounced, the land of the permanently unconscious Luciferian Buddhi men, the yogis. These yogis are represented by the Indian king Saltyk Stavrulyevich.

Volkh fears that he and his people will cause the unjust, unconscious Buddhi element which renounces the world, to be victorious for ever throughout the world. This is why he marches against them in the guise of a strong, self-conscious falcon, and defeats Saltyk as an unconscious weak raven, the bird that represents the force of metamorphosis of the astral body based in unconsciousness, as a lesser creature than the falcon, and representing all lesser and weaker creatures.

After his victory over Saltyk, Volkh Vseslavyevich marries his wife Azvyakovna and inherits India's gold, silver, horses, cows and warriors. This means that he inherits everything that could be saved of the Indian culture, and uses it to serve the Buddhi element on the basis of future self-consciousness, because it is right in principle. This is in the first place India's queen, the Indian attitude to find the Spirit and serve it.

137

The story of Volkh Vseslavyevich is therefore the story of a transformation — particularly from the perspective of the future — of the ethereal body into the Buddhi, preceding the transformation of the physical body into the Atma.

Volga Sviatoslavovich

At the funeral of King Volga Sviatoslav, who had reached the age of 90, the minstrels predicted that his son Prince Volga Sviatoslavovich, who was only a week and a half old, would perform even greater deeds than his late father. All the people present at the funeral stood up and shouted, 'Long live Volga! Long live Volga!'.

When the child was three years old, he always wore a harness and spoke in a loud, stentorian voice. No children wished to romp about with him, and no man dared to fight him. When he was about five years old he weighed more than a castle, and the earth trembled under his footsteps. When he was seven, anonymous tutors were commissioned by his mother to prepare him to become a king/priest. Within 60 months he was able to change himself into a falcon, wolf or any other animal. The day after his nineteenth birthday, Volga formed a guard comprising 29 men, and he led his soldiers in a hunt for *zubr* (aurochs). In order to help them catch sable, foxes and pine martens, he assumed the form of a predator, and chased the prey towards them. In order to attract the geese and swans towards them, he chased these slow-moving birds, assuming the form of a swift falcon. To help the fishermen catch their fish, he changed into a pike and drove the creatures in their direction. King Volga Sviatoslavovich ennobled Russian nature, and taught his guard and later his whole people to live together and from nature.

Commentary
The third story of the cycle of mythical bylini is the story about King Volga Siatoslavovich, Russia's third ancient bogatyr. He was named after his father and excelled in the same skills. This is clearly emphasized in the bylini about him. The fact that Volga was named after his father, and excelled at his father's skills, means that the strength and skills which he represents are passed down through the generations. I will return to this below.

In addition, the remarks made in this context about the spiritual trappings of Volkh Vselavyevich based on the past, also apply to Volga Sviatoslavovich. In fact the latter's name is almost the same as the former's. They are both called *Slav*, which means 'Bearers of the word', and they are both named after the River Volchov (Volga). In his book 'Russian Heroic Sagas and Legends', Boris Raptschinsky pointed out that Volkh and Volga are interconnected to a significant extent.

Volkh Vselavyevich was also omniscient and omnipotent. However, he

Volga Sviatoslavovich and Mikoela Selyaninovich.
Taken from 'Russian Heroic Sagas and Legends' by Boris Raptschinsky

was not primarily a magician and warrior but rather a king/priest and hunter, hunting for *zubr* (aurochs). Like Volkh, he had completely mastered his astral body — his emotional life. He too could transform himself into all sorts of creatures, representing very different aspects and characteristics, without becoming a victim as a result of these extreme experiences, as King Saltyk had been.

Volga was also able to change himself into a predatory animal — a falcon, a pike etc. — by means of his self-consciousness (in historical terms, a temporary self-consciousness) and with the help of the peasant Mikoela Selyaninovich, as we shall see in the next bylina. However, unlike Volkh, Volga does not do this as easily as writing a letter. This means that Volkh, Volga has spiritualized his astral body to become Manas, but unlike Volkh, he has not spiritualized his ethereal body to become Buddhi.

As a Manas person he represents the Persian culture of the past, where everything revolved around the astral body and the related unconscious imaginative consciousness; he represents the Slav culture of the future where everything will revolve around Manas and the related conscious imaginative consciousness, in so far as this culture is assimilated in the Slav-Manichean root race, in its own right, and referring back to Persia. The ancient Persian culture was therefore concerned with developing the Self in the astral body, and in connection with this, with ennobling nature. Unlike Volkh, Volga did not fight another nation (India) in order to resist the unwanted influences from that country, but he hunted the *zubr* (aurochs) in the footsteps of another nation, Persia.

This legend expresses the way in which he followed in another nation's footsteps by describing how Volga excelled at his father's skills. The footsteps of the Persian culture pass through the culture of the Caucasus, the culture of Rustaveli and others, to the eastern Slavs. It was described by von Skerst.

The *zubr* represents the strength of nature's former wilderness, when left to itself and/or misused, as well as its future wilderness and pollution.

As a hunter, Volga — assuming many different animal forms, together with his party of hunters, also assuming animal forms, for Volga taught them his skills — fought against the terrible process of the destruction of nature on the basis of mastering the animal forces of his own astral body, so that it could be spiritualized to become Manas.

Volga Sviatoslavovich symbolizes knowledge and the ability to make use of that knowledge to put an end to the Ahrimanian destruction of nature, and to return to an improvement of nature.

As mentioned in the chapter on early Russian history, Volga Sviatoslavovich has been identified with King Oleg of Kiev, who reigned from 879 to 912, and according to a legend was killed by a snake which came out of his dead horse's skull. In general, Volkh Vselavyevich was viewed as the first lord of Novgorod. The relationship between Volkh and Volga is reflected in mirror image by the relationship between Novgorod and Kiev:

Kiev is like Volkh from Novgorod marching against the enemy, while Novgorod is like Volga from Kiev creating order in its nature and culture.

Volga Sviatoslavovich and Mikoela Selyaninovich

The kingdom of Volga Sviatoslavovich encompassed the whole of (Russian) nature. Every year the knights brought in products, crops and cattle from all the towns and villages in the land. However, one day they told him that the citizens of the fortified towns of Gurchevyets and Oryechovyets refused to pay their tribute. Volga decided to march there himself, together with his guard comprising 29 knights. Two hundred *verst* away from the rebellious towns they could hear a peasant who was ploughing unceasingly. However, for two days they were unable to find him anywhere. On the morning of the third day they heard the peasant urging on his horse, but for many hours they both remained invisible. It was only towards evening that Volga finally perceived them — an ordinary peasant with his horse and plough. However, the plough was remarkably large and was made of oak and had a silver ploughshare, while the mare drawing it looked rather small and scrawny. The oversized implement ploughed furrows literally as large as canals through the black earth, with no beginning and no end. Volga greeted the peasant, introduced himself and his men, and gave him God's blessing for his tremendous task. Then he explained why he was on his way to the fortified towns.

The ploughman greeted him and replied: 'Oh, young Volga, I know the inhabitants of Gurchevyets and Oryevhovyets. They are insolent robbers. Some time ago I bought three bales of salt from them. Disguised as toll-keepers, they tried to make me pay again for the same salt. I refused, and they tried to rob me. In order to proceed on my way I had to kill off a thousand of those scoundrels.'

Volga suggested to the peasant that they become friends and punish the rebellious towns together. So they set off. After a while the peasant realized that his plough had been left unguarded. After consulting the king, three soldiers were sent back to hide the implement behind a bush. However, they returned without having done what they were told to, and admitted that they had been unable to move the plough; it was stuck fast in the last furrow. Volga then sent back his whole guard to carry out the task, but the guard also returned, having met with no success.

The peasant reproached Volga: 'Is this your strong guard with which you hope to force Gurchevyets and Oryechovyets to pay the tribute?' He added: 'I will go back myself and hide my plough.' He walked back and picked up the implement from the deep furrow with one hand and threw it into the bushes. Even Volga, who was as strong as an ox, stood and stared at this. He felt challenged, and suggested to the peasant: 'Let us see who can gallop fastest on his horse.' Volga on his giant steed lost. He called out: 'Who are you?' The peasant introduced himself as Mikoela Selyaninovich. When Volga offered him the sum of 500 roubles for the mare, Mikoela refused, saying: 'My little horse may seem very bony, but, O King, it is worth more than your entire kingdom.'

When they arrived at the rebellious towns, all Volga's warriors were killed in the battle which ensued. However, Volga and Mikoela in their turn defeated the rebels. Volga did not take any more grain and cattle than was owed him by way of tribute.

Commentary

The fourth and last story of the cycle of mythical bylini is the story of the encounter between the third ancient Russian bogatyr, Volga Sviatoslavovich, and the fourth, Mikoela Selyaninovich, as described in the previous bylina. The latter played a role in the story about Russia's first ancient bogatyr, Sviatogor. In both stories, Mikoela remains in the background, although he is a great hero. As Volga and Volkh Vselavyevich are in some respects identified with each other, the heroic deeds of Mikoela described here are indirectly also at the basis of the success of Volkh's deeds, as is shown in this bylina.

When Volga Sviatoslovovich had finished cultivating the whole of (Russian) nature, the citizens of the fortified towns of Gurchevyets and Oryechovyets did not wish to pay him tribute. The people of these towns were scoundrels, exploiters and thieves. In Volga Sviatoslavovich's cultivated kingdom they represented the asocial element which had also troubled the early Persian reformers of nature and culture. During the Ancient Persian culture the Turan element remained outside the borders of the cultural area of Persia, but in Volga's kingdom it was inside the borders of the cultural area of the Slavs, a reflection of Persia. This was in accordance with the principle that the Slavs assimilate everything that can be assimilated. [6]

This led to problems in the country. Volga Sviatoslavovich had to prepare to call the disobedient fortified towns to order, and in this way he was following in the footsteps of Volkh Vselavyevich, who was similar to him, but more militant.

In Volga as a magician/warrior, Volkh (magician/warrior) and Volga (priest/hunter) are united and become one.

When Volga was on his way to the fortified towns with his guard comprising 29 knights and was only 200 verst from the towns, he met a peasant with a gigantic oak plough that had an oversized silver ploughshare. Yet this fantastic plough was drawn only by a scrawny horse. The peasant was Mikoela Selyaninovich. He is the free Self man, who was engaged on the Slav version of the Grail: this did not involve a quest and ultimately finding the Grail as a chalice (the quest following from the Ceremonial Eucharist), but working the Grail as Christ's earth body (a task following from the Eucharist in Deed and Truth).

The attribute of the Slav task of the Grail is therefore not the sword which is used in the quest for the Grail as a chalice to pass through a world of injustice, but the plough made of oak (life force of the earth) and silver (moon force as the force of the Holy Ghost) with which the Body of Christ (the Earth, nature on Earth) is tilled or worked.

The *Grail sword* (of King Arthur, Parsifal, Gawain) represents the Western European driving force of the human Self to find the Grail, or to combine the Self with Manas to become the Holy Grail (the Self as the host in the chalice of Manas). In the context of the Western European quest, finding the Grail is tantamount to becoming the Holy Grail oneself; this is the strict mission of the Rosicrucians. This driving force brings to mind the Faustian saga.

Mikoela's Plough made of oak and silver represents the East European way in which Manas and the Self serve the whole world, as the violated and denigrated body of Christ, in order to purify the world and in the process involve the essential parts of the Self (the Self and the Earth as the host in the Chalice of a new Manas world) in which the individual Manas is assimilated. In the context of the Eastern European feeling of solidarity, working the Grail is primarily tantamount to turning the world into a Holy Grail (the Manichean mission). This feeling of solidarity brings to mind the Kitezh legend.

As stated above, ploughing is a way of piercing the earth. The earth has to be pierced so that the blood of the earth becomes ether in the atmosphere and can feed all the people who work on the earth. The blood of the earth is the blood of Christ, which was shed for all those who accepted him. St John said: 'He who eats my bread, walks over me (Christ).' In the first instance this is the peasant, the archetypal peasant of the world, Mikoela Selyaninovich. He provides food for himself and for others with his work on the body of Christ. His act of piercing the earth, ploughing with his plough, full of the life force of the earth and the lunar force of the Holy Ghost, is a way of looking after the earth, ploughing it so that it can breathe, for all of mankind.

In front of the plough Mikoela has a scrawny horse, though it is stronger than a giant steed. In general the horse represents the human personality, the lower part of the Self, the lower soul, and particularly the physical body. Mikoela's scrawny horse particularly represents all this insofar as it restrains the whole personal element. Because of this restraint, the personality appears to be weak, like the weak horse, however, it is in reality stronger than the healthiest giant steed, which is at the mercy of its drives. In this restraint a higher Self dominates over a lower Self.

In the Slav context Mikoela is the higher Self man, while his horse is the self-controlled lower aspect of the Self related to the physical body. Mikoela's lower Self draws the plough to serve the world, the plough of the mission of the Grail for which he, Mikoela, is predestined as a higher Self man. Just as Volga cultivates the (Russian) earth on the basis of astral control, Mikoela does this on the basis of self-control, controlling the lower Self with the higher Self. Volga's task of cultivating the land seems to be inferior to that of Mikoela — neither he nor his guard can lift the plough made of oak and silver, and Volga's giant steed loses a race against Mikoela's scrawny nag.

Mikoela is best and strongest in everything, because he has love, the strongest force on earth, the gravity of the world, the Self force of the world. In order to give weight to his task of cultivation, Volga needs the weight of Mikoela's love and his free Self. This applies particularly when Volga acts in the guise of Volkh, when he must become a warrior in order to make the rebellious fortified towns of Gurchevyets and Oryechovyets pay the tribute they owe. The inhabitants of these towns are described as robbers of salt, i.e. as robbers who kill the Self force of man. Thanks to Miloela Selyaninovich's help and his strong Self force, Volga is able to overpower the salt robbers. In doing so, he loses his guard, i.e. his victory is a Pyrrhic victory, as is any conflict between the Self and the Self force.

The story of the encounter of Volga and Mikoela and their fight against the salt robbers describes how working on, with, and in the earth on the basis of the Manas and the Self neutralizes the forces which turn the earth into a wilderness and cause man to lose his Self.

When we take another look at the bylini of this mythical cycle, noting only the intention of the individual stories and the progress in them, the following ideas on the four Ancient Bogatyri who play a role in them, emerge: Sviatogor represents the primeval force and will of the world. The bylina about him describes what becomes of this primeval force and will, from the age of Atlantis to Christ, and again from the sixth root race.

Volkh Vselavyevich and Volga Sviatoslavovich represent the wisdom and knowledge of the world in the same periods. The bylini about them reveal how the wisdom and knowledge of the world are combined in the Slav experience with the pre-historic Aryan cultures, the Ancient Indian and Ancient Persian cultures, and are projected onto the time of the sixth root race. Mikoela Selyaninovich represents the essence of labour, insofar as this labour is a caring activity, using the plough. He looks after and cares for

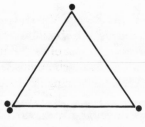

Primeval force/will (Sviatogor)

(Volkh Vselavyevich)
Primeval wisdom/knowledge
(Volga Sviatoslavovich)

activity in love
(Mikoela Selyaninovich)

(ploughs) the earth with the force of the Self (love) again in the periods mentioned above. Together these four heroes form a divine triangle of the will, wisdom/knowledge, and labour.

The divine triangle of the will, wisdom/knowledge and activity is an aspect of the Grail sun, as we shall see below. It is also the Mountain of Initiation, the Holy Mountain Sviatogor. This divine triangle of the will, wisdom and activity can also be represented with the point pointing downwards.

(Volkh Vselavyevich)   activity in love
Primeval wisdom/knowledge   (Mikoela Selyaninovich)
(Volga Sviatoslavovich)

Primeval force/will — Sviatogor

In this case the point of the triangle symbolizing the primeval force and primeval will, which is symbolized by Sviatogor, points down towards the earth. The triangle with the point of the force and the will pointing upwards represents the standing mountain, Sviatogor, at rest. The triangle with the point of force and will pointing downwards represents the upturned mountain, i.e. Sviatogor descending down to earth. The progress of Russia's heroes begins with this descent. The story of Sviatogor in relation to the other stories of the cycle of mythical bylini is the story of the standing triangle and the descending triangle. Therefore the story of Sviatogor is the story of the six-pointed star, the Star of Venus.[7]

The Heroic Bylini of Kiev

The Wedding of King Vladimir

There was feasting at the court of King Vladimir, the Red Sun. The poet knight Dobrynya Nikitich sang songs about Holy Russia's illustrious past. Then Vladimir announced: 'Like most of my bogatyri, I would like to be wed.' The aged boyar Bermyata Vasilivich pointed out to him the beautiful Apraxia, the youngest princess of the king of Lithuania. The old bogatyri Dunai Ivanovich, nicknamed 'the Silent' because of his tack and silent ways, was sent to the foreign court, together with the bard as a representative in order to negotiate.

When they arrived, Dunai suggested to his travelling companion: 'As I

145

served here for nine years in my youth, I will present the ruler of Lithuania with Vladimir's proposal of marriage. Meanwhile you can keep guard and watch out for any sign of betrayal.'

In a furious rage, the foreign king refused the proposal, and Dunai signalled to Dobrynya that he had been betrayed. The two bogatyri fought against all the enemy armies. They were victorious and Apraxia was taken from her chamber which was protected with three times nine locks, and obtaining her father's consent by force, she was taken off to Russia. However, Apraxia's older sister, the *polienietsa* (female bogatyr) Natasha, who constantly, vigilantly wandered round the steppes with her guard, suddenly became suspicious and followed them in the night. For safety's sake Dunai sent Dobrynya on ahead to Kiev with Apraxia, and stayed behind to wait for Natasha. There was a life-and-death struggle, and finally he defeated her. When asked, he explained that Apraxia had not been abducted, but had been given to King Vladimir in marriage by her father. Then Dunai asked Natasha to marry him, and she consented. When they arrived in Kiev, two wedding feasts were celebrated together.

Commentary

The first story about the first (Kiev) cycle of heroic bylini is the story about the wedding of King Vladimir, the Red Sun of Kiev, Russia's foremost younger bogatyr. Vladimir means 'famous for (his style of) ruling'. It is true that he did not rule in a particularly remarkable way as the historical Vladimir, but he did as the legendary Vladimir. As that Vladimir, he ruled in a typically Slav way, i.e. certainly not as a militant ruler or prime minister, or as an ambitious manager, but in a fatherly (or motherly) way, with the emphasis on small details. His authority was based on the principle that to rule is to serve. His wishes are followed because nobody wants to disappoint him — he is everyone's beloved father. Vladimir is obeyed because disobedience would give rise to a feeling of shame in a person's conscience, as though something particularly valuable had been intentionally neglected.

Like King Arthur of Logres, King Vladimir was at the centre of a circle of heroes or bogatyri, and like the former he was the founder of a Round Table. This may not be a well known fact, yet it can be found in any encyclopedia.

Like King Arthur, Vladimir sent his knights out to do good deeds, to help widows and orphans, slay dragons, and free the people who had been captured by these dragons from their lairs. However, in contrast with the court of King Arthur, there was no mention of a Holy Grail at Vladimir's court.

As mentioned in the outline of early Russian history, and in the discussion of the mythical bylini, Russia or Kiev Rus, the earth itself, is — and will always be — the Holy Grail. Therefore unlike Arthur, King Vladimir did not send his bogatyri out on a quest for the Holy Grail, in addition to performing all the other above-mentioned tasks, but sent them out to walk the Grail in the footsteps of Mikoela Selyaninovich. They were to work it as peasants. In fact, King Vladimir's first and most important bogatyr was a peasant, just like Mikoela Selyaninovich.

That the earth is the Grail is obviously not a complete and finished process, but is an ongoing creative process in which the earth becomes by stages a sun. The way in which this happens is the most typical characteristic development of the earthly Grail. The word 'Grail' can mean *gradalis*, 'by degrees'. In this context the sun is the image of earthly impurity which has been burnt away.

In the context of Slav development the two most important stages in the development of the earth as a Grail are firstly the development of Kiev Rus, Vladimir's Round Table, and the (historical) Christian communist city of Kitezh in preparation for the coming sixth culture and sixth root race. (This preparation obviously had to come to an end, and has already done so.) The second stage is the final manifestation of all this (a Manichean style manifestation yet to come), in a cultural and racial context.

Therefore the first stage of the earth becoming the Grail can be compared with the setting sun or red evening sun, while the second stage can be compared with the rising sun, or morning sun, again a red sun. In this sense King Vladimir was sometimes called 'the Red Sun'. This nickname again underlines the extent to which Russian legends (and early Russian history) are concerned not only with the past, but also and particularly with the future.

In the (Kiev) heroic bylini, everything is expressed in terms of the Christian element, an element which is primarily outlined in a cultural sense. Historically this is self-evident. The mythical bylini are set in the pre-Christian primeval era — or more precisely, they have the trappings of that age — while the heroic bylini are set in the post-Christian period when Russia was converted to Christianity — or more precisely, they have the trappings of that age. However, these facts explain more.

The Kiev heroic bylini are about heroes, young bogatyri, who to some extent represent the same powers as the heroes, the older bogatyri, of the mythical bylini (the forces of the physical, ethereal and Self elements, the forces of the Will, Wisdom/Knowledge and Love).

Just as the older bogatyri represent these forces in the context of the world of the Father, the world which was related and is still related to the formation of the races, the younger bogatyri represent these forces in the context of the world of the Son, of Christ. This context is currently concerned with cultural formation. It is only since the 'Alchemical Wedding' of Christian Rosenkreutz that this context has also slowly started to include aspects of racial formation, particularly the formation of the Slav race, which implies androgynous and eternal development.[8] In this respect it should also be mentioned that just as King Arthur's Round Table is usually considered to consist of twelve knights (or a multiple of twelve),

King Vladimir's Round table is considered to consist of seven bogatyri (or a multiple of seven).

Because esoteric numerology says that seven is the number that expresses those things that are manifest in time (periodically) — according to numerology, the number twelve does so in relation to space — the bare structure of the Slav Round Table also refers to the twofold character of its activity in time. Further information is given about the relevance of the number seven for the Slav Round Table in the commentary on the bylina 'How the bogatyri of Holy Russia met their death'.

Let us return to the wedding of King Vladimir. The king of Kiev Rus was seeking a wife; this was Princess Apraxia of Lithuania. The historical Vladimir had several wives, but never married one named Apraxia. However, the legendary Vladimir married a Princess Apraxia. What does this mean? In the Slav language Lithuania means 'foreign land' or 'western foreign land'. Apraxia is neither a Slav, Roman, nor Germanic name. The name is derived from the Sanskrit world 'Aparoksha'. Aparoksha means 'direct knowledge through perception'. This word is in contrast with the word 'paroksha', which means 'knowledge through reasoning'. The Greek word 'Abraxas' is probably also derived from Aparoksha. Abraxas means God, or the name of God as revealed in the cosmic rhythms, particularly those of the year.

It is clear that when King Vladimir asks (through Dunai Ivanovich), for the hand of Princess Apraxia of Lithuania the Slav-Rurik Call to the Varangians is continued and revealed in secret. This is a call for order in spiritual science, i.e. direct knowledge through perception, or the knowledge of God revealed in Nature. It goes without saying that after the fall of Kiev Rus, the unasked Princess Paroksha forces herself on Russian tsars and presidents.

It is interesting to compare the marriages of King Vladimir and King Arthur. The latter married Princess Guinevere, a sexual woman, of flesh and blood, as a (soul) princess. In this sense Guinevere serves as King Arthur's anima. This reveals the manifestation of the Self in the threefold soul. (This entails the development of the perceptual soul, the intellectual and emotional soul, and the consciousness soul, and King Arthur was ahead of Western European mankind in this development.) For the recognition and development of the soul, the Self uses a projection technique: the soul is projected onto a member of the opposite sex.

In this development of the soul and projection of the soul, the free love of the Self is removed from blood ties — which are related to physical development — and elevated into the erotic sphere in such a way that this eroticism is a foreshadowing and a preparation for the alchemical wedding between the Manas (which contains the soul) and the Self (the Spirit), i.e. the Alchemical Wedding of the Rosicrucians and the transformation into the Holy Grail.

Because of the particular character of the anima problem, the development of the soul is a highly individual matter. Thus the marriage of King Arthur and Princess Guinevere serves the process of the individual becoming of the Grail during the stage of the threefold development of the soul; for this development it is the anticipation of the anima and in this process it serves as a prototype.

King Vladimir married Princess Apraxia of Lithuania, the symbol of Western Self force and spiritual Self-knowledge. He himself represents the element of brotherly love and the astral physical aspect which serves in the development of Manas, particularly in a social context.[10] In contrast with the marriage of Arthur and Guinevere, his marriage symbolizes a social event, the continued sounding of the Rurik Call and the continued Answer to it.

Therefore it is a marriage which is not primarily concerned with the development of the soul in becoming the Grail of the individual self, but of the development of the whole Slav community towards becoming the Holy Grail. This community will eventually encompass all of mankind on earth. In becoming the Grail in a social sense, which is inherent in the development of the Manas culture and the Manas root race, the free love of the Self (seen here as the Self of King Vladimir) seems to be removed from the sphere of the anima and eroticism of man as an individual and elevated to the sphere of brotherly love, a truly social matter, because this love does not exclude anyone, while anima love must by its very nature be exclusive. In this love, which miraculously both forms the Manas and results from it, the Self and the Manas (in an individual but particularly in a collective sense) enter into an alchemical wedding and are transformed into the Holy Grail, which in this case is a world grail.

It is logical that we do not hear any more about Apraxia as a seductive woman, unlike the stories about Guinevere. Moreover, the marriage of Vladimir and Apraxia is not characterized only by the lack of eroticism and the problems of adultery on the personal plane. It is also characterized by a reversed polarization in the aspects represented by the two partners in a social sense.[11]

The element of spiritual science which has a powerful Self and is represented by Apraxia must be characterized as a male element, and in future it will be identified with Christ as the Self of the world and of mankind, i.e. the Holy Ghost. The astral element represented by King Vladimir, which embodies brotherly love and develops into Manas, should be characterized as a female element, and will evolve in future into a world Manas known as Sophia. An aspect of this reverse polarization is expressed in the Russian equality between men and women, and in the Russian custom of women proposing marriage to men.

All this can be summarized as follows. The marriage of King Vladimir of Kiev and Princess Apraxia of Lithuania serves as a primeval image of the Slav Rurik call, and the Varangian-Germanic answer to this call, as a primeval image of the spiritualization of the astral body to become Manas

149

through the Self and the interrelationship of the two in a cultural and racial context, which assimilates the individual development of Manas. Thus it serves as a primeval image of the social and universal development of the world towards becoming the Holy Grail, in which the individual development is only one aspect. All this is at a particular evolutionary stage, although it can also be seen in terms of a historical analysis of the future.

It is also interesting to compare the preparations for King Vladimir's wedding with those for King Arthur's. King Arthur's bride Guinevere was brought to the Court of Camelot by the great courtly knight and lover, Lancelot. The other great courtly knight and lover of Camelot, Tristan de Lyonnes, did not play a role in this. Vladimir's bride Apraxia was brought to Kiev by two knights, whose love was expressed in terms of brotherly love. These were the old Dunai Ivanovich — the opposite of Lancelot — and the young Dobrynya Nikitich, Russia's second main young bogatyr, the counterpart of Tristan.

Lancelot means 'scion of the land', or more freely translated, 'son of the earth', meaning the physical and ethereal material earth. He represents the life force of earth. He is the best knight in Camelot in all earthly matters. He burns with love for Guinevere as soon as he sees her. It is not surprising that as a sexual woman Guinevere in her turn loves this son of the earth, as well as loving Arthur, the son of the spirit. Lancelot is unable to carry out his individual Grail development because of his illicit anima love for Guinevere. By his very nature — his earthly nature — he complicates the problem of anima represented and experienced by Arthur with the aspect of adultery and the love triangle. Involuntarily he makes Arthur's mission more difficult: to experience the anima as the primeval image for the soul evolving to become androgynous. It is Lancelot's karma to represent, in the context of the earthly problem of anima, the prototype of the adulterer who exists almost as a law of nature.

It is King Arthur's destiny to be betrayed by the anima in the context of this problem, and yet to achieve Psyche, the alchemical wedding, as his individual development as a Holy Grail. In fact it is King Arthur's destiny to endure the heaviest burden, and yet to find and become the Grail, just like Parsifal, Gawain and Galahad.

Arthur, Guinevere, and Lancelot express the unfulfilled aspect of the problem of the anima, while the aspect of its fulfilment is expressed by Tristan and Isolde. As the true fulfilment of love does not coincide with the lack of it, there are two couples in the Arthurian legends (one of which involved a third person) who represent the matter of the anima. This is why there are not two great courtly knights who bring King Arthur's bride to him, but only one.

In contrast, as mentioned above, Vladimir's bride was brought to him by two knights, Dunai Ivanovich and Dobrynya Nikitich. They both excel in the virtue of brotherly love. In Dunai this is expressed in age-old astral forces based on family and tribal ties, which are unsuitable for transformation into

Manas. In Dobrynya it is expressed in astral forces of youth that wish to combine with the Self and are suitable for transformation into Manas.

Dunai Ivanovich means 'Danube, son of John', i.e. son of the watery element. Dunai is old, and the astral element concerned belongs to the past. Dobrynya means 'good heart'. The heart is the astral organ *par excellence*. However, it is a young and developing organ, and will only be perfected by means of those astral forces that can be spiritualized into Manas in future. Therefore Dobrynya also means 'youth'. The old son of water, Dunai, is the Slav opposite and counterpart of the young son of the earth, the Western European Lancelot, who is full of the force of life. The latter is said to be the best knight in the world in all earthly matters. The former believes that he is.

Lancelot is destroyed by what he represents in connection with the problem of anima. Dunai is destroyed by what he must represent in the context of showing his brotherly love, as we shall see in the following bylina. Lancelot transgresses in his love for Arthur's bride. Dunai the Silent restrains himself and is content with the sister of Vladimir's bride, Natasha. Natasha means 'reborn'. As the sister of Apraxia, she represents that aspect of Western European Self force and spiritual science that can be used to make the astral element of Dunai, which is not really suitable for Manas development, capable of this development by means of a process of rebirth.

The young, good-hearted Dobrynya is the Slav counterpart of Tristan, the Western European successful lover of the anima. Dobrynya is also successful. He excels in giving brotherly love, as shown by his name. He is Russia's second young bogatyr, and above all, Vladimir's most courtly and artistic companion at the Round Table.

Just as there is an exclusive element in love of the anima, which led to Arthur's bride being brought to him by only one knight, there is something inclusive in brotherly love, even in the sense that its progressive form coincides with its atavistic form. This explains why Vladimir's bride is brought to him by two knights or bogatyri.

The Contest between Dunai Ivanovich and Natasha Korolyevichna

During a drinking session, just after the wedding feasts, the bogatyri were boasting about themselves. Dunai Ivanovich even reckoned that he was the best knight in Kiev at absolutely everything: 'Didn't I bring Vladimir's bride, Apraxia, here from Lithuania? And for myself, his sister Natasha?' Natasha argued against him: 'You are boasting. Many bogatyri are much better than you at a lot of things. In any case, I am much better than you at archery, and I will prove it to you.' Then at 500 paces from Dunai, she shot an arrow through a ring on his head into the bull's eye of a target placed behind him. She did this three times.

Dunai was ashamed and wished to emulate her. His first two shots missed the target. Out of frustration he killed her on purpose with the third arrow, shot from close by. Immediately he came to his senses, and desperate with remorse, he called out again and again: 'Where the white swan (Natasha) has laid her red head on earth, there will lie the head of a falcon (himself).

Then he committed suicide. Their blood gave rise to the Danube and the Natasha, which was later called the Dnieper. For a while the two streams flowed on separately, but eventually they combined in one broad river. Where the two lovers fell, there are now two cypresses with intertwined branches.

Commentary

Most bylini in the Kiev cycle begin with a feast, as does the bylina about the competition between Dunai and his wife. These feasts are a reference to the arcane mysteries of Christ's Eucharist. In the final analysis, the tasks undertaken by the bogatyri can only be performed with the strength gained from the food of these mysteries, and in particular, the food from the mystery of Christ's Eucharist in Deed and Truth.

During this feast Dunai boasted that he was the best knight of Kiev in all respects. The representatives of the (astral) past are picked to say that they are the best when they are in the company of representatives of forces which are related to the future. This was also true of Dunai Ivanovich, but it is not right. It is an incorrect way of thinking typical of many conservatives. A similar mistake is often made by those who represent purely material things when they are together with representatives of spiritual matters: they boast about their material superiority, sometimes with justification, or their superiority is generally accepted. For example, it is justifiably said of Lancelot that he was the best knight in Camelot in all earthly matters. Certainly Dunai was not the best bogatyr in Kiev, in hardly any respect.

Natasha Korolyevichna points this out as the level-headed, strong representative of the aspect of Western European Self force, which could serve to rejuvenate Dunai, give him rebirth and development as Manas. Furthermore, she proves that she is better at archery than her husband, a sport which symbolizes effectiveness. Natasha's aiming at the future is obviously better than Dunai's repeated concentration on the past. This is proved in a William Tell-like duel. Three times Natasha shoots an arrow into a target placed over Dunai's head. Natasha's shots symbolize her attempts to change her husband's concentration on the past, and with the three shots into the target of his threefold spirit she is successful — at least in principle.

Dunai is furious about his wife's success because he in his turn is unable to change her direction, and he kills her. Immediately he is filled with remorse, for in principle he has changed. He kills himself from remorse.

Dunai and Natasha were buried next to each other. The Danube and the Dnieper sprang from their blood, and two cypresses with interlaced branches grew on their grave. This romantic conclusion indicates that Dunai's change in direction and his continued union with Natasha are perpetuated in the astral and ethereal aspects of the spiritual world. This perpetuation in the astral world is reflected in the material world in the source of the Danube and the Dnieper. The perpetuation in the ethereal world is reflected in the material world in the growth of the cypresses.

Dobrynya Nikitich and the Dragon Zmei Gorynchich

Dobrynya was the son of the boyar Nikita Romanovich and Afimya Alexandrovna. His father died after they had been married for two years, and his mother brought up the boy to be wise, to sing, and to be well-mannered, and she also saw to it that he was instructed in the art of military skills. As related above, Dunai Ivanovich took this excellent young man to the King of Lithuania, when he went there for Vladimir to ask for the hand of the king's daughter Apraxia. When he returned to Kiev, Dobrynya was not arrogant and conceited, unlike Dunai. He developed his skills to the full in singing and playing and became an excellent goesli player.

One hot day Dobrynya decided to cool himself down in the triple stream, the Putcha. His mother forbade him, because as everyone knew, the river spewed fire, sparks and smoke. However, the hero saddled his horse and left anyway with his shield-bearer. On the bank some beautiful virgins were waiting for him, advising him not to bathe naked. They said they could not endure seeing such a beautiful naked man, but they meant that they feared that his nakedness would awaken the fire of the river to devour him, and with him, them as well. Nevertheless, the bogatyr undressed and entered the water naked.

At first the stream seemed cool, but then Zmei Gorynchich, the three-headed robber of virgins, appeared with twelve trunks in fire, sparks and smoke, and called out: 'Some time ago it was predicted that I would be killed by one Dobrynya Nikitich. Certainly this is true, but for the moment he is in my power.' The beautiful virgins ran away. The shield-bearer fled with the horses. Dobrynya hacked off three of the dragon's trunks with a helmet which he found just in time. In order to escape death, Zmei suggested to the knight that they conclude a pact. Dobrynya fell for the trap. Then Zmei hastened to Kiev to avenge himself. He seized Zabava Puchatichna and carried her off to his lair under Mount Sorochin.

At first Dobrynya felt proud of his victory and also went to Kiev. When he arrived, he noticed his mistake: while he was forgiving his shield-bearer for his cowardly flight, he saw Zmei flying overhead with Zabava. He went to his mother and lamented, and then presented himself at Vladimir's court.

At the court the bogatyr Leontyevich was telling anyone who was interested what he had chanced to witness from afar of Dobrynya Nikitich's fight against Zmei Gorynchich, and what had happened after. In his view, Dobrynya was the obvious person to slay this dragon who devoured virgins. Therefore he advised Vladimir to charge Dobrynya with this task. Afimya Alexandrovna then showed her son a magic steed in their own old stables. She gave him the horse and a dragon-slaying whip which gave the horse gigantic strength when it was used.

Dobrynya departed for Mount Sorochin. First he slew Zmei's dragon offspring with the horse and the whip, and later, after three days and nights of fighting, he killed Zmei himself. The earth was torn apart, the chivalrous knight went down to Zmei's lair and freed 40 tsars, 40 kings, 40 princes, thousands of peasants and townspeople, and countless virgins. However, at first he could not find Zabava Puchatichna.

Finally, like Prometheus, he found her in a niche, chained to a rock. He freed her, and out of gratitude and love she wished to be his daughter, his lover, his wife. But he merely took her back to her uncle, King Vladimir.

Commentary

Dobrynya Nikitich, as the second main bogatyr of the heroic bylini of Kiev, and as the 'Good Heart' of Kiev Rus, represents the aspect of the emotions or the feelings of love in the triad comprising feeling, thinking and the will. This new triad forms the essential characteristics that are the foundation for the heroic bylini of Kiev, as it developed during man's evolution from the original divine mythical triad which had similar characteristics, and which formed the foundation for the mythical bylini.

A comparison between the two types of bylini clearly shows that Dobrynya Nikitich, and what he represents, corresponds to Volkh Vselavyevich and Volga Sviatoslavovich, and what they represent in a racial and physical context, as well as resulting from and anticipating them in a psychic/cultural context. In connection with this it should be noted that Vladimir, the Grail ruler of Kiev, does not play a role in the human triad, but symbolizes the circle or (red) sun which moves around this triad or triangle.

The bylina about Dobrynya Nikitish's first battle starts by saying that Dobrynya was the son of a widow. According to the tradition of the mysteries, this represents the son of man cut off from the divine Father forces that unconsciously influence him as he develops his own Self and Manas force. For example, Mani and Parsifal were also called 'widows' sons', and the later pseudo-Dmitri was another widow's son. Dobrynya's deceased father was Nikita Romanovich. Nikita means conqueror, popular hero, while Romanovich means with Roman, i.e. of chivalrous Roman roots.

His mother was Afimya Alexandrovna. Afimya is the Slav form of the Latin *Ave*, the reversed and Christianized form of Eva, the original mother. Alexandrovna is derived from Alexander, who turns away and separates herself from man. On her own, Afimya Alexandrovna raised and trained her son in the arts of chivalry and as a warrior, both in the service of the Russian people.

It is quite clear that the meaning of his parents' names forms the basis of Dobrynya Nickitich's function as Russia's Good Heart. As Dobrynya, he was Vladimir's greatest singer and goesli player, an artist who tuned the hearts of his companions on the Round Table with his songs and his music to equal the goodness of his own heart, and gave them courage to slay dragons. As Dobrynya Nikitich, he was the leading warrior of his people, with regard to the threats facing the Russian soul and Russian feelings and the victor over Zmei Gorynchich.

One day, against his mother's advice, he went to the Putcha, the river of the soul, in order to cool down. She and many others believed that the three-headed dragon with twelve trunks, Zmei Gorynchich, who regularly spewed fire and sparks, lived in this river, which was therefore to be feared. The dragon expresses the three egoisms derived from the lower Self, which are present in the (threefold) soul. These are: the egoism of perception; the egoism of the intellect and the emotions; the egoism of consciousness. The twelve trunks are a reference to the twelve influences of the zodiac which serve to outline this threefold egoism at the astral level.

Periodically the astral fire raises its head in the soul. Dobrynya wishes to bathe naked in the Putcha, i.e. to master his soul with his own strength. He wishes to become a truly self-conscious, higher-soul person to prevent his people from being eventually overwhelmed by the three egoisms of the lower soul. The Slavs are threatened by the egoism of the soul and ultimately by a lack of Self (when they do not wish to be connected with higher external Self forces, with the Self forces of Apraxia or Natasha of Lithuania (external in space), or with the Self forces of Miloela Selyaninovich (external in time).

Dobrynya did not listen either to his mother or to the beautiful virgins who advised him against bathing. He entered the water of his own accord and hacked off three of the dragon's trunks. In this way he neutralized three of the influences of the zodiac, the influences emanating from the signs of the zodiac representing fire: Aries, Leo and Sagittarius. However, he concluded a pact with the other nine influences of the zodiac, which do not seem to have such a negative effect.

In this context the bylina describes Dobrynya as stupid enough to conclude a pact with Zmei. Therefore the three eogisms of the soul can still be effective through the remaining nine influences of the zodiac that are still intact. The dragon of desire is devious and reveals himself, always, to be a diplomat.

Furthermore, Zmei breaks the contract. In other words, the planetary influences form a whole, and when part of it is neutralized, this can only be a temporary matter. (Therefore the threefold egoism of the soul reveals itself again, and can be identified as a complete dragon with twelve trunks.) The bylina then describes how Gorynchich seizes King Vladimir's niece,

Zabava Puchatichna, and keeps her in his lair under Mount Sorochin, the mountain of materialism, just as he had already done with 40 tsars, 40 kings, 40 princes, thousands of peasants and townspeope, and countless virgins. He chained her to the rock. Zabava means 'gift from God'. She was God's gift in the Putcha, the soul.

Zabava, or Prometheus, serves as a counterpart to Epimetheus, the force of thought and unconscious astral observation (based on unconscious inspiration). After capturing virtually all the forces that are present in humans (kings, princes, etc.), Zmei finally also captures the Prometheus force. When man wishes to learn to control his soul with his own strength, he loses the capacity of forethought, after losing many other things.

When Dobrynya returned to Kiev, his mother gave him a magic steed from the family stables, and a whip to go with it that could kill dragons. In this way she showed her son first of all the existence of an age-old, everlasting physical body concealed inside the ordinary, mortal, material body: the so-called crystal body or Phantom of Light (Atma), which was healed and saved from death by Christ so that it became a resurrected body. Secondly, she emphasized the strength of the will insofar as it is used in accordance with the word of Christ: 'Not my will, but thy will be done.' Used in this way, the will gives the magic steed (Atma) an enormous secret power a long time before it has fully developed. Therefore this enormous force can be traced back to Christ, to Christ as the future Self of mankind and above all, as the Lord of the Soul.

If necessary, this force can for a while replace the lack of an individual higher force of the soul and of the Self. (Dobrynya Nikitich acquires his own Self force only later on, when he marries a daughter of Mikoela Selyaninovich.) Meanwhile he performs his tasks with that which temporarily replaces his individual soul and Self force. This is thanks to the advice of his mother. It is therefore the result of being 'the son of a widow'.

Dobrynya Nikitich ultimately vanquishes Zmei Gorynchich and its offspring (the egoistic feelings and thoughts) altogether, rather than partially, with the enormous force of Atma which can be traced back to Christ, and with the help of his magic steed and giant whip. He liberates all the forces within him, i.e. within Russia, from the spell of the egoism of the soul and the attendant materialism. Finally he also frees Zabava Puchatichna. She represents the force of forethought and Manichean prescience, and wishes to bind herself to him permanently. However, Dobrynya does not bind himself to Zabava.

A fascination emanates from this Manichean prescience which could impede the further progress of the soul and could endanger its marriage with the spirit. This is particularly the case when the individual higher Self force has not yet been awoken, and one must rely on the higher Self force of Christ. Dobrynya brings Zabava back to her uncle from Vladimir, the representative of the Grail son.

(As the representative of Manichean prescience, i.e. not the intellectual prescience of the Self, Zabava must await Vasili Budimirovich under Dobrynya's care. Vasili Budimirovich is the Western representative of the aspect of peace of the higher Self who is intended for her. See also the bylini about Vasili Budimirovich.)

Dobrynya Nikitich and Natasha Mikoelichna

Dobrynya Nikitich became Vladimir's court singer. One day, at Vladimir's request, he sang about Volga the wise and Mikoela Selyaninovich. At the end of Dobrynya's recital the 60-year-old boyar Bermyata Vasilevich pointed out to Dobrynya that the song was not finished and that in the end Volga became Mikoela's guest and was spoiled by the latter's daughters. The pious but rather weak bogatyr Alyosha Popovich confirmed this, and said provocatively: 'Dobrynya, the eldest daughter Vasilisa has long been married to the merchant bogatyr Stavyor Godinovich from Chernigov, but the youngest daughter Natasha is still free. Natasha Mikoelichna says that she will only marry the man who defeats her in a duel. Why don't you challenge her?'

Dobrynya pointed out to Alyosha that it was not necessary to fight a woman to obtain her acceptance in marriage. Nevertheless, the chivalrous singer could not forget Natasha Mikoelichna, and set out to find her. He travelled to the west and followed a knight wearing the clothes of a woman, the polyenitsa Natasha Mikoelichna. She remained silent in every language. When he finally became irritated by this, Dobrynya struck her on the cheek with his open hand as hard as he could. She mumbled to herself: 'Am I being bitten by a mosquito?' Dobrynya felt that he was not as strong as she. Nevertheless, Natasha was won over by him, and she admitted: 'I used to visit Kiev secretly very often, and I saw you there. I love you, Dobrynya. If you will not have me as your wife, I must kill you.' They swore to be faithful to each other, and another wedding was celebrated in the capital city of Russia.

Commentary
After his fight with the soul dragon, Dobrynya Nikitich came into contact with Mikoela Selyaninovich through the suitable medium of emotional expression and song.

Just as King Vladimir and Dunai Ivanovich acquired Self force through their marriage to a representative of that force from outside the Slav sphere of Kiev Rus, in the sphere of space, Dobrynya acquired his Self force through his marriage to a representative of that force from outside the Slav sphere, in the sphere of time. As a younger bogatyr, he derives his Self force from the Self force of the daughter of the older bogatyr Mikoela Selyaninovich. In this respect the younger bogatyr resembles the older bogatyri Sviatogor, Volkh Vselavyevich and Volga Sviatoslavovich. In this way he acquires a Self force which is strongly directed towards the future.

Mikoela Selyaninovich has two daughters: Vasilisa, who is already married to the merchant bogatyr Stavyor Godinovich — this marriage will be discusssed later — and Natasha. Mikoela's second daughter has the same name as the second daughter of the King of Lithuania. Like the latter, she represents the force of the Self and the related spiritual Self insofar as this leads to a rebirth of the soul. However, she brings this force to Kiev Rus from the sphere of time (from the future), while Natasha of Lithuania did so from the sphere of space (from Western Europe).

Both Natashas are stronger than their respective husbands, the former messengers requesting marriage on behalf of King Vladimir. The Self is always the strongest force in man, and the messengers each in their own way also acquire this Self force through the efforts they make for their Grail King, so that he may bind himself to the (West European) Self force. They acquire this Self force in the 'Natasha form'.

Dunai Ivanovich was only able to assimilate this Self force in the Natasha form, which came to him from the sphere of space through his death. Dobrynya Nikitich was able to assimilate this Self force in this form into his life, as it came to him from the sphere of time.

As we have already seen, Dunai represented the emotional element of the Slavs insofar as this was directed back to the past, while Dobrynya represents this element insofar as it points to the future.

Alyosha Popovich and the Magician Tugarin Zmeiovich

Alyosha Popovich and his friend the bogatyr Jekim Ivanovich left Rostov to go to Kiev. Halfway there, a kalika (ancient bogatyr) told the priest's son that the magician Tugarin Zmeiovich was coming towards them. The cunning Alyosha suggested changing clothes with the kalika so that he would be able to surprise the magician and trick him disguised as a beggar. When Tugarin approached, Alyosha had no difficulty in beheading the magician with an unexpected stroke of his sword. Out of vanity, Alyosha put on the magician's cloak, took his winged horse, and hastened back to Jekim and the kalika. At first they thought that he was the enemy, and Jekim struck down Alyosha in fear and shock. The priest's son was mortally wounded, but the kalika cured him with prayers and meditation. The beggar from the time of Sviatogor was given back his rags and Tugarin, wearing his own cloak again, was taken back to Kiev. At Vladimir's court Alyosha was received with the highest praise. However, Tugarin slowly came back to life.

Out of fear, Vladimir prepared a meal for the magician. He ate and drank more than could be provided. In frustration Alyosha presented himself as 'a bite and a drink' on which Tugarin would choke. This resulted in a duel.

Alyosha prayed to God for storms and rain, so that Tugarin's horse would not be able to spread its wings, and the magician would be forced to fight on the ground.

This would probably make it possible for Alyosha to destroy Tugarin by trickery. As always, God granted the wish of the priest's son and provided terrible weather. As they started fighting on the ground, Alyosha called out: 'Tugarin, what now? Why did you bring your helpers along?' The magician looked round and Alyosha struck his head off again, this time for good.

Commentary

Alyosha Popovich is the third main bogatyr in the Kiev cycle of heroic bylini. He represents the third aspect, the aspect of thought in the triad of the will, feeling and thinking, the triad of essential human characteristics. His name means the all-wise son of a priest.

Even today, wisdom is associated in Russia with the status of the priest. The human aspect of thought, the human manifestation of the Self, corresponds to the aspect of the effect of the Self in the mythical triad: the will, wisdom/knowledge, (Self) activity — the aspect represented by Mikoela Selyaninovich. Thus Alyosha Popovich corresponds to Mikoela. However, it immediately becomes apparent that the mythical Mikoela as a bearer of the Self is a peasant, and therefore fulfils a function that corresponds with the aspects of the will, while the heroic Alyosha as a bearer of the Self fulfils a function as a priest that corresponds to the initiation of Sviatogor, the representative of the first aspect, the aspect of the will, in the mythical triad of essential characteristics. (Furthermore, with regard to the initiation of Sviatogor, it should be noted that this does not correspond with what Sviatogor represents either.)

In terms of what he represents, Alyosha is therefore an emanation of Mikoela Selyaninovich; in terms of the deeds which he performs, there is a relationship with Sviatogor.

Thus in relation to the above-mentioned three bogatyri, there is a triangular relationship between their essential character and their profession (see the diagram on p. 144). Anticipating the interpretation of the following bylini, it is appropriate to make the following comments.

The first bogatyr in the Kiev cycle of heroic bylini is the famous Ilya Muromets. He represents the first aspect, the aspect of the will in the triad of essential human characteristics, and he does so in the function of a peasant, i.e., in a function which corresponds with the aspect of the will. In what he represents Ilya Muromets corresponds to Sviatogor. In his profession he does not correspond to this: as a representative of the (mythical) aspect of the will, Sviatogor is not a peasant but an initiate. In his profession Ilya corresponds to the mythical older peasant, Mikoela Selyaninovich. Therefore with regard to these last three bogatyri, there is again a triangular relationship between their essential character (what they represent) and their profession (see the diagram on p. 144 and the table below).

The two triangular connections that cross each other only result because the first and third of the mythical older bogatyri fulfil a function that does not correspond with what they represent. It is this that particularly complicates the emanation of the three main heroic bogatyri in the three mythical ones. However, it is not only this aspect. There is another factor that complicates this emanation.

As we shall show, Alyosha Popovich is a representative of the typical Slav weakness, or lack of reinforcement by an external Self force (e.g. as in a character such as Apraxia or Natasha Mikoelichna). Therefore he is a weak representative of that aspect of the Self. Ilya comes towards him in his weakness. Ilya becomes and acquires a very special Self in a very special way, without any type of schedule or structure. He does not do so through the circumstances that he represents (rather weakly), just like Alyosha; nor does he do so by means of a marriage to a strong character such as Apraxia or Natasha, as do King Vladimir, Dunai Ivanovich and Dobrynya Nikitich. He does so, as will again become apparent later, by means of everything that is related to his will.

As stated before, the additional Self-bearing quality of Ilya Muromets further complicates the emanation of the heroic bogatyri in the mythical ones. It further complicates the two overlapping triangular relationships since Ilya Muromets corresponds to Mikoela Selyaninovich not only because of his function as a peasant, but also because of his extra Self-bearing quality (again see the table below).

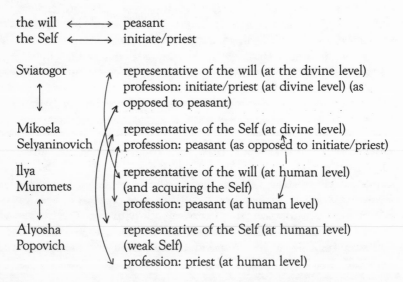

From where do these complications arise? The concept of the two overlapping triangular relationships with the additional complication described above is

160

based on the following esoteric facts that form the foundation for the bylini. Clearly it is not possible to explain these in detail here, but they can be briefly mentioned at this point. They should be read in conjunction with the notes and commentaries on the mythical bylini.

Within the framework of earlier Father mysteries, certain people were especially chosen to lead mankind. For this purpose they were transported at an early stage and very quickly to higher forms of consciousness, the forms of the imaginative, inspirational, and intuitive consciousness, on the basis of the premature and rapid development of their Self-consciousness. This development was known respectively as the threefold or fourfold initiation. This took place while mankind was still in a state of astral, ethereal and trance-like consciousness, while Self-consciousness slowly developed alongside.

It is clear that the accelerated development of consciousness in the mysteries reveals some differences from the slow development of the mass of mankind. This applies particularly with regard to the development of Self-consciousness and intuitive consciousness.

In the early (Father) mysteries these forms of consciousness developed separately (like those of the imagination and inspiration).[12] This means that in general a chosen initiate had no more than one higher form of consciousness foreshadowing the development of mankind. For example, he would be endowed either with Self-consciousness or with intuitive consciousness, as described above. Initiates with different types of higher consciousness had to co-operate together.

However, in the context of the slow development of consciousness, which most of mankind must pass through, it has become increasingly apparent since the early Middle Ages that a particular form of higher consciousness (Self-consciousness) cannot be acquired on a permanent basis separately from the other form of higher, or intuitive consciousness.

We will not discuss here the processes that reflect the essential characteristics of imaginative consciousness (related to higher thought processes and observation) and of inspirational consciousness (related to wisdom, artistic sensibility and the higher feelings). Again the process of reflection in the one case is the converse of the other. In both the mythical and heroic bylini they are taken together.

Let us return to the emanation of the first and third heroic bogatyri in the corresponding mythical bogatyri. If we view what the bogatyri represent (their essential characteristics) as 'what is reflected' and their profession as 'the mirror', Sviatogor illustrates the reflection of the essential characteristics and related matters: will → organization of the Self. Mikoela Selyaninovich reflects this as: organization of the Self → will. Alyosha Popovich does so as: organization of the Self → . . . → organization of the Self. Finally Ilya Muromets does so as: will → . . . → will.

As explained above, Sviatogor therefore symbolizes the 'Father-initiate'. He expresses how he exists as an initiate and how he is increasingly dependent on Mikoela. It was also explained how Mikoela Selyaninovich symbolizes the higher Self-man in and out of the early mysteries. He illustrates both the early Self initiate and the slow development of mankind towards acquiring a Self. He illustrates this as something that can succeed the exclusive initiation principle of the Father mysteries in a dignified way to become an inclusive initiation principle for all of mankind.

Alyosha Popovich symbolizes the contemporary autonomous Self man related to a) the development of the lower Self, which leads to contempt and mockery, but through which he also acquires the help of Christ if he desires it; b) the higher forms of consciousness, particularly intuitive consciousness, which must necessarily be acquired in the future. He illustrates the acquisition of the Self in a realistic way — in its weakness.

Ilya Muromets symbolizes contemporary man, who has acquired intuitive consciousness (based on an acquisition of the Self that is sufficiently prepared for this in karmic terms; he expresses Mikoela's acquisition of the Self). Ilya illustrates the Slav interpretation of the Grail. As a Self-man with intuitive consciousness and a Grail worker *par excellence*, he complements the weaker Self-man, Alyosha Popovich.

With regard to the last bogatyr who is concerned here, and whose essential characteristics and profession have been compared with those of several other bogatyri, two remarks should be made, and to some extent repeated, to clarify the following bylina about him. In the first place, Alyosha is presented as a bogatyr with a paradoxical character: he is both the most egocentric and the most Christocentric bogatyr. This is because he also represents the Self in its lower aspect, the aspect necessary for there to be a freedom of choice, which allows man to fail and act contemptuously, but which is still tolerated by Christ as the ultimate guardian of man's freedom of choice.

Secondly, in contrast with King Vladimir, Dunai Ivanovich and Dobrynya Nikitich, Alyosha Popovich does not have to bind himself to an external Self force as a representative of the Slav Self force — though admittedly this is now very weak, if present at all — yet it can be considerable as a thinking force through the lower aspect of the Self.

In order to fulfil his destiny, it is sufficient for him to join his friend, the bogatyr Jekim Ivanovich. Jekim is the Russian version of the Jewish names Jachin and Joachim. Jekim means founder, establisher. In the Self, Jekim represents the power of initiative. On the way to Kiev, Alyosha and Jekim meet a kalika. A kalika is something special, extraordinary. A kalika is an anonymous ancient bogatyr who does not play a role in the mythical bylini because he was converted to Christianity at an early stage. Thus a kalika is a pre-Christian representative of Christ and Christianity, who has moreover survived the ancient past and entered the era of the heroic bylini, usually as a beggar.

This kalika, an archaic representative of Christ, informed Alyosha and Jekim that the magician–dragon, Tugarin Zmeiovich, was threatening

Kiev Rus. Tugarin symbolizes the force of the Asiatic heathen gods who were worshipped by the Eastern Slavs before they turned to the Christian God.

As the most pious of the younger bogatyri, it is appropriate that Alyosha should slay this magician-dragon who constantly raises his ugly head, and should continue the initiative of establishing Christianity in Russia, together with Jekim Ivanovich. The bylina tells how Alyosha succeeds in his destiny, though not at the first attempt. He uses borrowed kalika forces and succeeds on the basis of all sorts of tricks derived from the force of the lower aspect of the Self.

Alyosha exchanges clothes with the kalika so that he can approach Tugarin as an apparently harmless beggar, and then strike him down in a surprise attack. Alyosha succeeds in surprising and cutting down Tugarin. Out of vanity and in order to show off to Jekim, he puts on Tugarin's magician's cloak after striking him down, and also takes his winged horse. This gives Jekim such a fright that he strikes Alyosha in turn, so that the latter has to be cured by the kalika.

This story expresses how early Christianity in Russia triumphed, thanks to a large number of dubious means derived from the activity of the lower aspect of the Self, and that particularly the external form and personal experience of this Christianity adopted many magic customs which remained from earlier heathen tribes. These customs were unsuitable in the original conversion to Christianity, and eventually had to be dispensed with.

Finally Tugarin, dressed in his own cloak, is taken back to Kiev. This means that the heathen teachings are finally unmasked very clearly, and presented to the Brotherhood of the Grail in Kiev for the protection of Christianity. For a while this helps to consolidate pure Christianity in Kiev Rus. However, gradually Tugarin comes back to life and swallows up the good habits of Christianity. Then Alyosha presents himself as meat and drink on which Tugarin will choke. In other words, the power of thought is offered to crawl into the skin of the dragon of the heathens, so that this dragon will be hollowed out from inside. Finally, Alyosha succeeds in slaying Tugarin with the help of external circumstances granted by God — Christ always hears the prayers directed towards him by the lower aspect of man's Self — and also by means of improper tricks. (The final part of this story is also a scenario of the future.)

The Cure of Ilya Muromets

During the reign of King Vladimir there lived in the village of Karacharov near the city of Murom a poor man called Ilya Timofejevich, who had been crippled from birth. He was the son of the peasants Ivan Timofejevich and Jefrosina Jakovlyevna. For 30 years he had been chained to his bed of pain

163

like a Prometheus. All he did was pray to Christ to be cured, and that one day he might be able to serve the world with health and strength. Visitors told him stories about King Vladimir's court in Kiev. His favourite stories were those about the dragons Zmei Gorynchych and Solovei Razbojniek. They threatened Holy Russia and seemed invincible.

One day, when the Timofejevich family were working on the land, three kaliki from the time of Sviatogor went past. They had the power of healing in their hands, and they said: 'Ilya, get up. You have acquired great skills in 30 years of being ill. Now you are better. Go and be a hero.'

Ilya got up, and the kaliki continued: 'Never start a fight with the bogatyri of ancient times: Sviatogor, Samson Samojlevich, Mikoela Selyaninovich and Volkh Vselavyevich. The first two are the basic forces of the earth itself, Mikoela is protected by the earth, and Volkh is too clever for you. Go to the field and wait for the first peasant who is taking a young and scrawny stallion into the town. Buy the animal, no matter how much it costs, feed it for three months on wheat and water, and then let it bathe in dew for three mornings. In this way the stallion will become the strongest horse on earth, and you will become the best bogatyr in the land'.

When the kalika departed, he broke some bread and drank a beaker of wine with Ilya, who was cured. Ilya then hastened to the land, where his parents were taking a nap. With amazing speed he finished their work for the rest of the day. Then he acquired a scrawny stallion as he had been told, looked after the creature according to instructions and bade farewell to his parents. They gave him their blessing on condition that he always do the right thing everywhere.

He went to the village priest and swore before God: 'I am going to Kiev along the shortest route, even if it passes through a large and hostile army. If I am challenged, I will not draw my bow, shoot an arrow, draw my spear, nor sully my club with blood. Nevertheless, I will be in Kiev in an hour and a half, and I will present myself to King Vladimir, the Red Sun. I will partake of my first meal when I am with him, and not before.'

Ilya took a handful of earth, placed it in a linen bag, and tied it round his neck to remind him of the land of his birth. He threw a crust of rye bread into the River Oka, saying: 'Than you, Mother Oka, for quenching the thirst of Ilya Muromets so often'. He bowed in every direction, mounted his horse and went on his way.

Commentary

Ilya Muromets is the first main bogatyr in the Kiev cycle of heroic bylini. What he represents was discussed above. Ilya is named after the Jewish prophet Elijah, who was personified in the peasant Naboth, and acted against King Ahab and Queen Isabel with the help of punitive weather conditions commanded by Yahweh. He also opposed the cultural decay caused by them, the worship of Baal enforced by them, and the annexations of land. (Naboth lost his garden and finally also his life.) Elijah means: Yahweh is my God.

Muromets means 'of Murom', the city in the woods of Murom before Kitezh-Philadelphia was built there. Timotheus was Ilya's second name. Timotheus means 'glory to God'.

The character of the Russian Ilya Muromets is strongly reminiscent of that of the Jewish Elijah. This is particularly apparent when the following conclusions of Rudolf Steiner about the Elijah character are examined:

1) The spirit of a people — the people of Israel — was manifest in Elijah. (This was the spirit of a people who were starting to prepare for the future development of Manas.)
2) The character of Elijah returns in the figure of St John the Baptist.
3) After being beheaded, St John can be identified in a particular way through the circle of the twelve apostles of Christ and with one of these in particular, St John the Evangelist.
4) The age-old Elijah–St John the Baptist individuality is rejuvenated by its identification with the youthful Hiram Abif–St John the Evangelist individuality. The latter acquires the strength of Elijah's age and maturity through this identification.
5) The latter returns as Christian Rosenkreuz. The spiritually rejuvenated Elijah returns in the figures of Raphael and Novalis.
6) Both Raphael, the painter of Madonnas, and Novalis, 'the Sophia poet', died at the age of 30–3 after a brief, predestined life of scientified and artistically coloured, spiritual experiences. In this way and by these means he prepared himself for a particular task in the future.

The sixth point is particularly informative. The Elijah–St John the Baptist individuality has both mental and scientified experiences as Raphael and Novalis (Novalis was a mountain engineer), as well as astral, emotional, and artistic experiences. These take place at an early age before the death of this individuality aged 30–3. What remains in the incarnations of Raphael and Novalis are the experiences related to the will, the experiences which this individuality has as Elijah, the peasant Naboth, at a much older age, well past 33.

It is certainly a challenging idea that the individuality of Elijah lives (or will live) in Ilya Muromets. [13] Nevertheless, the following considerations are a reason for accepting this. Firstly, Ilya is the same name as Elijah. As the first main bogatyr of Kiev, he is said to be a manifestation of the spirit of the Russian people, the spirit of the people who will develop Manas. Secondly, like Elijah, he is a peasant, and as a peasant — again like Elijah — he fights against the dragons of cultural decay, the worship of idols (like Alyosha Popovich) and the annexation of land. Like Elijah, he does this when he is older. Thirdly, as a man of will, a peasant, he is the counterpart of Raphael and Novalis, in whom intellectual — and above all, artistic and emotional — aspects played a role at a young age, a role in which the Madonna–Sophia element is central. He is their counterpart in the future, while Elijah was their counterpart in the past.

It may be assumed that the preparations of Raphael and Novalis for their future task carried out before the age of 30-3, will be fulfilled in the older Ilya Muromets and his mission.

For the first 30 years of his life Ilya was bedridden and his legs were paralysed. It is as though the force of the intellectual and emotional aspects of Raphael and Novalis were transformed and came to rest in his will, in his metabolic system and limbs, to be revealed in renewed glory at a predestined moment, in the glory of the Slav knighthood of the Grail.

At the end of this time Ilya is cured by the three kaliki and becomes Russia's first bogatyr. These three kaliki represent the forces of the triad of divine essential characteristics as they are converted to Christianity, and they therefore advise Ilya never to fight against the pre-Christian representatives of these forces. Indirectly they themselves are these representatives. (In the next bylina about Ilya Muromets, Samson Samolevich is presented as the physical aspect of what Sviatogor represented in relation to the will. His function is comparable to the function of Natasha of Lithuania in relation to Apraxia.) In addition, the kaliki explain how Ilya can acquire a horse and rear it so that it is like that of Mikoela Selyaninovich. As we saw above, this apparently weak, but actually extremely strong horse represents a physical/personal aspect of man, in which according to Christ, the most remarkable developments are achieved in weakness.

On the eve of departure the kaliki and Ilya Muromets celebrate a sort of Holy Eucharist. Then Ilya helps his parents for a while with their work on the land. With his superhuman strength he finds this very easy. He then hastens to King Vladimir's Round Table in Kiev, after swearing an oath that he will temporarily renounce violence. (According to spiritual science, evil is by definition goodness taking place at the wrong time. At certain times it must be spared in order to mature and be recognized.)

Then Ilya swears that he will reach Kiev in an hour and a half, i.e. in a time circle and a half (or halfway into the next cultural era). Until he arrives there he will not eat, and he will renounce all earthly material things. He places some of the earth of Murom in a bag and leaves. Russian earth, particularly the earth of the heart of Russia (initially this is Murom as the city preceding the future Kitezh) has more heavenly forces than any other soil in the world. Ilya the peasant takes some of the heavenly forces absorbed from this earth — as the body of Christ — with him to Kiev.

Finally, some comments should be made about Ilya's Self as described here in relation to the commentary on the previous bylina. It was show that, like Alyosha Popovich, Ilya Muromets has a certain amount of Self force. However, unlike the former, he does not have the naturally weak Slav Self force of the present; he possesses an aspect of the strong Slav Self force of the future (as also represented by Mikoela Selyaninovich). This is because this force is a premature reflection in his will of his previous incarnations resulting from his sickness and cure. As a transformed Raphael-Novalis character, he was suitable for this reflection during the time of King Vladimir's Round Table. He did not acquire his Self in the same way as King Vladimir, Dunai Ivanovich or Dobrynya Nikitich, through marrying Apraxia or Natasha, but acquired the Slav element of the Self of the future prematurely and without mediation by means of the process of the sickness and cure of the Self. In this respect Ilya was unique. That is why he is such a well loved character. The cure of Ilya's will, and particularly the development of his Self, continues, breaking down barriers, during his encounter with Sviatogor, as will appear in a later bylina.

In summary, it may be concluded that in the context of the heroic bylini, Ilya Muromets as a peasant and worker of the Grail represents the will, for his is the profession which corresponds to the will. Regardless of all comparisons, he is a bearer of the Self in a very special way.

Therefore the self in the Slavs is based on a fourfold element: a) relationship with the present Self force of the Varangian/Germanic tribes (King Vladimir — Apraxia) (Dunai — Natasha); b) relationship with the foreshadowing of the Self force of the future Slav root race (Dobrynya Nikitich — Natasha Mikoelichna) (Stavyor Godinovich — Vasilisa Mikoelichna); c) a weak manifestation of the individual Self (Alyosha Popovich); d) the Self of the St John-Raphael-Novalis individuality (Ilya Muromets).

Ilya Muromets Frees Chernigov

In the church of Murom, Ilya repeated his oath to renounce violence until his arrival in Kiev. Then he hastened on. Halfway to his destination his steed suddenly stopped and made a hole in the ground with his hoof. Living water bubbled up. Ilya cut a cross from an oak tree growing by the road and planted it in the earth next to the hole. He carved the following words onto the cross: 'Ilya Muromets, the son of a peasant and a bogatyr of Holy Russia, passed this way'. Later a chapel was built on that spot and animals fortified themselves with the water from the well.

In three leaps Ilya's stallion reached Chernigov, also known as Kitezh. Three Tsars were besieging the city. Despite his indignation Ilya did not resort to armed violence. However, he tore a giant oak from the ground, much larger than the one which he had used to make the cross, and with this and his horse, which trampled on everything, he defeated the three armies of the Tsars. However, as he had no dungeon, he set the three Tsars free. He found the inhabitants of the city in the cathedral of Chernigov preparing to die. The young peasant bogatyr explained to them what had happened and that they were free. In gratitude they asked Ilya to rule over

Ilya Muromets with the citizens of Chernigov.
Taken from: 'Russian Heroic sagas and Legends by Boris Raptschinsky.

their city, but he refused twice with the words: 'I am not a ruler and I do not wish to rest here. I am hastening to Kiev to serve Vladimir.'

He also refused their gold. The people of Chernigov told him that the shortest road to Kiev had been blocked for 30 years. There was grass growing between the stones. Three obstacles made the road absolutely impassable: the Brynski marshes, which sucked in every passer by; the dragon Solovei Razboniek Rachmaninovich, who had been laying in wait by the so-called Levanidov cross on the Smorodinaya for 30 years, all the while hypocritically whistling like a nightingale in an intolerable manner; and finally, by the seven old oaks, there was the dragon's impassable house, wife, three large daughters and six small sons. However, Ilya was not to be discouraged, and went on his way.

Commentary

As a tiller of the Grail, Ilya Muromets performs some holy tasks in relation to the earth: halfway on the road to Kiev from Murom, he finds living water and plants an oak cross in the ground. In this way he digs up the blood of Christ from the earth that once dripped onto the earth when Christ was hanging on the Cross of the earth. Then he reaches Chernigov, which some believe represents an earlier stage of the later Kitezh, just as Murom does.

Ilya frees Chernigov from all the threats that will destroy Kitezh later on. He does this without resorting to armed violence, but by means of the force of Christian resignation, which helps to vanquish strength with weakness. (This resignation subsequently characterizes Kitezh.) Ilya refuses the offer to become ruler of Chernigov: he has not come to rule, but to serve. His services are needed in Kiev. The people of Chernigov show Ilya that the shortest road to Kiev by which it can be reached in an hour and a half (one cultural era and a half). This has been impassable for 30 years (the time needed to prepare for the coming of Christ). It is blocked by three interrelated obstacles: the Brynski marshes that suck in everyone who passes by; the whistling dragon, Solovei Razboniek Rachmaninovich, who keeps guard by the Levanidov cross (the cross of brotherhood); and the family of the dragon consisting of his wife, three large daughters and six small sons, who live by the seven old oak trees. Ilya Muromets is not to be discouraged, and continues on his way to Kiev.

Ilya Muromets and Solovei Razboniek

Thirty verst before Kiev, Ilya Muromets went to the Brynski marshes. He quickly built a bridge over the swamp with oak trees torn out of the ground and approached the Smorodinaya, which sprang from nowhere, where the Levanidov cross stood. This is the cross where Vladimir's bogatyri had once sworn to each other to be brothers in spirit. A voice screeched: 'Who is the bold person who dares to ride past my nest?' Ilya picked some poppies and stopped up his ears with them so that he was unable to hear the roaring, hissing, and whistling of the dragon — this must be Solovei, the treacherous singer, a dragon or a giant.

Ilya did not fall down dead from the terrible din, like every other bogatyr who had ever taken up the fight against this 'nightingale'. Instead he urged his frightened horse to continue undaunted. In order to catch sight of this miracle of endurance, Solovei leaned too far out of his nest. Ilya forgot his promise of peace and shot an arrow into the dragon's right eye so that the latter fell out of his nest. The hero caught him, tied him up, put him upside down on his steed, and continued on to Solovei Razboniek's house. This house was seven verst long and built on seven old oak trees. On every spike of the railings there was a hewn-off head of a knight.

Solovei's wife, his three large daughters and six small sons saw the group approaching. The children thought that their father was coming home with another victim, but their mother could see more clearly. In order to save her husband, she sent her daughters to meet the peasant to distract him, but in vain. Ilya mowed them down and kicked them away. Solovei called out: 'Children, ask your mother to offer this peasant the magic gifts and conclude an agreement with him.

The mother, Akoelina Dudenchevina, then sent her six sons to Ilya with all the stolen goods she had. However, they changed into ravens and attacked the hero. Then Ilya grasped his whip and beat them out of the air. Finally, the mother and daughters went to Ilya themselves with the magic gifts. However, he was intransigent and took Solovei with him to Kiev. He made the family promise that they would stop robbing and killing. When he came to a house of God, he asked a priest for forgiveness for violating his promise to temporarily renounce violence.

From Karacharov, Ilya reached Kiev in an hour and a half, tied his horse and the giant Solovei to a post in front of the royal stables, and entered the palace. He was welcomed by King Vladimir, the Red Sun, and when asked, he told him who he was, where he had come from, and how he had been bedridden and paralysed for 30 years, but had recently been cured by three kaliki.

Finally he said that he had decided to serve Holy Russia in the name of Christ for the rest of his life, without seeking any reward for this. He related how he had taken the shortest road from Karacharov to Kiev to offer the king his services . . . Then the ever-suspicious Alyosha Popovich tired of his story and interrupted: 'How did you say you came here?' He pointed out to the court that the invincible Solovei Razboniek had cut off the shortest road to the north for 30 years. Ilya answered: 'What this bogatyr says is true. Or at least it was true, but I have defeated Solovei and brought him here. He is tied upside down to my horse. He was not invincible.

All the bogatyri went to the stables. The robber cowered. Vladimir challenged Solovei to prove the power of his terrible voice then and there.

Solovei answered: 'No one other than this peasant defeated me. I will listen only to him.' Ilya then commanded him: 'Solovei Razboniek, whistle, hiss, and roar with half your strength.' However, Solovei demanded food and drink first. After a gigantic meal, he whistled, hissed, and roared, but to everyone's despair he did so with all his strength. Ilya ordered him to stop, and when he continued to whistle, immediately killed him with an arrow.

Vladimir thanked Ilya and made him Russia's first bogatyr. The king had hardly finished speaking when Solovei's wife arrived unexpectedly with his three big daughters, six small sons and carts full of stolen valuables. Alyosha Popovich suggested to Vladimir that they accept the family's wish and take all this wealth in ransom for the father's body. Ilya ignored Alyosha's proposal, and on his own authority ordered the family to turn straight round with all the stolen goods: 'Akoelina Dudenchevina, take the body of your husband, bury it decently, and bring up your children properly.' The family slunk off. The bogatyri went back into the palace and made fun of Alyosha Popovich for misjudging the new bogatyr. At Samson Samolevich's suggestion, Dobrynya Nikitich picked up his goesli and sang to them all about Sviatogor and Mikoela Selyaninovich.

Commentary

The present Sardes culture, and particularly the forces inhibiting evolution in this culture, divides mankind — and in the first place, the Slav element — by 'an hour and a half', or one cultural period and a half, from the zenith of the future Philadelphia-Kitezh culture. Clearly, the greatest force that inhibits evolution in our time is the attraction of materialism, symbolized in this bylina by the swamps of the Brynski marshes.

The virulent effect of this materialism is an unavoidable pollution related to it. This pollution should not merely be viewed as a mechanical effect. It is caused by all sorts of demons; in a sense, it can be seen as a dragon. The most serious form of pollution is not even chemical pollution, but ethereal pollution. The latter indeed forms the basis for the former. The ethereal world is the world of rhythm and sound, the world of the creative word and the world of life. Any materialist thoughts and feelings are a burden on this world of rhythm and sound, this world of life, and pollute it long before materialistic deeds following from feelings cause pollution in the world's chemical sphere.

Ethereal pollution moves rather like a living force or dragon underneath mechanical pollution, making the latter transcendant. The link between the two is formed by noise pollution, i.e. the form of mechanical/chemical pollution which manifests itself in the chemical sphere with the characteristics of the ethereal sphere: rhythm and sound. Because of its unique linking function, noise pollution serves as the prototype of all pollution.

In this bylina, noise pollution is presented in the form of the dragon Solovei Razboniek Rachmaninovich. Solovei (Solveig, in Norwegian) means 'fighter for one's home, for one's own affairs'. Razboniek (Radbod, in German) means 'advise and command'. Rachman (Abram in Hebrew) means 'raised up father, patriarch'. All these meanings indicate an invigorating and independent influence on the world and many, many subsidiary influences. Solovei is sometimes called 'the nightingale', whose song pleases some while it tortures others. The nightingale aspect of this dragon represents the element in noise pollution which is produced by 'light music'. This light music often pleases materialist man more than the bird lover likes the song of the nightingale. On the other hand, this light music can be torture for spiritual man, preventing him from hearing the harmony of the spheres and achieving inspirational consciousness.

Solovei keeps guard by the so-called Levanidov cross, planted on the bank of the Smorodinaya, which springs up from nowhere. The Levanidov cross is the cross of brotherhood, while the Smorodinaya symbolizes the principle of love — the love that increases as one gives more of it away. The whistling Solovei, who pollutes the world with his noise, keeps guard by the cross of brotherhood on the bank of the river of love, in order to set people against each other by being irritated with each other about him. Therefore he stops people from loving each other.

The dragon (sound) pollution 'ploughs with his family'. He has a wife, Akoelina Dudenchevina, three big daughters and six little sons. They live in a house which is seven verst long and is built on seven old oak trees. The dragon's wife represents the lower Self of man (not to be confused with the higher Self — of Ilya — and what is represented by characters like Apraxia and Natasha Mikoelichna), insofar as this is drawn along by the egoistic effects of pollution. In this context Akoelina Dudenchevina (Alexandra the Wolf Woman) signifies something like a restrainer of the (male) higher Self (of Ilya). His three big daughters represent the three characteristics of man's soul, again insofar as they are affected by pollution.

Finally, his six small sons represent the three human bodies and their related physical aspects (the material body with the seed of Atma, the ethereal body with the seed of Buddha, and the astral body with the seed of Manas), again insofar as they are subject to the consequences of pollution. The house of the dragon family, represents the earth, as it was created by the seven divine impulses, now at rest in the form of oak trees of the seven divine hierarchies.

To summarize: the dragon Solovei Razboniek personifies pollution in terms of world materialism. He does not evoke love in the essential characteristics of man, but hate and irritation. As a result, these characteristics are dehumanized; they become demonic, like dragons and the wife and children of a dragon. This is the central problem of the fifth cultural period, and it is the main problem that impedes man's progress to the middle of the next cultural era. On his way to the future Kiev with the whole of mankind, Ilya Muromets, like Raphael or Novalis, and using their means, fights against Solovei Razboniek after only an hour and a half.

None of King Vladimir's bogatyri ever succeeded in defeating Solovei. None of them could endure his whistling. Ilya succeeds. He consciously uses the forces that are sensitive to noise (poppies). He uses them almost in a homoeopathic way, and in this way manages to endure the din made by Solovei. Although he does not do so entirely without violence, and in weakness — i.e. using only the purely artistic means of Raphael or Novalis — as he had sworn, he does defeat the dragon. He shoots an arrow through its right eye and strikes the aspect which gives life to Solovei — the spirit of Ahriman. Then, with the whip of his single-minded will to clear the road to Kiev, Ilya strikes down the six sons of the dragon who attack him from the air in the form of ravens. This means that he frees the physical and spiritual aspects of man from their addiction to the nightingale aspect of Solovei; he destroys all the logical arguments (ravens) that rise up from the human, physical, and spiritual figures; arguments like 'after all, in itself the nightingale of light music cannot hurt anyone or anything'.

When the lower Self of man, and particularly the threefold nature of his soul, prepares itself like a bride, to present Ilya with the pleasures of materialism (for there is an aspect of pleasure in materialism, as well as an aspect of burden) in the form of magical gifts, the hero does not accept these. He does not take the wife and daughters of the dragon and what they have to offer, for he serves only the archetypal Madonna, the Sophia (the perfect soul married to the spirit) of Raphael and Novalis. Ilya clubs Solovei and takes him to Kiev upside down; in other words in such a way that his evil is turned to goodness. He makes Solovei's wife and children (human nature) promise that they will no longer exploit the world. He reaches Kiev and the Round Table of King Vladimir in the allotted time — an hour and a half. He tells his story and presents Solovei, who had been considered invincible, to the bogatyri.

In order that they will identify Solovei as the dragon of (noise) pollution — particularly the intellectual and cynical Alyosha Popovich — Ilya orders the beast to whistle, hiss, and roar with half his strength after it has eaten its food. However, the dragon immediately produces such a din with all his strength that Ilya is forced to shoot him dead almost immediately. This means that Ilya wishes to give the good aspect of materialism a chance in Kiev, provided that the pollution could be reduced by half. However, this did not work, and furthermore materialism proves to be too costly in terms of life force (the dragon eats too much). Materialism is rejected, the dragon is well and truly killed.

When the dragon's family arrives in Kiev, having followed the father to redeem the father's body with the means of materialism, Akoelina Dudenchevina is given her husband's body with the words, 'Bury your husband honestly (materialism had its uses) and bring up your children properly (spiritually).' Finally, Dobrynya Nikitich sings the song of the encounter between Sviatogor and Mikoela Selyaninovich, the song of the free human Self and of love, which weighs more than all matter.

Ilya Muromets and Sviatogor

Accompanying himself on the goesli, Dobrynya Nikitich sang to King Vladimir's bogatyri about the ancient Sviatogor. How he lived on the Holy Mountains (the Carpathians) because the earth could no longer withstand his weight, and how one day he got up and met the peasant Nikoela Selyaninovich with his bag full of gravity. He concluded: 'It is said that in the end, Sviatogor disappeared completely into the ground and died.' However, the well informed boyar Mermasta Vasilevich denied this and said: 'No, he returned to the mountains and is still there.' This version of the story gave Alyosha Popovich the idea of challenging Ilya Muromets. He asked him: 'Isn't it just the thing for you to go and find out? In this way he thought that the newly arrived hero would disappear from sight for a while on a journey that was bound to be fruitless.

Ilya was aware of the ambiguous nature of Alyosha's proposal, but he wanted nothing more than to learn about the world, and test his strength. He asked Dobrynya to accompany him on his travels. They saddled their horses, and the next day the pair travelled west and soon reached the Levanidov cross in the Levanidov meadow. They swore an oath that they would always remain brothers in spirit, and they exchanged crosses. Then they travelled in the direction of the Carpathians. They discovered traces on the ground, and Ilya asked Dobrynya to follow them while he climbed the Holy Mountains himself.

He reached a plateau by means of a secret path, and just in front of him he saw the giant bogatyr asleep on a giant steed that was slowly walking along. He called the giant and challenged him to a duel, but the latter did not wake up. Even striking him with a club did not wake up the giant, let alone tip him out of his saddle. When he was struck for the third time, he merely mumbled: 'Russian flies bite rather painfully.' He opened his hand, seized Ilya, put him and his horse in his pocket, and rode on, still asleep. After walking for 48 hours, the giant's steed became tired. It stumbled and sank to its knees on the ground.

As a result, the oversized knight woke up despite himself, cursing his stallion. He took Ilya and his horse out of his pocket, and asked: 'Who are you?' Ilya told him who he was, how he had become a member of Vladimir's Round Table, and that he was looking for Sviatogor. It appeared that the giant was Sviatogor himself. Ilya and Sviatogor made friends. They continued their journey together, and one day they found an enormous coffin lying across the road, inscribed with the words: 'This coffin is intended for the person who fits it.' The giant had a premonition that this referred to him, and hesitating, he wished to try the coffin for size. Ilya also had a premonition that it was intended for Sviatogor, and therefore he got in first, beating the giant to it. The peasant's son proved to be too small. Then the giant lay down in the coffin, which fitted him like a glove.

Ilya did not wish to close the lid, so Sviatogor did so himself. Immediately the coffin and the lid fused together. Sviatogor called out with great regret: 'Woe is me, I am buried alive. Ilya, rip the planks off, one by one.' Ilya tried, but in vain. Then Sviatogor suggested: 'Take my sword and smash the coffin to smithereens.' Through a crack in the coffin, the old giant gave Ilya his breath, and thus his strength, to lift the sword of ancient days, but the sword was counter-productive. Every time Ilya struck a blow, it did not make a hole in the coffin, but produced an iron hoop. Sviatogor sighed: 'I am suffocating. It is obviously God's will that you succeed me. Keep my sword, but bind my giant steed to the coffin.'

So died the giant bogatyr and his giant steed. Ilya, now the successor of Sviatogor, decided to return to Kiev. He assumed (correctly) that Dobrynya would already have arrived back.

Commentary
When Dobrynya Nikitich has finished his song about Sviatogor, after the killing of Solovei Razboniek, Alyosha Popovich challenges Ilya to find out whether Sviatogor is still alive (as some believe, such as the boyar Bermata Vasilevich).[14] Ilya accepts the challenge and leaves. He wishes to test his strength and learn about the world. With regard to his imminent encounter with Russia's first ancient bogatyr, this has the following significance.

Through himself, his profession, and what he represents, Ilya wishes to turn to good use in the future everything that Sviatogor represents, as well as his profession and everything related to it. Thus he does not wish Sviatogor merely to represent and reveal his character from the point of view of the past, but also — as indicated in the discussion of the mythical bylini — from the point of view of the future.

The dual nature which has often been mentioned, i.e. that the aspect represented by the (first) mythical bogatyr (bogatyri) and their profession, oriented both to the past and the future, only becomes a true fact through the strength and knowledge inherited by Ilya from Sviatogor. It is this inheritance that cures Ilya's will to an ever greater extent: towards a Self-consciousness of his previous incarnations. This coincides with what he represents and his profession. It is because of this that he increasingly acquires an intuitive consciousness based on (higher) Self-consciousness. It is in this way that he renews the Sviatogor mysteries for the future, for the sixth root race era.

In this way he also repays the advance for his cure by the three kaliki (one of whom represented the heathen Sviatogor element in a pre-Christian Christian sense). However, first Sviatogor must die. His connection with the Self of Mikoela Selyaninovich will not save him from death. Indeed, the archetypal peasant, as we saw above, represents both the developing Self of pre-Christian man in general and the Self of the chosen individual who was a participant in the pre-Christian mysteries. However, with regard to Sviatogor as an initiate, he represents the latter in particular. This last form of representation as an aspect of ancient initiation systems particularly needs to be concluded and replaced by the new path to Self-consciousness in Christ, which incorporates all men. On this path towards Self-consciousness Apraxia, the two Natashas, Alyosha Popovich and Ilya Muromets serve as milestones, the latter in a special way, as he continues the line representing Mikoela's Self.

Therefore Ilya goes in search of Sviatogor in order to acquire knowledge and test his strength: the strength of his will, and especially of his Self. He asks Dobrynya Nikitich to accompany him on his journey, for this singer had proved to King Vladimir that like Dunai Ivanovich, he had acquired Self force from outside the geographical territory of the Slavs. He had also proved that he had acquired this force for himself outside the current period of the Slave culture. At the Levanidov cross, the cross of brotherhood, the two bogatyri promise to remain brothers in spirit for ever.

Upon reaching the Carpathians, the cradle of the Slav culture, they decide to separate to continue searching for Sviatogor. Ilya finds him riding his giant steed, asleep. Thus Sviatogor is certainly still alive, but he is asleep. Three times Ilya tries to wake up the sleeping giant. This means that he is trying to instill new life into the Father mysteries of Sviatogor which still exist, though in a very weak form. However, he does not succeed. Indeed, the mysteries merely assimilate him — Ilya, and what he represents — for Sviatogor puts him, and his horse, in his pocket.

Nevertheless, after walking on asleep for two hours, when the Father mysteries have simmered quietly through the first two post-Christian cultures, the time comes at the end of the fifth cultural era that the mysteries have become so heavy that they are derailed, and therefore temporarily wake up only to die away for good in the end (in their old form).

Sviatogor and Ilya find a sign of this imminent process of death on their way, along the path of the development of mankind: they find a coffin. Clearly this coffin, the symbol of destiny, will not fit the young Ilya, but fits the old Sviatogor. The latter crawls into the coffin, and with some misgivings closes the lid. In his last death spasms he asks Ilya to smash the coffin into smithereens. Ilya tries to do so, knowing that the mysteries that Sviatogor represents are also future mysteries. However, every time he strikes the coffin he does not split it but creates an iron hoop. Then Sviatogor sighs: 'Ilya, take my sword (the symbol of my strength) but bind my giant steed (my physical body, related to what I represented and practised) to the coffin.' Then the giant bogatyr and the giant horse both die.

Ilya, now the successor of Sviatogor, turns back to Kiev on his thin horse, and after yet another adventure on the way, finds that Dobrynya Nikitich has returned there.

In this bylina Dobrynya remains very much in the background, although he is clearly present. He is present as someone who has acquired a Self, but he is in the background because the consolidation of Ilya's Self is not 'a marriage requiring any form of mediation'.

176

Ilya Muromets and Idolich

When Sviatogor's strength had passed to Ilya, the latter asked himself as he rode back to Kiev how he could test his newly acquired powers. He met a kalika and suggested that they fight a duel. However, the kalika, who introduced himself as Ivanich, and saw what strength had passed to Ilya, pointed out to him that there was no honour for a bogatyr in such a duel. He would do better to fight the dragon Idolich, which had appeared in the neighbourhood of Kiev once again. Alyosha Popovich and Dobrynya Nikitich were there, but Alyosha was too scared, and Dobrynya too much in love with his wife, to fight the dragon. As Vladimir himself was too weak to march against the dragon, the beast was entering Kiev unimpeded and devouring and drinking all the supplies. Ilya reproached Ivanich: 'You do not wish to fight a dual with me, and it is clear that you have not fought the dragon either. This is rather strange. You are one of the ancient race, a kalika, perhaps twice as strong as I am. However, if you do not wish to do anything, let us exchange clothes. I will go to Kiev and you stay here by this big rock and wait for me.' The ancient mendicant monk agreed to Ilya's proposal.

When he arrived at Vladimir's court, the disguised hero bowed down before all those present, except Idolich. He introduced himself as a kalika from Murom. Gradually the dragon became suspicious. He asked the visitor whether he knew Ilya Muromets, and whether this greenhorn 'first bogatyr' ate a lot. Ilya damned the monster and the monster threw himself at the kalika, who was now recognized by everyone as Ilya. The peasant struck the dragon's dagger out of his hand. As it flew round, it killed twelve boyars and injured many more. Ilya dragged Idolich away from the palace and then out of Kiev, for it would not do to sully Russia's capital city with a dragon's blood. In a field out in the open the bogatyr who had acquired Sviatogor's strength used the dragon's body as a club to batter down his own army of idols.

When he had done this, he beheaded the dragon. For a while Vladimir's army continued to fight some of the remaining phantoms, but finally they were also defeated. Then Ilya returned to Ivanich.

Commentary

Riding back to Kiev after his encounter with Sviatogor, Ilya meets the kalika Ivanich. The latter advises him to liberate Russia from the dragon Idolich, the dragon of the heathens, who had once been defeated by Alyosha Popovich when he was wearing a less dangerous (historical) coat. Now he has settled in Kiev in a new guise and no one can stand up to him. He must be defeated with the force of 'Christian Self-consciousness'. However Alyosha does not have this to a sufficient extent, and Vladimir and Dobrynya do not have it in themselves. Just as Alyosha exchanged clothes with the kalika (possibly also Ivanich) to give him the courage to fight against Tugarin, Ilya now exchanges clothes with Ivanich. Then he resumes his journey to Vladimir's court.

Who is the kalika Ivanich (Jekim Ivanich, 'the taker of Initiative?' his name means 'John'). There is an element in him which serves both as supplement and a counterpart of Ilya's character. While Ilya represents the character of Novais-Raphael-St John the Evangelist, it seems that this Ivanich represents the character of Christian Rosenkreuz, helping the former from a hidden place while remaining in the background himself. This aspect of the interpretation of this bylina is only presented here as a possibility.

In what respect does Idolich correspond to Tugarin Zmeiovich, and in what respect is he different? Idolich means lord of the collective idols, a collective of phantoms (spirits of deceit that lead to an unbrotherly division of material foodstuffs), spectres (spirits of the 'evil law' that encourage an unequal treatment of one's fellow man in the legal domain), and demons (spirits of intolerance which encourage lack of spiritual freedom).

These three groups of idols together form a heathen collective of idols, encompassing the Slav world, a 'dragon of the heathens', when they arise from the philosophy and life created by the Slav Rurik and the three following unasked for Answers to it: a) the 'Golden Orda' of the Asiatic Tartars, forced on Russia by the Khans (the order of Lucifer); b) the Varangian-Germanic (Anglo-Saxon) materialism, which was introduced into Russia by Tsar Peter the Great (the order of Ahriman) and prepared by the Jesuits (see Chapter 5) c) the combination of a) and b), appearing in the form of Soviet communism, which was smuggled into Russia by Western Freemasons' lodges (the order of Lucifer-Ahriman).

The threefold curse of the lack of liberty, equality and fraternity is brought about by Tartarism, materialism and Soviet communism, because of their very nature and because the Call for liberty, equality and fraternity made by the Slav culture is reversed.

The above-mentioned three groups of idols, as we derived from the Slav-Rurik Call and the elements a) and b) can be identified as Smei Tugarin. He symbolizes the dragon or heathen dragon consisting mainly of either a dragon's trunk (symbol of the will of the Mongols) or of a dragon's head (symbol of the intellectual, materialist drives of Western Europeans). This 'half dragon', which often appeared in Russia's past, could still be defeated by someone like Alyosha Popovich. The above-mentioned three groups of idols, as derived from the Slav-Rurik Call, together with the element c), can be identified as Idolich.

When Ilya reaches Kiev dressed as a kalika, Idolich wishes to test his own strength against that of Ilya. He asks whether the latter eats a lot (has a lot of Christ strength). He asks this in order to decide on his approach to the newcomer, whom he rightly suspects is Ilya. However, it is not easy to decide on this, for Ilya appears as an indeterminate, kaliki-like background figure. To avoid any risk, the dragon throws himself on the bogatyr. They come to blows. Ilya strikes Idolich's dagger out of his hand, and during the fight it kills twelve boyars and injures many more. This means that the fight between (the representative of) Christian communism and (the representative of) heathen communism is concluded by the Slav world of form and labels represented by the boyars (which is derived from other peoples).

Idolich is killed by Ilya outside Kiev, i.e. outside the actual holy centre of the Slav Grail. Some groups of individual idols are slain by the other bogatyri. Ilya returns to Ivanich.

It is clear that the defeat of Idolich expresses the way in which Alyosha Popovich's weak Self force is supplemented by the strong Self force of Ilya Muromets.

The Dispute between Ilya Muromets and King Vladimir

After years of wandering and fighting over dragons apart from Idolich, Ilya finally succumbed to the advances of a foreign heathen princess. While he was staying at her father's court, she visited him at night and they became lovers. However, after several weeks of ecstasy, some noblemen informed him that since his departure Russia had again been attacked by enemies. Ilya regretted his relationship with the princess and returned to his native country. Again he wandered round for many years restoring order and peace, but this time with the memory of the heathen princess in his heart — a memory like a question without an answer, a memory that slowly and mysteriously transformed his erotic longings into a Christian brotherly love. Burning with that love, burning too strongly, he returned one day to Kiev in disguise.

At the court there were great celebrations. He introduced himself as Nikita Zoalieshanien, a peasant from the north, as poor as a church mouse, and asked for a place at the table. He was granted a place at the back, but was not content with this. He cursed the celebrating bogatyri, accusing them of being ravens and telling them to make room for him. Vladimir was furious and ordered three bogatyri to remove the stranger, but they were unable to do so. Ilya (Nikita) remained sitting without moving. Six knights and then nine knights were unable to push him aside. The king was perplexed.

Then Ilya roughly pushed his attackers aside, stood up of his own accord, and left. He slammed the doors and gates behind him so hard that they fell from their hinges. When he was outside he shot a magic arrow onto the domes of the roof of the palace, setting them on fire. In a stentorian voice he called out over all the city: 'Hey there, poor citizens of Kiev, come here and collect the gold from the domes of Vladimir's palace. Buy as much wine as you can with it in the tavern, and

179

celebrate.' The poor people of Kiev came to him, thanked him for the gold, and had a feast. But their hearts were not really in it. They mumbled: 'How will Vladimir punish us?' Ilya answered; 'Citizens, don't worry. Tomorrow I will be king, and I will share out the riches of Kiev more fairly than Vladimir.' Meanwhile, Vladimir was informed about what was happening outside.

Dobrynya Nikitich suggested: 'This Nikita Zoalieshanien is probably our own Ilya Muromets. Only he could do what this Nikita has done.' Then because he was Ilya's brother in spirit, Dobrynya was sent as a delegate to talk to the rebel. He found Ilya in Kiev's largest inn, where the people were calling out: 'Long live our new ruler!' Dobrynya was shocked by Ilya's fiery mood, and cautiously approached him from behind with the words: 'Brother in spirit, remember our oath under the Levanidov cross. The younger brother will obey the elder, but he will also give him advice which must be heard. Come with me to the court and take up the place which is yours by right.'

Before returning, Ilya demanded that Vladimir should lay on a feast for the people. If he would not, then he, Ilya, would push Vladimir off the throne. Dobrynya relayed the message. Vladimir agreed to the proposal, fearing Ilya's capacity to lead the people against his authority. The feast in the palace developed into an enormous feast of the people, where the peasant bogatyr was acclaimed by them. Ilya returned to the court and was offered the place which belonged to him, but now the hero refused and said: 'King Vladimir, I had intended to kill you because of your injustice towards the people. It is only because of the influence of your true messenger that I have decided not to do so. However, I will remain standing to see whether you will give the poor people food and drink from your own cellars.'

After this, the servants fetched meat and wine from the cellars of the palace. After a while Ilya helped them to carry it away. This was too much for King Vladimir. As the peasant was going into the cellars yet again, he ordered some of the boyars to slam the doors behind the rebel and lock them. However, all the bogatyri now openly took Ilya's part and demanded that he be set free. Vladimir refused. Indignantly the noblemen left Kiev, leaving their lonely ruler behind with Ilya locked up in the cellars below.

Commentary

It is not really surprising that the bylina 'The dispute between Ilya Muromets and King Vladimir' — the bylina about the attempt to introduce a form of Christian communism rather like Kitezh in Kiev — follows the bylina 'Ilya Muromets and Idolich', the bylina about the overthrow of heathen communism.

Ilya finds the strength for this attempt after a time of fortifying sinfulness, a temporary erotic relationship with a heathen princess. The erotic love that he discovers is the fuel that is transformed into brotherly love, the basis for

180

true Christian communism. As we shall see, he finds this erotic love with the woman who forms his anima as a sort of messenger (a sort of Kundry) of the Grail as a world Grail.

In the guise of a poor peasant Ilya presents himself at Vladimir's court one day, and asks to be given an important place at the table. This is refused him. Then he incites the citizens of Kiev to use violence to divide Vladimir's riches (food) among themselves, in other words, to achieve something which characterizes Christian communism. Dobrynya Nikitich, Ilya's brother in spirit, is sent out to calm down the 'poor peasant', who has meanwhile been identified and to bring him back to court to negotiate. However, Vladimir betrays Ilya and locks him up in his cellar. Everyone leaves court.

The fact that it is actually the Grail King of Kiev who is presented in this bylina as the person preventing what is implied by Grail communism in Kiev is because this ruler as a historical person was so different from the character as represented in the legends, and has a long way to develop. This difference is related to the difference between the Christian communism of Kiev and that of the later city of Kitezh, as regards the maturity and development and quality of its ultimate goal. Kiev is the first step towards this communism in the form of a Grail movement, while Kitezh is the final form, the social conclusion of this Grail movement both in a historical and future context.

Ilya Muromets and Tsar Kalien

Vladimir's daughter lamented both the departure of all the bogatyri, and Ilya's unjust incarceration. She looked after him secretly. Vladimir was troubled by his conscience but did nothing. Spies informed Tsar Kalien that a virgin who read the Bible was leaving Kiev's Church of the Sacred Heart. The more she read, the more she cried. Kalien suspected that this indicated that there were problems in Russia's capital city. When his questions about what was happening were answered, he marched on Kiev with his entire army. Arriving at the unprotected city of Kiev, he ordered every warrior to place a stone on top of one another. In this way a mountain was built higher than the highest peak of the Carpathians.

Kalien climbed to the top of the mountain of stones, looked out over Kiev, and announced: 'This city will be mine.' Then he ordered his armies to surround the city. Meanwhile Kalien's messenger Ahmed delivered a letter to King Vladimir with the following demands. 1) All the crosses must be taken down from the churches. 2) In future all the churches will be used as stables for Mongolian horses. 3) All the streets must be cleaned for the Tartar entrance. 4) Kiev will provide a feast for all the Tartars. If the king surrendered the city and complied with these four demands, it would be spared.

Vladimir read the letter, went up to the roof of the palace, and saw the enormous mountain of stones and his city which was surrounded. He prayed to God for salvation, and asked his wife and daughter for advice. His daughter told him that Ilya was still alive, and that she had been looking after him. She advised him to free Ilya. Vladimir hastened down to the cellars of the palace and found Ilya, who was reading the Bible by candlelight. The ruler apologized for imprisoning him, and for everything that had happened, set him free, and asked: 'Are you prepared to save the mothers, children and widows of Kiev? I implore you to do this, not for myself and for my family, but for the poor people of the city.'

Ilya answered: 'Vladimir, you are the judge between us. I will do what I can. May God help me!' Then the peasant knight mounted his horse, broke through the enemy lines, and called up Russia's bogatyri with a voice that sounded far over the horizon. He soon met Samson Samolevich and several other warriors, and explained that Kiev must be saved from Tsar Kalien and his hordes.

He explained that this was not for Vladimir, who had set him free out of desperation, and not for his family, but for the poor townspeople. However, Samson and his companions refused to help. Then Ilya marched on Kalien's army alone. For three days and nights he fought them without ceasing. Finally he was so exhausted that he had to accept Kalien's proposal of holding one day of truce. However, the Mongol had a trick up his sleeve. On that day he undermined Ilya's camp. Fortunately Ilya's horse noticed the danger just in time and warned his master. Ilya immediately sprang back to the attack. Three times the horse and the knight sprang clear as the earth suddenly caved in, but the third time Ilya fell back.

He was captured, bound, and taken before Kalien. He made such an impression that Kalien offered to take him into his service, celebrate with him, and offered his two daughters in marriage. Ilya refused, and Kalien ordered his guard to behead the hero out in the open. However, as soon as he left Kalien's tent, Ilya whistled for his horse, which ran up to the bogatyr. Ilya immediately jumped onto his back and shot an arrow with a message asking for help in the direction where he thought Samson Samolevich must be.

Samson and the other knights sped to Ilya's aid. The latter took the body of a giant Tartar as a weapon and swung it round to great effect. Meanwhile Kalien, who suspected nothing, was dreaming that he was entering Kiev as a triumphant victor. His dream did not last long. Ilya woke him up roughly, hitting him soundly, when the bogatyri had made short shrift of most of the army. Kalien was carried through all of Kiev as a prisoner, and then taken before Vladimir. However, the king was full of remorse, and he dealt mercifully with the aggressive easterner. They concluded a mutual agreement not to attack each other, and Kalien was allowed to leave. Vladimir gave every bogatyr his own castle, except for Ilya who refused his reward. All the citizens were treated royally, and Kiev celebrated for three days and three nights.

Commentary

When Ilya Muromets is in prison and the bogatyri have left Kiev, King Vladimir reaps the bitter harvest of his deeds, which were in such strong conflict with Christian communism, and corresponded so closely with the first aspect — the Turgain aspect — of the vanquished Idolich.

The Mongol Tsar Kalien (in other versions of this bylina he is given other names, such as Batu Khan) approaches Kiev with his hordes (Orda). His spies had gathered what was happening in Kiev on the basis of the behaviour of the virgin who serves as the image of an undervalued and therefore weakened form of Sophia (Manas). Kalien means 'the enemy' (who builds the Unholy Mountain, and uses the unholy Tartar principle of initiation). The enemy must be interpreted here as the external limiting aspect of Turagin-Idolich, in other words, the most material and violent aspect of (Mongol) heathenism.

The lack of liberty, equality and fraternity which are brought by Tugarin-Idolich, are outlined under Kalien and his Orda in the following four external demands imposed upon Kiev Rus. 1) All crosses must be removed from the churches. This command is the external image of lack of spiritual freedom. 2) All the churches will be used as stables for the Mongol horses. This command is the external symbol of the inequality before the law of Mongols and Russians, based on equating the Russian house of the Spirit and the Soul (the church) with the Mongol house for a horse (the body, or stable). 3) All the streets must be cleaned for the Tartar entrance to the city. This means that the influence of the Tartars needs a prepared place in the material world. This command serves the previous two commands. 4) Kiev must prepare a feast for all the Tartars. This command is the external symbol of the lack of brotherly love in dividing the fruits of the earth, so that everything goes to the Mongols for their welfare, leaving nothing for the Russians to survive on.

Finally King Vladimir is forced by circumstance to free Ilya, who has been kept alive by one of the king's daughters, and to ask him to march against Kalien. Ilya accedes to Vladimir's request, not for the sake of his king, but for the sake of the people.

Ilya and Kalien do battle for three days and three nights. Three historical periods — the Tartar domination, Tsarism, and the period of Soviet communism — strive for supremacy against the Christian influence in Russia and the Mongol influence.

Initially Ilya appears to lose the battle, after three skirmishes in which his life is saved, and which can be historically identified as the times when the above-mentioned systems were changing. The skirmishes relate to: 1) the appearance of Dmitri Donskoi; 2) the appearance of Dmitri Ivanovich; 3) the appearance of Tolstoy, Dostoevsky, and Solovjev, who together form a precursor of Russia's Demetrius force. This is discussed in more detail in the next chapter.

Kalien captures Ilya and offers him his two daughters, as he is rather impressed by Ilya's appearance. They symbolize the twofold Mongol spiritual inheritance: order through domination and welfare through centralization. Ilya refuses Kalien's daughters.

When the Mongol Tsar then wishes to have Ilya beheaded out in the open, the other younger bogatyri, led by the older bogatyr Samson Samolevich (the representative of the physical aspect of Sviatogor, the aspect remaining after his death), hasten to help the threatened hero. Together they defeat Kalien. Kalien's life is spared and a non-aggression pact is concluded with him.

From a historical perspective this means that the defeated Kalien by no means signifies the end of the Mongold heathen threat. From the perspective of the future this means that ultimately Slavism will increasingly adopt Mongol aspects (and transmute them) instead of destroying them. (This is a facet of 'the last Kitezh'.)

The bylina concludes by relating how after the defeat of Tsar Kalien the bogatyri and citizens of Kiev are royally rewarded. The question whether this reward can serve as a manifestation of the Christian communism that Ilya wishes to introduce in Kiev Rus is wisely left unanswered: the age of Great Kitezh in particular has not yet dawned, either historically, or in the future.

Ilya Muromets and the Falconer Sokolniek

After Ilya's victory over Tsar Kalien there was peace in Russia for a long time. Then new hordes attacked Kiev. To repel them the bogatyri established a guard on the border. For three years this had consisted of Ilya Muromets, Dobrynya Nikitich, Alyosha Popovich, Grisha the son of a boyar, Vaska Dolgopolisty, the three brothers Zbarodovich, and four knights from Zalyesh.

One night Ilya was unable to sleep because of the cawing of a raven. He woke up Dobrynya, and the two bogatyri left the guards' tent to see what was happening outside. In the ground Dobrynya noticed the tracks of an unknown horse. The noise woke up the other bogatyri. They were ashamed because they had not noticed anything. Dobrynya was the most alert as he was not too sleepy, too young, too ignoble, or too ill-mannered to track the unknown horseman, so he was sent out by the others to investigate. At midnight he caught up with the stranger, who could only be compared to Ilya. On his left, next to his steed, a hunting dog was leaping about, on his right shoulder there was a falcon, and a lark and a nightingale were flying and singing around his helmet. Dobrynya asked him why he had ridden straight through their camp. The stranger silently threw himself on the singer-knight, who was barely able to flee back to his brothers in spirit. Ilya stripped Dobrynya of his bogatyr status for his cowardice.

Then Alyosha presented himself for a confrontation with the stranger. However, as soon as he was within reach, the giant flattened him. Then Ilya himself stormed after the aggressive falconer. The colossus let his animals go, and a titanic duel took place between the pair of them. They fought three times. It was a draw when they used spears, a draw when they used clubs, and a draw when they used swords. Then they fought with bare fists. Ilya stumbled over a stone, and the falconer threatened to kill him with a dagger in a cowardly fashion. But first he mocked Ilya: 'Why old man, do you want to fight me, a young bogatyr?'

This insult gave Russia's first knight such sudden strength that he struck his opponent senseless with a single thump on the heart. Before deciding to behead him, Ilya was suddenly filled with a vague premonition, and he pulled back the visor from the face of the defeated man. This brought the stranger back to consciousness. He taunted: 'Crazy fool, if things were the other way round, I would have killed you long ago. I am the son of Latygorka, the queen of the Latyr Sea, where the water is always black. Sokolniek is my name.'

Ilya realized that this Sokolniek must be his only son. He ordered him to return to his mother and convey his greetings to her. The hero continued: 'But let us first take a rest.' However, Sokolniek was unable to sleep and thought of Latygorka's advice: 'Fight every bogatyr except Ilya Muromets. He will kill you, and then I will be alone.'

Dissatisfied with being conceived by this Ilya, who seemed as full of integrity as he was corrupt, Sokolniek grabbed a hunting whip once Ilya's breathing showed that he was asleep. With this he attacked his father. At first, Ilya did not wake up, but when he was struck on the heart protected by a cross on his chest, he opened his eyes. Then he attacked his son and tore him to pieces.

Commentary

In the first place, every person as well as every group and all nations have a doppelganger. The falconer Sokolniek is the doppelganger, the 'son' of Ilya Muromets. When Ilya is presented as the prototype of what he represents and what he is as a bearer of Self — when he is in fact presented as the main representative of Slav culture (this historical and future culture) — the doppelganger of that Ilya is also Sokolniek.

The doppelganger of man can be described as that part of his being that is a creation of the Luciferian-Ahrimanian evil and stands just as far below the essential human characteristics as the angel of destiny stands above it. At birth, the doppelganger enters the human being from the depths of the earth, from that part of it to which he is bound. At his death man retreats from the human figure into the depths of the earth — for in

185

principle he does not tolerate death. Just as the angel of destiny wishes to protect man from evil, while taking into account human freedom, the doppelganger wishes to keep man from what is good and force him to join with evil — to bind him to himself. If the doppelganger succeeds in this, man loses his Self and becomes a Tartaros being, unsuitable for being taken up into Kitezh. The doppelganger exists in the human body (except in the physical body) even throughout the process of death. In the Slav part of the earth in particular, there are cosmic forces which weaken the doppelganger beings — in contrast with what happens, for example, in the American and Mongolian areas of the earth.

As the performance of the doppelganger in man is limited by the latter's birth and death, it is logical that this doppelganger plays a role in erotic love, and death, which casts its shadow in the form of post-coital sadness. In fact, it is precisely this erotic love that enables the doppelganger to become even more active. This occurs particularly in the experience of this form of love 'as an anima complex', the experience in which a man identifies his inner soul with a woman in the outside world, so that his soul can come to life. For as opposed to women in the Arab and Western European cultures, no woman can permanently fulfil this role of identification.

Isolde's achievement for Tristan and Guinevere's potential achievement for either Arthur or Lancelot — if there had been no triangular relationship — are exceptional cases in the spiritual culture of Western Europe. If the role of identification is not fulfilled, and if the anima complex is experienced strongly enough, this may lead to the woman becoming a *femme fatale* for her partner. Horror of horrors, she proves to have borne an evil son in a secret psychological sense, who wishes to avenge the unacceptable failure of his mother (thus Mordred in the Arthur legends).

This evil son emerges as the image of the death of the soul, threatening the emotions, because the woman was unable to arouse life in the soul. All the sins of the soul that result in death coincide in the feelings in the form of that son. Therefore the doppelganger manifests himself in that son through the experience of the anima complex as a *femme fatale*.

When man transcends the above-mentioned experience of love, the 'mother and son' (the anima as the *femme fatale* and the doppelganger of the earth) rest in the soul of man. When man truly transcends this experience of love, that which remains of it in the soul forms the best fuel for brotherly love. However, when the moment arrives that this brotherly love leads to the development of higher forms of consciousness, particularly the development of higher forms of life, (to becoming a Grail), the 'mother and son' are reborn, the mother as the evil Grail messenger (an evil Kundry), and the son or doppelganger as an evil guard (an evil Klingsor or Mordred, Arthur's incestuous son).

The experiences of Ilya Muromets described in the last two bylini fall under the psychological pattern outlined here. Once again, it should be noted that Ilya Muromets means everything which he personifies and represents for all Slav culture, and what he is as an exceptional Self. It means that his anima as a *femme fatale* develops as a messenger of the Grail as the Slav Grail, and therefore the world Grail, and that his doppelganger reveals itself as the evil guard of the whole Slav culture, which will one day encompass the whole world. This also means that his experience of the anima complex as described here is based on an experience like that of Tristan de Lyonesse.

One day, when it is Ilya's turn to guard the borders after the defeat of Kalien, he follows the tracks of the falconer who has ridden straight through the camp of the bogatyri in the night. Dobrynya Nikitich and Alexander Popovich had briefly pursued the falconer, but when they had apprehended him he had struck them down. When Ilya follows the falconer and apprehends him, there is a threefold fight for life and death, a fight involving the body, spirit, and soul. At first, Ilya is in danger of losing, but then he puts the enemy out of the fight with a blow on the heart.

Driven by a strange premonition, Ilya does not kill his attacker, and the latter calls to the hero: 'Don't you recognize me? I am the falconer Sokolniek, the son of Latygorka, queen of the dark Latyr Sea. If I had won, I would have killed you.'

Sokolniek means falconer, as well as person of violence. That he is a falconer signifies some planning in his violence; this is the planning of the hunter. With this planned violence, an exaggerated power of thinking and the will, the doppelganger aims to remove man's Self. The doppelganger has large reserves of will and thinking powers. However, he does not have any strength of feeling. Thus Ilya is able to fell him with a blow to the heart.

Latygorka means firstly the woman of the bed (via Latyrus); and secondly black archetypal mother (via Lilitoe or Lilith, the archetypal wife of Adam before he was united with Eve). Latygorka is the queen of the dark Latyr Sea. This means that she is the queen of night and the dark astral world.

As stated before, in his youth Ilya Muromets had a relationship with a heathen queen. It may be said that now Ilya projects the image of his soul when he was young onto a woman who represents the female (astral) element of evil. This element of evil, the black aspect of Isis, once lived in Elijah's opponent and enemy, Isabel (Isis-Baal). This will be discussed further in the commentary on the following bylina.

Ilya understands that Sokolniek must be his 'son', his doppelganger, and that therefore he is also the 'son' of his former lover. In this respect he understands that with regard to everything that he represents and is, Sokolniek is also the doppelganger of the whole of Slav culture, and that therefore Dobrynya Nikitich and Alyosha Popovich were also able to meet him, though without being able to tackle him. Ilya sends Sokolniek back to his mother. He is unable to kill his son, but he pays for this. It darkens the hero's consciousness so that he falls asleep. Then Ilya wakes up again when Sokolniek wishes to strike at his father's heart, just as his father had

187

struck him where his heart should be, though there was only evil there. Thus he kills his (Russian) doppelganger after all.

The Three Journeys of Ilya Muromets

Ilya Muromets was tired of the intrigues at King Vladimir's court and he set off on a journey. He came to a crossroads where there was a sign on a tree which reead: 'He who takes the first road will be rich. He who takes the second road will soon be married. But he who takes the third road will not return alive.' As Russia's first bogatyr cared nothing for wealth and felt too old to marry, he chose the third road, since he was not afraid of death. After three verst he was attacked by a thousand robbers. Ilya said to them: 'Look, all I have is a cross worth a thousand roubles, a skin worth 1500 roubles, and a hat worth 300 roubles. My horse has never been valued, but the saddle is not worth much more than 2000 and the harness is not worth more than 500 roubles. So just have a look at the person before you.'

He shot down a giant from the forest with an arrow from his bow. The tremendous thud caused all the robbers to fall to the ground, and they all fled, apart from the robber chief. He remarked: 'Only Ilya Muromets is able to fell a giant of the forest in that way. You must be he. Will you become our chief?' Ilya refused, and urged the robber chief and his band to be converted. Meanwhile, he thought to himself: 'So the sign was lying about this road. I took the third road and I am still alive. I will try the second road and see whether I marry.'

When he took the second road, he came to a palace. Twelve maidens and a queen came up to him. The last one caressed him and invited him to join them at dinner. After the meal Ilya asked the queen whether she could show him a bed for the night. However, he did not trust the bed that was offered. He took the queen into his arms and laid her on the bed. Immediately she fell through it into a cellar below. He climbed down after her, and in the cellar he found 40 boyars, 40 bogatyri and 40 tsars. He reproached them: 'You simple-minded fools — to be seduced by such an evil queen. But now you are free. Return to your families.'

Then the queen said: 'Don't you recognize me, Ilya Muromets? I am Latygorka, the ruler of the dark Latyr Sea. Once I was your lover. Do you remember? You murdered my only child. You are not as innocent as you look, Ilya.' The peasant-knight answered: 'Oh Latygorka, how much that troubles me. For he was also my son. But he had only himself to blame for his death. He attacked me, his own father, while I was asleep. You were, and I see that you still are, an enchantress, and our son was a scoundrel. Now you will die.' He had her torn to pieces by three horses, and thought to himself: 'In this respect too the sign at the crossroads was wrong. I am still unmarried. Now I will take the first road.'

Along this road he soon encountered a stone weighing 270 poed, inscribed with the words: 'Anyone who is strong enough to roll me aside can go down into the cellar below and take the treasures stored there. Ilya succeeded in doing this and took a dish full of gold, a dish full of silver, and a dish full of pearls. When he returned to Kiev he used this treasure to build three cathedrals and feed the poor. He thought to himself: 'The sign at the crossroads was completely wrong. I am, and always will be poor.'

Some versions relate how he returned to the stone, crossed out the words which had proved to be wrong, and wrote down his own versions. On his way back to Kiev, an invisible angel caught up with the hero and took him to a cave where he was turned to stone. It is said that his skeleton can still be seen there to this very day.

Commentary

In a sense the last two bylini about Ilya Muromets belong together. The bylina 'The three journeys of Ilya Muromets can be viewed as a sequel and as a counterpart to the bylina 'Ilya Muromets and the falconer Sokolniek'.

Whereas Ilya was confronted with his doppelganger in the first of these bylini, in the second he once again encounters his anima as the *femme fatale* who had borne his doppelganger. He encounters her as an evil Grail messenger. This is particularly the case because it was his destiny in his youth to experience the anima complex through a woman who represents the female side of evil in the form of a heathen princess, instead of through a woman as a holy madonna (like the experience of Novalis), or through an arbitrary woman (which leads to nothing). His anima first took the form of a *femme fatale* and then that of an evil Grail messenger, in his case not merely because the mediating woman was unable to fulfil the anima identification role, but particularly because she proved to be the model of evil, the princess of night.

As stated in the commentary on the previous bylina, the figure of this evil woman, which also serves as the anima/*femme fatale*/Grail messenger of the Slav culture, just as her son serves as its doppelganger, can be traced back to the person of Isabel, the wife of the evil king Ahab of Israel who was Elijah's opponent.

All this is based on the rather relentless law of incarnation that decrees that two arch-enemies, whatever the reason for their enmity, will attract each other in the next incarnation as lovers in the context of the anima complex. Thus in Chinese the word for anima love is exactly the same as the word for implacable arch-enemies. In the figure of Ilya Muromets, the person who once lived in Elijah-Naboth, and, as Novalis, was bound to Sophie von Kühn, the representative of female goodness (the soul), Sophia, now has the opportunity to be united with Latygorka of the Latyr Sea, the representative of female evil, the dark sea of desire.

This bylina reveals what Ilya must endure from her as a *femme fatale*/evil Grail messenger, as the central temptation in a threefold scene of temptation reminiscent of the three temptations of Christ in the wilderness.

On his constant travels, Ilya comes one day to a crossroads where a sign tells that the first road leads to material wealth, the second to a happy marriage, and the third to death. The road that promises material wealth represents the road of Ahriman temptation. This temptation is greatest for the Anglo-Saxon people. It culminates in the ultimate derailment of technology. The road that promises happiness in marriage represents the road of Luciferian temptation. This temptation is greatest for the Slav people, and culminates in the ultimate derailment of eugenic life. Logically this is the temptation that Ilya Muromets is most involved with. The road that promises death represents the road of Asurian temptation. This temptation is greatest for the central European people. It culminates in the ultimate derailment of physical life.

Ilya first resists the temptations of the third road. He does so by defeating a thousand robbers who wish to rob him of his cross, his fourfold personality, his hide (the symbol of his soul), and his hat (the symbol of his spirit). He kills the robber chief, rather than being killed by him. When Ilya tries the second road, he comes to a Klingsor-like palace where Latygorka, his former lover, approaches him in the form of a *femme fatale*/evil Grail messenger. Latygorka, 'the woman of the bed', tries to tempt Ilya into the 'cellar of the subconscious' by means of 'the experiences of the bed' of her magic. This is the cellar of sexual, anti-Grail forces and effects. Ilya resists her enchantment, and she herself falls into the cellar of the subconscious.

This means that Ilya liberates the astral forces of his own being and of the Slav culture, which have been called upon to become Manas (or the Grail) from the dungeon of unconscious drives. These forces are presented here as Slav forces in the form of boyars, bogatyri and tsars. Ilya kills Latygorka, and in this way proves that he has resisted the temptation of the second road.

In the Parsifal sagas and the Arthurian legends, the hideous messengers, Kundry and Lady Ragnell respectively, are not killed but are freed from their demonic drives. They are transformed into 'the individual Sophia, the Manas soul' of the Grail hero Gawain. Ilya kills Latygorka firstly because for him she is primarily a Grail messenger in a racial supra-individual sense, and secondly because insofar as she is also such a messenger in an individual sense, like Kundry and Lady Ragnell, she is already united with him from a previous life in her aspect of immortality.[15]

Ilya has acquired such strength from his experiences on the last two roads of the crossroads of his trials that he finally takes the first road and succeeds in rolling away a stone that blocks the entrance to the cellar of material possessions. Ilya has become so strong that he takes all these goods and gives them to the common people. Some story tellers relate how Ilya is then turned to stone.

This story points out that the hero, and everything he represents and is, has become the new principle of the Holy Mountain, which encompasses all people of good will, through enduring the threefold temptation in the desert of the threatened Slav culture. This is the principle of initiation, which will culminate in the figures of Sviatogor and Mikoela Selyaninovich insofar as they are heroes of the future. That Ilya is turned to stone also indicates that the new 'Holy Mountain principle' acquired by him is still at rest and is the music of the future.

We will conclude the commentaries on the bylini about Russia's first young bogatyr with the following point. Gradually it has become clear that the corpus of Russian bylini in the form of legends contains the essence of anthroposophical teaching relating to the acquisition of Self-consciousness.

It is certainly true that the Slav bylini contain all of Western European spiritual science based on the Self force and Self-consciousness. However, they refer to this in a way which certainly is not about the Self and spiritual science, but is instead astral and legendary. Therefore the aspect of Self and spiritual science are not in fact, but only in principle contained in the bylini and in the Slav culture described in them.

The circumstance that the Russian bylini contain an authentic but rather special bearer of Self such as Ilya, as well as bogatyri whose Self force is derived from or represents something else, is therefore related to the fact that the Slav culture both contains (indirectly) and does not contain its own Self force.

The Self of the Slavs
consists of:

the Western
Varangian Self force
of characters such as
Apraxia and Natasha
of Lithuania

The St John Self of
Elijah–Ilya is derived
from *before* (in the
background there is
the Self principle of
Mikoela
Selyaninovich).

and the future Self
force of Natasha and
Vasilisa Mikoelichna

In the future the Self
of Mikoela
Selyaninovich will
manifest itself (united
with and assimilated
into the Self of Ilya
Muromets).

and the Self of Ilya
Muromets

this Self moves from
west to east and
from past to future.

The Betrayal of Alyosha Popovich

Once again the bogatyri were at Vladimir's court, boasting about their deeds while they ate and drank at a feast. Then the ruler spoke: 'I have just received a letter from Nievyezha Black Raven in which he challenges one of us to a duel. Knights! Which of you will propose someone to go to Nievyezha in my name and to defeat him and his armies at our borders?' Ilya Muromets suggested that Dobrynya Nikitich should go, on the one hand because experience had shown that the Black Raven had always fled from Ilya himself so that he could not be properly defeated once and for all, and on the other hand because Dobrynya was the strongest and bravest after him.

The minstrel-knight agreed to this mission, asked the blessing of his mother (Afimya Alexandrovna) for this quest, and without saying a word, he took his leave of his sleeping wife, Natasha Mikoelichna. But just as he wanted to ride away, his mother and his wife, who had woken up, came after him. Natasha asked: 'Why did you leave me asleep, and when are you coming back?' Dobrynya answered: 'I wanted to spare you the sorrow of parting. Wait for three years. If I have not returned, wait another three years. If I am not back then, you can assume that I am dead, and you may remarry, but do not marry Alyosha Popovich, for he is my brother in spirit.' Dobrynya departed. The two women stayed behind, weeping and full of fearful premonitions.

Three years passed, and Dobrynya did not return. Another three years passed, and Dobrynya was still away. One day the mother and daughter were sitting by the window, sadly looking down the road, when they saw a stranger approaching. He knocked at their door. When Afimya opened the door and invited him in, he introduced himself as a nameless wanderer, and told them: 'I was wandering through the steppe and in the distance I saw a flock of ravens circling over a fallen knight. I rode on and saw that it was Dobrynya Nikitich. He had a wound on his forehead and his eyes had been pecked out.' The wanderer departed, and the women were beside themselves with grief.

After several months, many young men vied for Natasha's hand, but in vain. Finally Vladimir and Apraxia asked her: 'Why don't you remarry? A flower like yourself should not remain alone. You'll become old before your time. Why don't you marry Alyosha?' Natasha said that first she would wait for Dobrynya for six more years. If he had not come back by then, she would remarry. Natasha waited in vain for another six years. Then she married Alyosha Popovich, who revealed that he had been the above-mentioned wanderer.

During the wedding feast at Vladimir's court, a wild horseman rushed towards Afimya Alexandrovna and told her that Dobrynya was still alive. He added: 'I am his brother in spirit, and I bring you and Natasha his greetings.'

The mother answered: 'That cannot be true. Six years ago Alyosha brought us the news of his death. At the suggestion of the king and queen, Natasha is marrying someone else today. There is a feast at the court.'

The stranger asked her: 'Give me your son's minstrel and jester clothes, and his goesli. I am going to the feast, for that was what your son wanted me to do if I arrived in Kiev during a feast.'

He entered Vladimir's court as a minstrel, a skomoroch, and suggested making music. He was granted permission and started singing a song about Russia's past. He sang with such feeling that he was asked to stay, and was even given a place to sit opposite the bride. Then he asked Vladimir: 'Let me fill a beaker of wine and give it to someone of my choice to drink.' Vladimir consented, and the stranger filled a beaker of wine and passing it to the bride, he said: 'Hail, beautiful bride. If you drink this, you will learn a secret, and if you do not drink, that secret will be kept from you.'

Natasha drained the beaker and Dobrynya's ring rolled out of it. She turned completely pale and called out: 'King Vladimir, my husband is not sitting next to me but opposite me.' She got up unsteadily, and knelt before the disguised Dobrynya, begging him: 'Forgive me, forgive me for not obeying you, but I obeyed the king and queen and am on the point of marrying Alyosha.' Dobrynya answered: 'I am not surprised about you dearest, but about Vladimir and Apraxia, and above all, about Alyosha. I was fighting for your honour, my king, and for the honour of all those present, against Nievyezha the Black Raven and all his armies. I defeated and killed them all, but it took twelve years because there were so many of them.'

Vladimir and Apraxia cast down their eyes. Alyosha went down on his knees to beg for forgiveness. Dobrynya forgave him his desire for Natasha, but not the lies about his death which he told her and his mother. He punished the priest's son for these lies so severely with a club that Ilya had to restrain him from fratricide. Dobrynya and Natasha left to go to mother Afimya to explain everything to her. And Alyosha groaned: 'Everyone marries, but God forbid that anyone ever does it again as I did. It seems as though the only people who are happy in love are Dobrynya Nikitich and Stavyor Godinovich.'

Commentary

Dobrynya Nikitich appears to be the most suitable person to defeat Nievyezha, the Black Raven. Nievyezha means bore or scoundrel. He symbolizes the principle of the inevitable, small, but never-ending guerrilla skirmishes in which the Slav cultures are engaged, insofar as he opposes the unasked for Answers to his Rurik Call, particularly the unasked for Mongol Answer to it.

Nievyezha is as clumsy as Dobrynya is elegant. They are opposites. Therefore the latter fights the former for twice six years. Dobrynya Nikitich takes responsibility for engaging in combat with the never-ending guerrilla presence for twelve years, the entire period of Mongol aggression. This leads the bachelor Alyosha Popovich into the temptation of desiring Natasha Mikoelichna, who has been separated from her husband for a long time. Alyosha's desire is understandable. As a representative of the naturally weak Slav Self force, he is well able to use some strengthening of this force from outside. But it is precisely because he is himself a Self bearer that such reinforcement is a sign of weakness and shame.

Dobrynya had advised his wife that if he were killed by Nievyezha, she should not marry Alyosha. Alyosha uses trickery to give the impression that Dobrynya is dead, though this is not true. Then, with the permission of Dobrynya's mother Afimya, King Vladimir, and Queen Apraxia, he succeeds in persuading Natasha to marry him, against Dobrynya's advice. Dobrynya returns on their wedding day. He brightens up the occasion as a skomoroch or pre-Christian minstrel. Obviously he declares himself to Natasha. He punishes Alyosha. In other words, with the force emanating from what Alyosha is and represents, he underlines that the latter should be an independent bearer of Self. But the latter groans: 'Apparently only Dobrynya Nikitich and Stavyor Godinovich are happy in love.'

In this way he indicates the happiness inherent in being united to an external Self force, external particularly in the realm of time. The happiness of such a unification is only granted to Dobrynya Nikitich and Stavyor Godinovich.[16] Both are married to a daughter of Mikoela Selyaninovich, the representative of Russia's future and ancient Self force.

In the commentary on the bylina 'The wedding of King Vladimir', the Slav Round Table was compared to its Anglo-Saxon counterpart. Various younger Kiev bogatyri — King Vladimir, Queen Apraxia, Dunai Ivanovich, Dobrynya Nikitich — could be viewed as corresponding to Anglo-Saxon heroes, respectively, King Arthur, Queen Guinevere, Lancelot, and Tristan. Such a correspondence can also be seen between the Slav Alyosha and the Anglo-Saxon Mordred (whose eye fell on Guinevere, just as Lancelot's did). Both are traitors. However, Mordred is an absolute traitor, a Judas, a representative of evil, while Alyosha is only a partial traitor, a Peter, who betrays despite the fact that he knows it is evil.

Mordred is the betrayer of the Round Table, and of King Arthur, through the latter's wife Guinevere, to achieve the death of all the Self force and processes of the realization of the Grail. Alyosha betrays only his brother in spirit, through his wife Natasha, in unjustly reinforcing his weak Slav Self forces, and indirectly in the services of the process of working the Grail (though again unjustly).

Dunai is not the double of Lancelot, but rather his counterpart, with regard to the question of the anima, and Alyosha does not act as a double either for Mordred in the sphere of treason and death. Again he is more like his counterpart.

Michailo Ivanovich Potyk

As the bogatyri were eating and drinking merrily at a feast in King Vladimir's court, they began to boast about themselves yet again. Vladimir announced: 'All the bogatyri are very dear to me, but I love Ilya Muromets, Dobrynya Nikitich and Michailo Potyk the most of all. They once added the countries around the Black Sea to our kingdom, and thanks to Michailo they even came back with so many geese, swans, and ducks that the citizens of Kiev ate meat for weeks. But it's all gone. I will request the marvellous archer Michailo to go to the south once again to supply us once more with geese, swans and ducks.'

Michailo took his steed and hastened down to the Black Sea. He shot down a tremendous amount of game in the adjacent water meadows full of reeds. Just as all the game had been collected, and he was on the point of returning to Kiev, he saw an unearthly, beautiful, milk-white swan sitting on a floating log. Her head was golden, and round her neck she wore a necklace of pearls. When Michailo wanted to shoot, she turned her eyes upon him and talked to him in a human voice: 'Do not kill me, Michailo Ivanovich Potyk. I am Avodtya Lichodjevna, daughter of Lichodyej Lichodyevna (i.e. the villain, the son of a heathen villain) from Podolia. If you will let me live, I will be your wife.' The swan hopped from the log, swam to the shore and in front of his eyes changed into the most beautiful princess that Michailo had ever seen. He wanted to kiss her, but she confessed: 'My lips are still unclean, for I am the unbaptized daughter of a heathen. Take me to Kiev to be christened, and then let us marry and love each other.'

Michailo placed the princess in front of him on his horse, and with her and the game he had shot he hastened back to Kiev. Vladimir wished to reward him royally, and Michailo asked: 'In honour of my wedding to the White Swan Princess, whom I will keep for myself, give every citizen in Kiev the right to drink as much wine, mead and beer as he likes for three days and three nights.' Avdotya Lichodjevna was baptised with the name Maria, the White Swan, and married Michailo Potyk. The couple promised each other: 'If one of us dies, the other will stay buried alive next to the deceased for three months.' After the wedding feast they lived together as man and wife.

A year and a half later Michailo was sent by Vladimir to the court of Tsar Buchar, where he forgot Maria. With the heathen powers of magic which she had inherited from her father, she conjured up in her imagination such a terrible disease that she actually died. Dobrynya Nikitich set out to Michailo to tell him about the death of his wife. Michailo returned to Kiev with Dobrynya. He asked Dobrynya and Ilya Muromets to help him fulfil the promise he made when he married. The three bogatyri asked a carpenter to to make a coffin as large as a room, order iron tongs submerged in holy water, three iron, three lead, and three copper stakes from a blacksmith, and collect food and drink for three months. The couple were

195

buried together. A rope connected the coffin to the clocktower at the cemetery. This clock could be heard throughout Kiev.

The very first night, on the stroke of twelve, a large snake slithered to Michailo's coffin with her young. The snake licked away the iron bands, licked the piece of wood, wormed her way in and said: 'What a delicious meal we will have, children, with this body of a young woman, and this living body of a hero.' Michailo grabbed his sacred tongs, keeping the speaking snake's head away from his with them, while beating the creature's body with the iron rods. But this was in vain. Even the lead rods did not hurt the snake. Only the copper rods, which had been made in a monastery, made the enormous snake hiss: 'Do not kill me. Let me go. Then I will bring you some Life-restoring Water from the sea to revive your wife, Maria the White Swan.

Michailo let her go and took the young snakes as hostages. When the mother returned with the life-restoring water for the sake of her young, Michailo tore them to pieces. When she sprinkled them with the water, they immediately revived and fled together with their mother. Then Michailo sprinkled it three times over Maria the White Swan. She came back to life, and Michailo tugged on the rope connected to the clocktower and rang the bells. Kiev was shocked, and the tower guards, Dobrynya Nikitich and Ilya Muromets, dug up the couple while everyone looked on. They lived a long and happy life. When Michailo died, Maria asked to be buried alongside him.

In some versions of this bylina the couple did not live a long and happy life. Maria the White Swan forgot that she had been baptised and her love for Michailo, and fled from him in the direction of Lithuania. However, the bogatyr pursued her, and long before she reached the border he forced her to return to Kiev. She pretended to be sorry, and one day gave Michailo some wine with herbs to drug him. When he fell asleep, she locked him up in a rock and fled again. Ilya Muromets and Dobrynya Nikitich heard that Michailo had been taken captive, and freed him with the help of a kalika, who broke the rock with the help of a magic spell. Again Michailo pursued his wife, and in Lithuania Maria once more poisoned her husband and imprisoned him. This time Natasha of Lithuania married the bogatyr. In a fit of fury he finally killed Maria and married Natasha.

Commentary
This bylina is about a unique bogatyr, Michailo Ivanovich Potyk. Michailo means: who is like God. This implies a form of leadership and a path which leads to the deification of man. Ivanovich means the son of, or someone who is united to John. Potyk means the eternal wanderer, and also in the form of the name Potok, an eternally flowing stream. In his foreword to this bylina in his book *Russian Heroic Sagas and Legends*, Boris Raptschinsky states that this hero, in accordance with the dramatic content of the story about him, is described as both a younger bogatyr, a member of King

Vladimir's Round Table, and an older bogatyr, particularly kalika.

Mikoela lives outside time; he lives in a number of eras at the same time. (Obviously this applies at the same time as the fact that this bylina in terms of time relates both to Russia's past and Russia's future.)

In addition, in his foreword Raptschinsky states that in Russia Michailo is presented as a drinker of green mead (the beverage of immortality), and also as the Great Archer of God, whose will is aimed at what God intends for the world and mankind.

In connection with this, and in view of the meaning of this bogatyr's names, Michailo can be seen as the personification of the archangel Michael, the silent, direct spirit of time in the early Jewish and Greek cultures, and the present Rosicrucianism of St John in Western Europe, which will continue in the future of the world and mankind as an eternal stream. This bylina reveals how the archangel Michael, as a spirit of time, will also unite with the future Slav culture in the spirit of time, and was united with the earlier Slav culture as a preliminary step.

One day King Vladimir asks Michailo to supply Russia once again with geese, swans, and ducks, the creatures that symbolize the forces of destiny taken in hand by man himself by means of the freedom of thought, the triple soul, as a manifestation of the free Self. King Vladimir asks Michailo to do this precisely because, as the archangel Michael, he is the guardian of man's freedom.

In the story, when Michailo agrees to Vladimir's request, he has a comparable experience to that of Ilya Moromets with Latygorka of the Latyr Sea (Ilya's last and most important adventure). This is followed by an experience comparable to that of the ancient bogatyri, Volkh Vselavyevich and Volga Sviatoslavovich, when they controlled the ethereal astral fire of the serpent, which led to the capacity to transform themselves into all sorts of animals.

As he is hunting for geese, swans, and ducks, Michailo meets Avdotya Lichodyevna, daughter of Lichodyey Lichodyevna (the villain, the son of a heathen villain). The meaning of the complete names of this prince therefore corresponds with the meaning of the name Latygorka, Ilya's lover and anima/*femme fatale*.

Michailo meets Avdotya inthe form of a swan seated on a log, the epitome of what he is hunting. He meets her as the strongest force of destiny, which must come into the reach of free thinking. He also meets her as 'his own' anima/*femme fatal*, and the anima/*femme fatale* of the Slav culture (in the form of Mongol heathenism). Therefore like Ilya Muromets, Michailo has an experience of anima, and in this way corresponds to the latter. However, his experience is not exactly the same as that of Ilya.[17] One could say that it supplements Ilya's corresponding experience.

In comparison with the many things that Ilya is able to do in relation to Latygorka — transforming the anima love into fraternal love, and then killing the doppelganger apparently conceived from the anima, as well as killing the anima/*femme fatale* itself (on the basis of a unification with the Sophia achieved in a previous incarnation) — Michailo, as a personification of a superhuman archangel, is able to achieve something with regard to Avdotya that in a sense transcends Ilya's achievement and is also a counterpart to it. Within the framework of a single life he transforms the anima as a *femme fatale* (as a Grail messenger), and also transforms Avdotya as the mortal soul into the Manas soul, into Sophia (Maria the White Swan) and marries her.

In this way he experiences in an almost impossible way something in the woman as an anima/*femme fatale* that was also experienced in Tristan and Novalis in an exceptional way in woman as 'pure anima', the woman who is able to fulfil her identification with the anima permanently. He thus achieves something exceptional, which the strange, mysterious Gawain also achieves in the Arthurian legends in relation to Lady Ragnell, alias Kundry. It should be noted that while Kundry is merely the messenger of the Grail as an individual Grail, Avdotya is so of the Grail as a world Grail. It should also be noted that Gawain's companion Parsifal knows that he is predestined for Kondwiramur. This is a reminder that since ancient days and in secret Ilya has been united with the Sophia. Therefore the Eastern European Grail legends are comparable to the Western European ones, and for those who know the latter, the following remarks may be made.

Just as Michailo Ivanovich Potyk corresponds to Ilya Muromets in the context of the Slav Grail mysteries, Gawain relates to Parsifal in the context of the Anglo-Saxon Grail mysteries. Thus the couple Michailo–Ilya (Michael–John) in the former mysteries corresponds to the couple Gawain–Parsifal in the latter mysteries, at least in the context of the theme of the anima. The wedding of Michailo and Avdotya based on her transformation into Maria the White Swan is in a sense repeated in the dramatic course of their marriage. The marriage is renewed after Maria dies, comes back to life, and is once again united with her husband. The process of marriage, death and 'remarriage' refers to experiences that occur by definition when the imaginative consciousness is transformed into inspirational consciousness.

The story goes as follows. The promise that the marriage partners initially make when they get married is: 'If one of us dies and is buried, the other will spend three months buried alive with the partner who has died.' A year and a half after his marriage Michailo has to leave his young wife to serve King Vladimir. After a while Avdotya/Maria believes that her husband has forgotten her, and she kills herself. When his wife is buried, Michailo returns to Kiev. He is buried alive with her in a coffin as large as a room, containing a pair of iron tongs, three iron, three lead, and three copper rods, and enough food and drink for three months. A rope connects the inside of the coffin to the church clocktower of the cemetery.

The buried hero's life is soon threatened by a serpent and her young. He controls and punishes the creature with the help of the iron tongs and the copper rods. By holding the serpent's young hostage, he forces it to fetch some life-restoring water from the sea. In this way Michailo finally brings his bride back to life. When he rings the bells in the church clocktower and is dug up with Maria, he takes his bride again, this time for ever.

All these images, which describe what Michailo can do with regard to the conception of his doppelganger and the subsequent murder of the doppelganger and his mother — refer to explanations about the creation, on the basis of the control of the fire of the serpent, of imaginative consciousness (the initial union of the spirit as the groom and the soul of the bride in the transient astral area) and inspirational consciousness (the permanent union of the spirit and soul in the ethereal area). They therefore also refer to the experiences of the older bogatyri, Volkh Vselavyevich and Volga Sviatoslavovich. However, in the latter the experiences that led to the above-mentioned conditions of consciousness were not described from the point of view of the theme of the anima and the 'Alchemical Wedding', but from the point of view of the acquisition of the magical capacities related to these conditions of consciousness.

This can be explained in more detail as follows. The image of the marriage vow between two partners means that the imaginative consciousness on the basis of the initial union between the spirit and soul only lasts if it leads to the even greater inspirational consciousness. As stated above, this trans-formation from the imaginative consciousness into the inspirational consciousness is experienced in the sense of initiation as a process of death (within the twofold marriage process). It is the same process of death of the 'three days in the sepulchre' of the old mysteries and of Jesus.

The image of Michailo's departure abroad, where he forgets his bride, and that of Maria's desolation and death, refer to the process of death experienced in terms of the loss of the sparkle in the anima because of the inevitable routine of life and all the emotional experiences referring to death that result from this, despite the transformation of the soul.[18]

The complex image of the burial of the partners in the coffin as large as a room with all its trappings, and the taming of the sudden appearance of the serpent of life and death, the force of 'serpent power' in the sacral chakra, into a force that brings life again to the soul for good in an inspirational way, refers to the transformation of anima love into fraternal love as very briefly experienced in the context of certain changes of the body and character.

This can be described in even greater detail. The iron tongs with which the serpent's head is held away (raised up) symbolize the will to self-domination, which is a necessary possession in this matter of burial and change. The three copper rods symbolize the capacity of the threefold soul to sublimate the erotic urge (of the young serpents), for without this the serpent fire could not be lit unpunished. The forces of the threefold body, symbolized by the three lead rods, and those of the threefold spirit, symbolized by the three iron rods, are less suitable for this sublimation. The living water represents the food of the Grail that the raised kundalini serpent was able to take. It is the food that permanently gives life to the Soul in an inspirational way, binding it again permanently to the spirit. Via the cord tied to the bell, the symbol of the central marrow, and the church bell, a symbol of the brain, all this is revealed and made manifest — it is exhumed. All this takes place in a period of three months, in a process of three stages: death, entombment and resurrection.

There are several different versions of the end of this bylina. They reveal that ultimately Maria the White Swan is an unfaithful wife to Michailo, so that in the end he has to kill her, just as Ilya killed Latygorka. These variations reveal the enormous risk of failure contained in the brief transformation of anima love into brotherly love — with the possible derailment in the processes of changes in character.[19] It is not possible to explore these risks further here. However, they mean that the anima/*femme fatale* experience of Michailo disappears, and the only thing that remains is the pattern in which Ilya experiences her through several lives. In that case, Mikoela is united with Natasha Michoelichna in order to serve Russia, and she is the Self force of Dobrynya Nikitich derived from the future, and the distant past.

Stavyor Godinovich and Vasilisa Mikoelichna

Once again there was feasting at the court of King Vladimir. The bogatyri, boyars and merchants were boasting about their deeds so that there was a tremendous tumult. Only the merchant Stavyor Godinovich from Chernigov was silent, and remained silent until Vladimir asked him whether he had nothing to boast about. Stavyor replied: 'What should I boast about? My parents are dead. It's true that I could buy the whole of Kiev with my money, but what's money? And what are clothes? Nor can I boast about my horses. They have themselves to thank for their beauty and speed. The only thing I could boast about is my wife, Vasilisa Mikoelichna. She's so beautiful and so wise that she could give everyone here an inferiority complex. Even you, King Vladimir, would do whatever she asked you to. Well, this wonderful woman has come to me. Perhaps that means something. Maybe I could boast about that.

Obviously these words were not very popular. The king was so put out that he commanded: 'Bogatyri, put this conceited man in prison, and fetch his wife from Chernigov to see whether she can make a fool of us.

The tidings of Stavyor's capture reached Vasilisa in Chernigov before the bogatyri arrived. She disguised herself as a man, took her enormous horse and rode towards Kiev with her husband's men. When she met the bogatyri coming to get her, Vasilisa called to them: 'Stop! We are the delegates of Tsar Kalien on our way to Vladimir to demand tribute. Who are you?' The bogatyri answered: 'We are bogatyri, ordered by King Vladimir to go to

Chernigov for Vasilisa Mikoelichna. Her husband's possessions must be confiscated, and she must come with us to Kiev.' Vasilisa answered: 'We come from Chernigov, and have heard that she has fled to Lithuania with all her servants and possessions. We don't know why.' The bogatyri returned to Kiev in dismay and told Vladimir about Vasilisa's flight and the approach of Kalien's delegates.

Vasilisa entered Kiev with her retinue, went to the king and told him: 'Take heed, King Vladimir. I am Vasili Mikoelich, Kalien's delegate. He demands a tribute from you for the last twelve years. And I demand the hand of your beautiful niece, Zabava Puchatichna.' Vladimir promised to pay the tribute, but when Zabava was hastily called, she refused to marry the stranger. 'Don't you see, king,' she called, 'that this delegate is not a man but a woman?' Vladimir promised that he would test Vasili to prove his manhood. He had him fight against the seven strongest wrestlers in the land. Kalien's messenger defeated them all. However, Zabava insisted that Vasili was a woman. Then Vladimir made him compete against his twelve best archers. Vasili won with no problem, but Zabava continued to insist. Then the king, who was Russia's best chess player, challenged the messenger to a game of chess, wagering the whole of Kiev on the game. Vasili won. Vladimir bowed his head in shame, and said: 'From now on the whole of Kiev belongs to you.' However, Vasili answered: 'I do not desire Kiev. I wish to marry Zabava.'

On the following day, the day of the marriage, the bridegroom became rather melancholy. When the king asked him what was the matter, Vasili answered: 'I don't know. Perhaps a song would make me more cheerful — by the great merchant minstrel Stavyor Godinovich, for example. Why is he not here? He was invited to the feast, wasn't he?' Stavyor was taken from his cell and passionately sang some of the oldest bylini of the land. Feeling more cheerful, Vasili suggested: 'Give him to me. What a singer! If you give him to me, I will forget Zabava and make sure that Kalien withdraws his demand for a tribute.' Obviously Vladimir agreed to this proposal.

The delegate took Stavyor with him/her to the camp and asked: 'Don't you recognize me, Stavyor?' But the merchant was too overcome. Then Vasili put on Vasilisa's clothes again and fell into her husband's arms. In his turn Stavyor explained why Vladimir had imprisoned him, and asked her to come from Chernigov. They went to the king and told him about Vasilisa's disguise. Zabava called out: 'Do you see, king, that I was right?' Vladimir agreed shamefacedly, and also agreed that Stavyor had every right to be so proud of his wife: the whole court had been fooled. Then the merchant and his wife journeyed back to Chernigov.

Commentary
As we know, Mikoela Selyaninovich has two daughters, of whom one, Natasha, the 'Reborn', is married to Dobrynya Nikitich, while the other, Vasilisa, the 'Royal One', is married to the hero of this bylina, a rich

merchant from Chernigov, Stavyor Godinovich (which means 'the crowned One', 'the Winner of the race' as a food friend — from the names Stephanos and Godwin). The two daughters represent the Self force of the Slav culture derived from the future with the related spiritual science. But Vasilisa, who is described as having many skills and being very wise, particularly represents the latter. It should be remembered that something similar applied with regard to Apraxia and Natasha of Lithuania as representatives of the Self force rooted in Western Europe.

Stavyor complements Dobrynya Nikitich through his wife Vasilisa. Just as the (future) spiritual science belongs to the future Slav Self force, Vasilisa belongs to Natasha. In this way Stavyor complements Dobrynyam, the soldierly artistic representative of the emotional and intellectual soul. It is not so much because of what he owns himself as a phenomenally rich merchant, and because of what he can do, that he complements the essential artistic soldierly aspect of the soul in a mercurial way — particularly the intellectual and emotional soul — but through his wife.

The merchant from Chernigov is all too well aware of this. Therefore at Vladimir's court this is the only thing he will boast about. He will only boast about his wife, not about his parents (his ancestors), his money or clothes (his position and image in the world), or his horses (his personality). King Vladimir and the other bogatyri do not like this, and Stavyor is put in prison.

Then Vasilisa, disguised as one of Tsar Kalien's male messengers, travels to Kiev and demands the hand of Vladimir's niece, Zabava Puchatichna, a female Slav Prometheus who in principle clearly complements the aspect of Self represented by Vasilisa, and was another possible marriage partner for Dobrynya Nikitich, though she was destined for another, as we shall see.

Vasilisa emphasizes her demand to the reluctant prince and his niece by defeating seven wrestlers and twelve archers in a context, showing that she has greater planetary and zodiacal virtues than anyone else. She also beats King Vladimir at chess, showing that she is in better control of the spirit, so that the whole of Kiev becomes hers. By winning all these contests she gives meaning to the name of her unjustly imprisoned husband. She asks where he is. Stavyor is taken from his cell and sings to the bogatyri as beautifully as Dobrynya Nikitich. Vasilisa recognizes her husband and relinquishes her claim to Kiev and Zabava, while claiming the singer.

In this way Stavyor has indirectly fulfilled the meaning of his name through his wife. Therefore on the basis of what his wife represents, he is a worthy counterpart to Dobrynya Nikitich.

The Death of Stavyor Godinovich and Vasilisa Mikoelichna

The merchant Stavyor Godinovich from Chernigov had once again displeased King Vladimir, and was sent to the distant island of Bushan to fight the king's enemies there and govern the inhospitable land. However, this mission amounted to exile. Stavyor carried out his king's commands and defeated all his enemies. However, he was so sad about the way he constantly displeased the king that he committed suicide. He threw himself onto his sharp spear, far away from Chernigov and Kiev.

His wife, Vasilisa Mikoelichna, heard of the desperate deed and lost the desire to live. She rode to the battlefield in Bushan, where she plunged a dagger into her fair bosom, to the dismay of her entire guard. She fell down dead on Stavyor's body and the two of them were buried together.

Commentary
Obviously everybody is secretly jealous of someone who is always best at everything, particularly when this is because of his wife. King Vladimir banishes Stavyor Godinovich to the desert, banishing the force of the soul which represents today (Stavyor) and the spiritual science of the future (Vasilisa). He wishes to lose this force because it supersedes the development of the present, thereby paralysing it. This leads to the temporary death on a voluntary basis of Stavyor and Vasilisa and what they represent.

The question arises why Dobrynya Nikitich and Natasha Mikoelichna (and Vladimir himself and Apraxia) escape the cruel destiny which falls upon this couple. Obviously this is firstly because the spiritual science of the future is superior to that of the current one in Western Europe, and secondly because it is not so much the corresponding Self force that leads to this paralyzing effect, but spiritual science itself — in the same way in which secret wisdom that has been divulged paralyses creativity.

Solovei Budimirovich from Venice

A number of foreign ships were moored in the harbour of Kiev. The merchant-singer Solovei Budimirovich was seated next to his mother Ulyana Vasilievna on the foredeck of the most beautiful ship. He sang and played on his goesli. Then he stood up and commanded his 300 followers: 'Place three gangplanks onto the steep bank, one of gold, one of silver, and one of ebony. Take the gifts, and follow my mother and myself to the palace of King Vladimir, the Red Sun.'

Solovei took the golden gangplank, his mother the silver, and his retinue the ebony. When they reached Vladimir, he offered his gifts. The king accepted them and asked who he was. The visitor answered: 'I am Solovei Budimirovich, a merchant from the trading city of Venice. I have come here to trade. However, to be honest, I must confess that my journey has another purpose of which I cannot yet speak. Will you grant me leave, sire, to stay here for a while and build three dwellings in the woods behind your palace?' The merchant was given permission to do so, and immediately ordered his retinue to build three houses with golden domes in the appointed place.

They had to be completed before the next dawn.

The woods bordered on the home of Zabava Puchatichna, who was very surprised to see the dwellings that had suddenly appeared when she looked out of her window the next morning. Full of curiosity she went to take a look with one of her ladies-in-waiting. At the first house they could hear money being counted. At the second house they heard a woman praying for her son's happiness. At the third house they heard many people singing and one, Solovei, strumming.

Quietly they crept into the third house and were completely overwhelmed by the wealth that abounded. The whole dome of the ceiling was made of lapis lazuli and supported by twelve pillars made of jade. The marble floor was so smooth that it reflected the golden sun and silver moon inlaid in the ceiling. Solovei and his 300 followers noticed the astonished ladies. Solovei took hold of Zabava's fair hands and greeted her. Then she greeted him. Head over heels in love with the handsome merchant at first sight, she offered herself to him as a bride, according to Slav custom. However, although Solovei had also fallen in love, as a Western European it irked him that she had not allowed him to take the initiative in this passionate affair (as it were, unexpectedly transcending him) and he said: 'Where I come from, the ladies wait for the men to ask them to marry.' With tears of shame in her eyes, Zabava broke away from him and returned home.

Then Solovei again went to King Vladimir and announced that he was ready to tell him of his second reason for coming to Kiev. His second reason was none other than to ask the king for the hand of his beautiful niece, Zabava Puchatichna, who was so full of initiative. Her fame and beauty had reached as far as Venice. Zabava was summoned, and blushingly and joyfully agreed to Solovei's proposal of marriage. The marriage was blessed in Kiev's Sacred Heart Church, and after the wedding feast the bride and groom returned to Venice.

Commentary
In his book *Heroic Sagas and Legends* Boris Raptschinsky points out that the younger bogatyr Solovei Budimirovich, a singer-merchant who does not come from Russia but from Western Europe (Venice) is sometimes held to be as important as Ilya Muromets. He is characterized as helping Russia in her greatest need. However, the bylina concerned here does not explicitly state this. Therefore the question arises in what way and in what sense Solovei is such a help. Moreover, it is not possible to consult any other bylini in this respect because they have all been lost.

As shown in the discussion of the bylina Ilya Muromets and Solovei Razboniek, Solovei means: fighter for the home or for personal matters. Budimirovich means: a) son of the commander (through the name 'Bode') and b) the son of the bearer of the spirit of Light and Love, the ethereal body spiritualized to Buddhi on the basis of the forces of the emotional and intellectual soul.

Solovei Budimirovich comes from Venice, where he is a merchant-singer. He comes from the city of Venus, which was a sort of trading centre at the time of Kiev Rus, where the most important Western European cultural influences met (Anglo-Saxon, Roman, Varangian, Greek, and Latin). As a merchant-singer, and as a representative of Mercurius (the intellectual forces) and Venus (emotional forces), he excels in those things that characterize the Western European city of his origin. He represents Venice in everything that is represented by that city-state.

What exactly does this city represent with regard to the Slav culture? Venice, as the city of Venus, protects and represents part of the Varangian Western European answer to the Slav-Rurik Call for order, which was initially retained in the spheres of Mercury and Venus. It concerns the part of Western European Self force and the related spiritual science to do with peace and the restraint of the drives of the lower self, i.e. the part of the Self that almost by definition cannot be united with the potential Manas culture of the Slavs through the Varangian's Martial urge to expand. Yet this is where it must go. Therefore it concerns a part of the Varangian Answer to the Rurik Call which must eventually seek its own peaceful road to the east, a road of Venus and Mercury — because, of course, this is also part of the Answer.

As stated above, it is Solovei Budimirovich who represents this aspect of the Varangian Answer for order, characterized by Venus. He brings this with him to Kiev, together with his mother Ulyana Vasilievna. He brings it there as the son of a widow, only on the basis of the king's daughter dedicated to Jupiter (via Jovilius).

As stated above, Solovei is considered to be as important as Ilya Muromets, for reasons which will become clear. Because of his profession as a singer-merchant, he is related to Stavyor Godinovich, and via him also to Dobrynya Nikitich (another widow's son). He also corresponds with Alyosha Popovich in what he personifies — a particular aspect of the Self — and because of what he is, a particular type of bearer of Self. The final correspondence is the most fundamental.

When Solovei arrives in Kiev with his ship, he puts out three gangplanks to the quay; one of gold, one of silver, and one of ebony. This indicates that when he arrives in Kiev his emotions, intellect and will are attuned to the culture of Kiev Rus, so that he can successfully make his contribution and take what is intended for him. He informs King Vladimir's court that he has come to Russia for a secret purpose, and also to trade. If the king permits this, he wishes to start this trade by enriching Kiev and Vladimir's wooded gardens with three beautiful temples. The three temples represent Solovei's character. King Vladimir's niece Zabava and her ladies-in-waiting note that the first temple contains the contents of Solovei's ship — they hear money being counted. Therefore the first temple is full of material goods related to Solovei; it represents Solovei's (physical) personality. (The ship or ark has traditionally been used as a symbol for the physical body.)

205

The ladies-in-waiting notice that in the second temple Solovei's mother is praying for her son. Therefore the second temple is a temple of the soul — it represents Solovei's soul. Finally the ladies-in-waiting see that Solovei himself is in the third temple. He is singing while his retinue are strumming on their instruments. Therefore this last temple is the symbol of Solovei's Self. These three temples — Solovei's whole being as a foundation for the aspect of Self which he represents — are for Kiev Rus.

Thus Zabava Puchatichna, the Slav Promethus force in female form, is united with Solovei Budimirovich, the peaceful aspect of the Varangian Self force, for the benefit of Slav culture. In this way the bylina reveals how the Slav Prometheus force, the force of the predestination of the Slav Manas character (which is manifest in female form in relation to the Self), i.e. the force of imaginative anticipation, is united with the most peaceful aspect of the Western European Self force, and not with another aspect of that force. It should be recalled that the power of the Manichean imagination is immediately destroyed by the slightest trace of Self violence.

Therefore Zabava is not destined for any of the Russian younger bogatyri, who represent other aspects of the Slav Manas character, but for Solovei Budimirovich and what he represents. In this way they both characterize a particular aspect — the aspect of Manichean anticipation — of the total multi-faceted union between the Slav Manas character and the Varangian/ Western European Self.

This is also a union with reverse polarization with regard to sex and the character of the couple in contrast with the union of King Vladimir and Apraxia, Dunai Ivanovich and Natasha, Dobrynya Nikitich and Natasha M., Stavyor Godinovich and Vasilisa M. Moreover, this polarization can be explained in terms of the female quality of Manas, which was mentioned before. For a while this aspect creates some difficulties for the union between Solovei and his bride, for who proposes to whom? Thanks to Solovei Budimirovich, the force of the love which he contributes to his Self from the Buddhi, the Slav Manas can anticipate and the Slav Manas culture can be a culture of anticipation. Therefore it is not surprising that this Venetian bogatyr is sometimes considered to be as important as Ilya Muromets. However, essentially he is the Western European counterpart of Dobrynya Nikitich, and above all, of Alyosha Popovich.

Finally, the description of Solovei's and Zabava's home in Venice indicates that the Slav Rurik Call and the Varangian Answer to it is not merely a matter that benefits the Slav culture (with Self force); it also benefits the Varangians by involving the Slav cultural aspect of Manichean anticipation. This benefit to the Varangian culture was Solovei's second purpose for his trip to Kiev.

In conclusion, the bylina about Solovei Budimirovich shows how apart from Russia's first and second bogatyri — Ilya Muromets and Dobrynya Nikitich — Russia's third young bogatyr also has a complimentary bogatyr, although the latter could also serve to some extent as a counterpart for Dobrynya Nikitich.

Dobrynya Nikitich and Vasili Kazimirov

Once again there was feasting at King Vladimir's court. Countless bogatyri, princes, and boyars were gathered together. Halfway through the meal, Vladimir suddenly stood up, walked around restlessly, and called out in despair: 'Which of you would be prepared to go to the distant land of Polovtsen for me to pay Tsar Batu the tribute I owe him? Over the past twelve years I owe him 40 wagons of silver, 40 wagons of pears and 40 wagons of gold, plus 40 times 40 falcons, 40 times 40 sable pelts and an equal number of black hunting dogs and grey stallions.'

After a very long silence the young Vasili Kazimirov offered to fulfil this rather dishonourable task. After making this offer the hero left the feast sadly and went outside. On the road he met Dobrynya Nikitich, who had been missed at the feast. The minstrel–poet stopped him with the words: 'What's the matter with you, Vasili? You look as miserable as sin.' Vasili explained the nature of his mission to Dobrynya. The master of the sword and goesli answered: 'What! Instead of taking all this treasure to that cur Batu, we will demand the same amount of treasure from him.'

They returned to the court like crusaders and brothers in spirit, and explained to the king what they planned to do. Moved by this, Vladimir wrote a demand to Batu to give his delegates the goods concerned, rather than demanding the goods from them. The king handed this document to the heroes and blessed them. Dobrynya and Vasili took the first horses they came across and hastened to the land of Polovtsen. When they arrived, they ignored all the guards at the gate and forced their way through to Tsar Batu. They called out: 'Greetings, you dog, Batu. We are the bogatyri Dobrynya Nikitich and Vasili Kazimirov from Kiev. We bring you King Vladimir's tribute in this letter here. Read it.'

Vasili handed Batu the demand. The Tsar read it and answered: 'Wonderful! You will not be leaving here again, certainly you won't, Vasili Kazimirov.'

Vasili answered him: 'That is entirely in the hands of the Mother of God, Batu, and furthermore I trust in the strength of my crusader-brother, Dobrynya Nikitich.

Batu, who was amused by Vasili's answer, wished to test Dobrynya's strength, and invited the latter to play dice and cards with him. Three times the warrior-singer defeated the Tsar of Polovtsen. Extremely annoyed, Batu announced: 'Nevertheless, despite the fact that Dobrynya has won the game, you will not be free, Vasili.' To Dobrynya, he added: 'We will see whether you can also defeat me at archery.' But Dobrynya also proved to have a greater skill than Batu with a bow and arrow. Furiously Batu hissed:

'Whatever happens, Vasili, you remain my prisoner, and he ordered his army of Tartars to overpower the two Russian bogatyri.

Vasili grabbed an enormous axle from a wagon made of white oak, and Dobrynya used his bare hands to start killing off the Tartars. This frightened Batu so much that he called out: 'Hey there! Leave me a few soldiers. You've beaten me and I admit it. You can go where you like. I will pay King Vladimir the tribute he demands from me, instead of demanding it from him.'

Dobrynya and Vasili returned with the 40 wagons of silver, the 40 wagons of pearls and the 40 wagons of gold, and with the 40 times 40 falcons, the 40 times 40 sable pelts, and an equal number of black hunting dogs and grey stallions. From Vladimir and the entire court they received the highest praise.

Commentary

The bylina 'Dobrynya Nikitich and Vasili Kazimirov' is an example of a bylina about a younger bogatyr as well as one of the three principal heroes of the heroic bylini: Ilya Muromets, Dobrynya Nikitich and Alyosha Popovich, and the three heroes who complement them, Michailo Ivanovich Potyk, Stavyor Godinovich and Solovei Budimirovich, as well as Dunai Ivanovich, the precursor of Dobrynya Nikitich. Vasili Kazimirov represents a new element.

While the three main heroes represent the triad of essential human characteristics — the will, intellect/emotion or knowledge/wisdom, and activity of the Self — Vasili Kazimirov represents four different human characteristics together with three other heroic bogatyri. In the esoteric knowledge of the East and in Theosophy the characteristics of the Self are summed up in this order: a) harmony through conflict; b) concrete knowledge; c) absolute devotion and idealism; d) ceremonial magic.

According to this, everything that is revealed is characterized by these seven characteristics. In Anthroposophy the three essential characteristics correspond to the medieval trivium of fine arts: astronomy (the will); grammar (intellect/emotion); and dialectics (activity of the Self). The four characteristics of the Self correspond with the medieval quadrivium of fine arts: rhetoric, geometry, music, and arithmetic (a more precise correspondence is arbitrary).

It is the idea that the existence of the world and of man is outlined in three essential characteristics and four characteristics of the Self that is at the basis of the importance of the number seven for King Vladimir's Round Table.

In this bylina it is immediately clear that the younger bogatyr, Vasili Kazimirov, represents the first characteristic: harmony through conflict, a characteristic that relates to the essential characteristic of emotion and intellect (love and wisdom), represented by Dobrynya Nikitich. Vasili means 'royal' (from the Greek: *basileios*). Kazimirov means 'son of a man of peace, bringer of harmony'.

According to Khan Batu, the ruler and representative of the Tartars as a people with no higher Self and other spiritual aspects, King Vladimir owes him the following tribute: 40 wagons of silver, the symbol of the complete Buddhi; 40 wagons of pearls, the symbol of the complete Manas (the perfect threefold soul in its alchemical union with the higher Self); 40 wagons of gold, the symbol for the complete Atma (reflected in the higher Self and therefore intuitively conscious); 160 falcons, the symbol for the completely developed lower Self as intellectual capacity; 160 sable pelts, the symbol for the ethereal body in which the life force has become a death force (dead fur); 160 black hunting dogs, the symbol for the astral body as a pure body of desire; 160 grey stallions, the symbol of the material body as the bearer of the whole fourfold personality. The number 40 refers to the principle of completeness; the number 160 (4 × 40) to the principle of complete development.

Therefore Khan Batu expects King Vladimir to surrender all the seven aspects of man because he, having no Self, is not a man. However, these seven aspects can and may not be surrendered. Because of what he represents, Vasili Kazimirov is the most suitable figure for reversing the roles between Khan Batu and King Vladimir: it is only by means of the one suitable method, harmony through conflict, and with the help of the only suitable essential force, emotion/intellect or wisdom/love, that man can escape the forces that try to remove his Self. The development which the human character must undergo is a source of conflict with the forces of evil. Nevertheless, the human character can only follow the path of the Holy Grail and work in harmony with and with the help of wisdom and love, and at the expense of the 'path of hell'.

Thus Vasili Kazimirov and Dobrynya Nikitich go to Khan Batu to arrange the above-mentioned matter of repayment of tribute. At Batu's court this matter is arranged in such a way that two competitions are held between Dobrynya Nikitich and Khan Batu for the sake of Vasili Kazimirov. One is a card game, a symbol of the forces of destiny coming into their own, and one is an archery competition, a symbol of the forces related to initiative coming into their own with the use of the free will. Dobrynya wins both these competitions three times, in other words in the spirit, soul, and body. Initially Khan Batu is aggressive, but eventually he peacefully agrees to pay Vasili, (King Vladimir) 'the sevenfold tribute', i.e. 'the total sevenfold human essence'. This comes to them in harmony through conflict.

How the Bogatyri of Holy Russia Met their Death

Once upon a time as the sun was setting, King Vladimir's seven bogatyri were riding through the steppes of Russia towards the River Sarfat. They were: Gordienko Bludovich, Ivan Gostiny, Vasili Kazimirov, Samson Samolevich, Alyosha Popovich, Dobrynya Nikitich, and Ilya Muromets.

They arrived at an oak tree by a crossroads and decide to spend the night there. One road led to Kiev, one road led to Novgorod, and one road led to Volkhov on the Black Sea.

Early in the morning, while the others were still asleep, Ilya got up, went to the river to bathe and pray, and saw an army approaching (Mongols? Tartars? Strangers?), an army larger than anyone had ever seen. He called the other bogatyri. They mounted their horses and threw themselves on the enemy. The earth trembled. In a battle lasting three hours they slew countless foes and were victorious. Then they called out together with reckless overconfidence: 'Our arms are not yet tired. Our horses are still raring to go. Our swords are still sharp.'

On top of this, Alyosha Popovich exaggerated: 'Even if the armies of heaven appeared before us, we would defeat them too.' He had hardly finished speaking when two knights appeared, who called out: 'Let the seven of you take up arms against the two of us. Do not be put off by the fact that you're in the majority.' The bogatyri did not recognize the two strangers. Alyosha stormed towards them and hacked them in two. But instead of dying, they doubled, and there were four knights. Then Dobrynya Nikitich threw himself at the four strangers, hacking them in half. But this time eight knights sprang up. When Ilya Muromets mowed down these eight, there were sixteen knights before him. The more enemies the bogatyri hacked to pieces, the greater their army became.

Russia's bogatyri battled against the growing army for three days and three nights, until they were exhausted. In utter dismay they finally understood who their opponents were. They fled to the mountains for protection, but just before they reached the mountains, they turned into stone monoliths. To this very day there is a row of giant rocks in front of the Holy Mountains. This is how the bogatyri disappeared from Holy Russia.

However, one day they will be liberated from their petrified state, together with the mythical bogatyri, and they will return and save Russia, this time for good. (See also the bylina contained in the Epilogue.)

Commentary
The final bylina in the Kiev cycle describes how the temporary historical culture of Kiev Rus comes to an end, eventually to develop into a future definitive culture. The Kiev bogatyr character doomed to temporary disappearance, i.e. the members of King Vladimir's Round Table, is presented again and again in the form of seven main bogatyri — a group of seven which clearly emerges as a comparison with: a) the threefold character of the archaic ancient bogatyri; b) the twelvefold character of King Arthur's Round Table and the Parsifal-Gawain duo in the Central European stories of the Holy Grail.

The seven bogatyri who meet their death in this bylina are:

1) Ilya Muromets, the human representative of the first essential characteristic of strength and will. In addition, as a particularly strong bearer of Self, he compensates for Alyosha Popovich's weak Self force.
2) Dobrynya Nikitich, the human representative of the second essential characteristic of love/wisdom, i.e. the emotions and the intellect.
3) Alyosha Popovich, the human representative of the third essential characteristic of active intelligence, and (lower) Self force (activity of the Self).
4) Vasili Kazimirov, the human representative of the first personal characteristic of harmony through conflict.
5) Ivan Gostiny, the human representative of the second personal characteristic of concrete knowledge.
6) Gordienko Bludovich, the human representative of the third personal characteristic of absolute devotion and idealism.
7) Samson Samolevich, the human representative (as well as the divine representative, as he is presented in some bylini as an ancient bogatyr — an ancestor of Samson, like Michailo Potyk) of the fourth personal characteristic of ceremonial magic (strength).

It is not really possible to explain how the last three personal characteristics are attributed to the last three bogatyri as shown above. On the one hand this is because it is not possible at this point to explore the huge body of esoteric science on these personal characteristics, and on the other hand because little is known about the last three bogatyri. However, there is another remark to be made about attributing the personal characteristic of ceremonial magic to Samson Samolevich. This is that this bogatyr is regarded as an emanation of Samson, the superhumanly strong founder of Israel whose strength depended on the ceremonial condition that his hair should not be cut. Furthermore, for this theory to be valid it is by no means necessary for there to be a complete correspondence between the bogatyri and particular characteristics. It is sufficient to determine on the basis of a few correspondences (and there are at least four) that the sevenfold nature of the Slav younger bogatyri as a whole corresponds in human terms with the total of seven characteristics characterizing what has been revealed. In this respect the first three bogatyri certainly correspond with the first three characteristics, the essential ones.

The commentary on the bylina 'Dobrynya Nikitich and Vasili Kazimirov' showed how these seven characteristics are presented in Anthroposophy in the form of the seven medieval fine arts. These arts in turn refer to the seven Greek muses and they correspond to particular virtues. (Establishing a precise correspondence leads to arbitrary results). Therefore the bogatyri who meet their death in this bylina in general also correspond with these arts and with these virtues. Furthermore, in the doctrines of the medieval Roscrucians and in the later Theosophy and the teachings of Alice Bailey, it frequently happens that the characteristics concerned are related to the seven planets (excluding the mystery planets and excluding either the sun or the earth), and to their astrological arts and virtues. Therefore the seven main bogatyri of King Vladimir's Round Table can also be related to these, though it is the sun and not the earth which falls outside these relations because King Vladimir himself represents the sun as 'the Red Sun'.[20]

Suffice it to say that King Vladimir's Round Table is based on the number seven and can be viewed as a system of seven planets circling round the sun (Vladimir), or as seven rays of that sun. The sun is the Grail Sun. This Grail Sun and Round Table can also be represented as the inscribed or circumscribed circle of a triangle, a double triangle with a square superimposed on it. In this configuration the sun represents King Vladimir, the triangle the three main younger bogatyri of the group of seven and what they represent. The double triangle represents these bogatyri, together with the three bogatyri who complement them, while the square represents the other four of the seven characteristic bogatyri and what they represent.

harmony through conflict
Vasili Kazimirov

concrete knowledge
Ivan Gostiny

love/wisdom
or emotions/intellect
Dobrynya Nikitich
& Stavyor Godinovich

activity of Self
Alyosha Popovich &
Vasili Budimirovich

absolute devotion
and idealism
Gordienko Bludovich

ceremonial magic
Samson Samolevich

strength and will
Ilya Muromets   Michailo Potyk

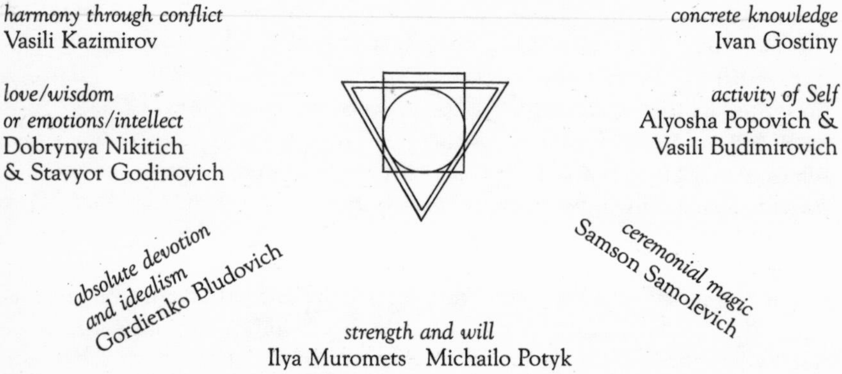

The double triangle of the three (plus three) leading younger bogatyri corresponds with the triangle shown on p. 144, formed by the three (four) ancient, mythical bogatyri and what they represented — the triangle that was described as the Holy Mountain of Sviatogor.

Insofar as these mythical bogatyri and what they represent are related to Russia's ancient past, and insofar as they were a preparation for Russia's future on the basis of the mysteries, particularly of the future Slav root race era, they were depicted as the Holy Mountain with the peak pointing downwards. Insofar as they, and what they represent, are related to Russia's future, particularly the development of that future sixth Slav root race era, they were depicted as the Holy Mountain with the peak pointing upwards. Insofar as they represented both the past and the future at the same time — which is the cast most of the time — they were represented as the six-pointed Venus star.

A similar explanation applies with regard to the double triangle shown here, i.e. in relation to the three (six) leading younger bogatyri. Insofar as

212

they and what they represent are related to Russia's past, particularly as a preparation for the future Slav cultural era, they are depicted as a double triangle with the apex pointing downwards, as shown on the left. Insofar as they and what they represent are related to Russia's future — particularly the development of the sixth Slav cultural era — they are depicted as a double triangle with the apex pointing upwards. Again, where they represent both the past and the future at the same time, as is usually the case, they are depicted as the (double) Venus star or (double) six-pointed star. [21] In the double triangle with the apex pointing downwards the Grail Sun is the evening sun — Vladimir the Red Sun as the evening sun. In the double triangle with the apex pointing upwards, the Grail Sun is the morning sun — Vladimir the Red Sun as the morning sun. In a sense, the morning sun also represents the earth becoming a sun (Grail).

Because the number seven in spiritual science indicates a division of time and a reference to Manas, the sevenfold nature of Vladimir's Round Table once again emphasizes the fact that they are both related to the past and to the (Manas) future. The sevenfold nature of Vladimir's Round Table, and the fact that its knights are workers of the Holy Grail as a world grail distinguish it from King Arthur's Round Table. The latter is usually presented as having a twelvefold nature consisting of knights engaged in a quest for the Holy Grail as a Chalice, and endeavouring to turn their own selves into a Holy Grail. In spiritual science the number twelve is used to provide space, and refers to the astral body.

←——— the constellations of the day correspond to the knights of King Arthur's Round Table who find the Holy Grail: Galahad, Parsifal, Gawain, Bors, Arthur, Lancelot.
←——— the constellations of the night correspond to the knights of the Round Table who do not find the Grail.

Therefore King Arthur's Round Table is characterized as a brotherhood of knights whose members endeavour individually to purify the astral body, which corresponds to the twelve constellations of the zodiac located in (astral) space. In other words, it is a knighthood related to Christ's ceremonial Eucharist mystery, a knighthood primarily engaged on a Rosicrucian mission, as described in the introduction to the Kitezh legend.

In summary, King Vladimir's Round Table is characterized as a knighthood working together towards the creation of world Manas, clearly based in individual astral purification. This process takes place within the sevenfold division of time. In other words, it is a knighthood related to the mystery of Christ's Eucharist in deed and truth, a Manichean knighthood, primarily on the basis of a Rosicrucian mission.

In addition to the stories of the West European and East European Round Tables, there is also a central European story about Parsifal and Gawain (and the Lohengrin saga). Admittedly that story is related to the stories of King Arthur's Round Table, for in it Parsifal and Gawain also play a major role. On the other hand, it is also a story in its own right. In this story there are two heroes. It is concerned with the aspect of duality in relation to the Grail. The duality of the Parsifal-Gawain story is related to the duality of the central soul of man, the soul of the emotions and the intellect.

The explanation of the bylina concerned here does not require any further exploration of this idea. However, it will be clear that the duality of the Central European story of the Grail is also present in the stories of the two Round Tables. As stated above, Parsifal and Gawain play a major role in the stories of King Arthur's Round Table, also in relation to the two aspects of the central soul of man, although it is integrated here into the twelvefold nature of the individual astral element. The corresponding major role is played in the stories of King Vladimir's Round Table by Dobrynya Nikitich as the counterpart of not one but two mythical bogatyri (Volkh and Volga).

To return to the seven bogatyri of Holy Russia who meet their death, the bylina begins with the words: 'Once upon a time as the sun was setting, King Vladimir's bogatyri were riding through the steppes of Russia . . .' This is a reference to the end of the preparation for the future Slav cultural era (and the future Slav root race era), the demise of King Vladimir as the red evening sun. The seven representative bogatyri of Kiev arrive at a crossroads. One of the roads leads to Kiev, the capital of Kiev Rus. One of the roads leads to Novgorod, a herald of Kiev Rus like St John, and the portal of Kiev Rus. One road leads to the Caucasus, the place where the seed of the ancient Persian culture is kept (in the Caucasian Grail mysteries) to bear fruit in the fields of Kiev Rus, first on a temporary, and finally on a permanent basis.

It is not possible to follow these roads immediately towards the future. The army of the angels of destiny, disguised as a Tartar army, advances towards the bogatyri of Russia (though not yet in the sense of a Selfless Tartar army). This army is initially defeated by the latter. However, the angels then advance on the bogatyri in the form of only two knights, as Lucifer and Ahriman, though they are unrecognized. The battle between the seven bogatyri and the two forces of evil runs an unpredictable course, according to the laws of destiny reflecting the material world.

Each time Lucifer or Ahriman is hacked down, he doubles in strength and new angels of destiny appear in an amazingly rapid mathematical progression: 2, 4, 8, 16, 32, 64 etc. In the same way, forced asceticism leads to extreme actions. After a few dozen times, their numbers are in the billions. This is an image of reproduction in such a consistent and large-scale sense that the Self force or Spirit must necessarily disappear from those who are reproduced. At the end of this series the angels of destiny incarnate these selfless beings, turning them into Tartaros people, an army of Tartars without a Self.

As we saw in the outline of early Russian history, Kiev Rus declined and fell, and was forced to do so by the Tartaros people. The bogatyri were killed by them in the sevenfold division of time. Why did this happen? The reason was so that it could once again rise up and prepare for the Kitezh of the sixth culture, and even the Kitezh of the sixth root race. This Kitezh will be permanently embedded in the Svetli Jarr, and its inhabitants will be able to assimilate even the selfless elements.

This brings an end to the Kiev cycle of heroic bylini, the Grail cycle, and we will continue with some other heroic cycles parallel to that of Kiev, and with commentaries on these.

The Heroic Bylini of the Other South Russian Cycles

King Roman Mstislavich

Halfway through a feast at the court of the old king Chimbal of Lithuania and Poland, his two young nephews Liwik came into the hall. 'Hail King!' they called. 'We have just returned from a journey through the kingdom. We noticed that the people are praising the victories of your enemy and contemporary, Roman Mstislavich, more than yours. Give us forty thousand knights and your blessing to defeat him.' Chimbal answered that he had concluded a peace treaty with Roman, and that in any case Russia would be invincible in war. He refused to allow the princes, whom he thought of as dolts, to attack Galicia, and advised them instead to conquer Lifeland, the watery kingdom of the Teutonic Knights.

The Liwik nephews had no option but to follow this suggestion and conquer the weak country of Lifeland for Chimbal. However, they were still dissatisfied, and assembed a large army of knights anyway. Without the knowledge of the king, they mounted a cowardly attack on Roman Mstislavich of Wolhynia and Galicia, just as the latter had left his country to deal with the ever-troublesome and godless Polovtsas. Obviously the nephews were initially successful in Galicia, where there was a minimal military presence. They took Roman's weakly defended castle, plundered it, ravished the women who had been left behind, and took captive his beautiful young wife, Natasha Dmitriyevna and her two-year-old son.

When Roman had defeated the heathen Khan Bunjak of the Polovtsas and returned home, a courier came to meet him with the news of the cowardly surprise attack by the Lithuanian army. Roman swore that he would avenge himself on the treacherous nephews. Without waiting for his large but exhausted guard, he hastened to the enemy camp with several brave bogatyri. He led his men into the woods and ordered them: 'When you hear a raven cawing in an oak tree, saddle your horses quickly; if you hear the raven again, mount your horses; if you hear him for a third time, quickly leave this ambush and attack the enemy.' Roman changed himself into a grey wolf and charged forward. Then he changed himself into a white stoat and gnawed to pieces the enemy bows and arrows, as well as all the harnesses of the enemy horses. Finally, he crept to the tent where his wife and son were held captive.

He heard his wife mumble: 'Oh little boy, if only your father were young and strong, he would be able to free us.' However, the little boy saw the stoat and recognized his father in the creature. He called out: 'But mother, father is right here. He is in that white stoat.' The guards heard this. They raised the alarm and within a minute the whole of the Lithuanian army was chasing the stoat. Before anyone could catch him, he changed into a raven, flew to an oak tree and began to caw. Then he cawed again, and then a third time. None of the Lithuanians were able to shoot down the bird, for all the bows and arrows were broken.

Then the small Russian élite corps stormed into the panic-stricken camp. The bird changed back into King Roman and under his leadership his men wiped out all the Lithuanian knights. He freed his wife and child and took them to safety. The Liwik princes were captured and Roman berated them: 'I did not fight the godless Polovtsas only for my own land and people, but for all Christian peoples, trusting in your uncle's word that he would cover my flanks. You have betrayed me.' He put out the eyes of the elder prince and cut off the legs of the younger. Then he put him on the elder's back and said: 'In this way the lame will lead home the blind. Go back to Chimbal, who was unable to stop you.' Chimbal, who had been informed of the ambush of his nephews Liwik, executed the two villains at their own request.

Commentary

Apart from Kiev and Novgorod, there were several other small centres of culture in Kiev Rus which were also the source of their own epic cycles about younger bogatyri. Examples include this bylina about Roman Mstislavich and the Song of Igor, the only bylina transcribed long ago.

Roman Mstislavich is the king of Wolhynia and Galicia, King Vladimir's regent over these domains. His name means 'the Roman' and also 'the famous man'. He is married to Natasha Dmitriyevna. Her name means 'the reborn daughter of the son of Mother Earth (Demeter)'. They have a two-year-old son whose name is not mentioned, but who can be identified as a grandchild of Demeter through his mother.

Roman's kingdom is attacked by Lithuania and Poland; admittedly not by the ruler of those countries, King Chimbal, but by his nephews Liwik, who have misled their uncle with their military exploits. Chimbal means 'representative of a higher strength of the people', in this context the strength of the Polish Lithuanian order. Liwik means 'representative of a lower strength of the people', in this context the aggression and overconfidence of Poland and Lithuania. Thus Russia is attacked by the evil, aggressive forces of the West European cultures via the peripheral Slav culture, and Roman's wife and child are taken hostage. In this way Russia is given the wrong Answer by the Varangians to its Rurik Call.

It is curious and perhaps not entirely a coincidence that this bylina outlines a political and military pattern of action in the form of a legend — one of the incorrect Varangian Answers to the Slav-Rurik call is described. Later the West European Jesuits tried to establish a foothold in Russia via Poland through the pseudo Dimitri Ivanovich, who was in a sense also an unnamed child and a descendant (son) of Demeter.

The correspondence between this bylina and the later historical question of Demetrius provides even more food for thought when we remember that this bylina is set at the end of Russia's early history, and therefore refers to a close future. (Where the future reflects the past, the most recent events always appear first in that future.)

By using powers similar to those of the ancient bogatyri, Volkh Vselavyevich and Volga Sviatoslavovich, Roman was able to defeat the foreign aggressors and free his wife and son after his initial military defeat. By recognizing the powers of his father, the son plays a major role in this. The nephews Liwik are condemned by Roman to be blind and lame, and are sent back in this state to King Chimbal, who has them killed.

If, as I believe, it is true that this bylina refers to later events around (the pseudo) Dimitri Ivanovich, it is clear that the madness of Ivan the Terrible was at the root of the dramatic developments relating to his youngest son in the same way as Roman Mstislavich's imaginative powers are responsible for the saving of his child (wife and people). Therefore if it is true that Demeter will have a grandchild after the 'pseudo-Demetrius' as her son, this bylina shows how his father can help him to succeed by using powers that spring from the imaginative and inspirational consciousness.

King Igor's Campaign

King Igor Sviatoslavich of Novgorod-Seversk marched against the godless Polovtsas against the will of the ruler of all of Russia and all the frightened city rulers, supported only by his younger brother Vsevolod. He was tired of the taxes they imposed and the atrocities they committed. When he bade farewell to his beautiful wife Jaroslavna, the sun suddenly disappeared behind a pitch-black cloud. This was a bad omen. However, he cheered up his wife and the guard waiting for him with the following promise: 'I swear that I will drive the enemy back across the Don, unless he kills me. Then I will scoop water from the river with my helmet to cleanse me of his thick blood. God reveals omens in nature, and perhaps they are meaningful, but I will fight, for I will not longer tolerate the Mongol yoke. Follow me.'

To everyone's dismay, a flock of crows suddenly assembled at the head of the army. Nevertheless, the army departed. Igor waited for Vsevolod in

Putievl, the castle of his son Vladimir, and at Kursk, Vsevolod's guard joined the troops. This time it was not a cloud but the moon that blotted out the sun, in order to give Diev, the spirit of the nomads of the steppes, the opportunity of passing on the news of their arrival by cawing to the east. Nature waited with bated breath.

Despite these increasingly black omens, Igor defeated the considerable vanguard of the Polovtsas between the Dnieper and the Don. The Russians acquired countless valuable and many beautiful Polovtsa women with their high cheekbones. However, the enemy Khans Gzak and Konchak had escaped to lead the remaining Mongol army. There was a second battle on the river Kajala. In this decisive battle, which lasted two-and-a-half days, all the Russians including Igor and Vsevolod fought the Asian hordes to the death, or until they were unconscious.

Shortly after the departure of the Slav guard, Jaroslavna travelled east to hear the news from the front as speedily as possible. One day the Mongol courier Ovloer informed her that the Russians had been defeated and that Igor and Vsevolod were amongst the wounded captives. They were very heavily guarded by the Khan. However, Ovloer was secretly a Christian, and he promised Jaroslavna at any rate to free Igor. He succeeded, and not long afterwards the king rejoined his delighted wife in the castle of Putievl. Her happiness was complete when — miracle of miracles — her son Vladimir, whom she had presumed dead, returned home with the beautiful daughter of Khan Konchak.

Commentary

This story about the campaign of Prince Igor is both a transcribed song — an adaptation of the song *Slovo o polkoe Igoryevye* as well as a bylina. The hero of the story, Prince Igor, can be considered both as an ancient bogatyr, because of his emotions and intellect, as well as a younger bogatyr, because of the nature of his deeds.

In the last instance the story of Igor Sviatoslavich of Novgorod-Seversk describes how, despite its heroic resistance, the Slav culture was nevertheless completely overrun by its enemies, in this case the Mongols, though it ultimately emerges as the victor, almost by means of sorcery (annexing enemy territory in the process). The enemy of the Slavs, in this case the Mongols, is not presented this time as an unasked for Answer to the Slav-Rurik Call, or as the anima/*femme fatale* of the Slavs, as it was in previous bylini in other cycles. It is described as the conqueror of the Slavs, though eventually assimilated into Slav culture. This is clear from the conclusion of the bylina. The beautiful daughter of Khan Konchak, who defeated Igor, travels to Novgorod-Seversk in order to marry Igor's son Vladimir, and live with him there.

In this way the story describes a third aspect of the complex relationship between the Slav culture and its enemies. It describes an archaic and martial type of metamorphosis that culminates in the Christo-centric assimilation characterizing the citizens of Kitezh after undergoing many meta-morphoses. In this respect it is curious that Igor's greatest supporter is called Vsevolod, the same name as the later prince and lord of Kitezh. Igor means 'farmer' (from the Greek *georgeos*), i.e. farmer as worker of the Grail, and as the bearer of the strength of the Archangel Michael (as St. George). Vsevolod means 'courageous conqueror' (from Sigisbold) and 'there according to God's will', (through Sibylla and Dios boulè).

The sorcery that turns the tide for the Russians in their battle against the Mongolian Khans Gzak and Konchak is obviously the power of Christianity. One of the Khan's couriers, a certain Ovloer, is secretly converted to Christianity and saves Igor and his son Vladimir.

A final remark should be made about this and the previous bylina. While the complex Kiev cycle of bylini — the Grail cycle — describes the whole foundation and structure of the Grail aspect of future Slav culture (and of the historical Slav culture), and while the Novgorod cycle of bylini served and will serve as an expression of these, as indicated in the outline of early Russian history, the last two bylini illustrate some important subsidiary aspects.

The bylina of Roman Mstislavich expresses the problem of the wrong Varangian Answer to the Slav–Rurik Call in a mythological sense; it outlines the so-called Demetrius problem (as a mythological blueprint) and a direction that a possible solution could take. The song of Igor illustrates how destiny turns the unasked for Mongol Answer to the Slav–Rurik Call against the Mongol culture itself; it describes what could be called 'the Ovloer effect'.

The phenomenon of the Ovloer effect seems to be in contradiction to the phenomenon of the Tartar overthrow of Russia (Kitezh). Obviously this contradiction is an illusion. The problems of the Slav culture in relation to the Tartar culture, like all phenomena, are of the nature of a wave with peaks and troughs. The peaks in this movement are characterized by the above-mentioned effect (and subsidiary annexation effects), while the troughs are characterized by what is described in the Kitezh legends and in the final Kiev bylina about Russia's overthrow.

The Heroic Bylini of Novogorod

The Youth of Vasili Buslayev

In the rich trading city of Novgorod lived Buslay, a rich man who lived an honourable and peaceful life. When he was 19 his wife Mamelyfa Timofeyevna bore him a son whom he named Vasili. The father died before the boy was seven years old. The mother had her son taught by a master to read, write, and sing very well, but when he weas 12 years old Vasili had had enough of education, and developed to become Novgorod's strongest and cruel street-fighter. Furious citizens regularly came to visit his mother. She urged him to assemble a band of soldiers to fight the unbelievers as his father had done, instead of doing evil.

Vasili interpreted his mother's advice in his own way. He wrote down on strips of paper: 'Anyone who wishes to eat and drink as much as he likes, come to me. Vasili Buslayev.' He folded the strips of papers into arrows and shot them into the town. Then he took a large number of barrels of wine from his father's stores, filled up a beaker with the contents of a bucket and a half, and placed it outside. It did not take long for the guests to arrive. Vasili took hold of a club weighing 12 poed and said: 'Anyone who can lift this beaker with one hand, drain it in one gulp, and withstand a blow of my club on his head without falling over can be my friend and may come in to celebrate with me.' Everyone left discouraged, except for the latecomer Kostya Novotorzianien who managed to lift the beaker with one hand, drained it in one gulp, repeated this once again, and bore Vasili's blow on his head without falling over, merely saying: 'I will just empty a third beaker.'

The two lads entered the house and made friends. Then, through the window, they saw Potanya the Cripple approaching. He also achieved and endured what Kostya had achieved and endured. The next few days another 27 strong lads achieved and endured the same. Celebrating day after day, they formed Vasili's band of men. The hero continued to feed and clothe them generously. The people of Novgorod wondered where it would all lead.

During a meeting about this matter, a stranger struck his staff on the ground three times and suggested: 'Let us too give a feast and not invite Vasili and his band. Of course, he and his followers will come anyway. Then we will offer the leader a flagon of green wine with the words: "Anyone who is a friend of Great Novgorod, drain this flagon." If he accepts it, he obviously has no evil intentions towards us. If he refuses it, we should watch out.'

They all agreed, and a great feast was prepared. Vasili and his band arrived uninvited, exactly as the stranger had predicted. The aggressive young fighter was offered a flagon of green wine with the words 'For anyone who is a friend of the city.' Vasili accepted the beaker and called out, 'Long live Novgorod'. He drank the wine in a single gulp, and everyone was relieved. However, befuddled by the alcohol, he became aggressive later in the evening and threatened: 'Whatever you do, you are, and will always be fools. You will all be in my power and pay tribute to me.'

The furious citizens doubted this. Then Vasili suggested holding a duel on the bridge over the Volchov between him and his band, on the one side, and an army of townspeople, on the other. If the latter won, they could take his head, but if he won, everything and everyone in Novgorod would belong to him. The drunken Vasili went home and boasted about this bet to his mother. He predicted: 'Tomorrow will prove to all those unbelievers in Novgorod that Vasili Buslayev is the boss over everyone.' His mother locked him up.

The next morning Vasili's band awaited their leader in vain, and then decided to fight the townspeople without him anyway. The band was heavily outnumbered and in danger of losing, but Mamelyfa Timofeyevna's housekeeper, who was doing the washing in the Volchov, saw what was happening to the band. She ran back home and freed Vasili from his bedroom. Hastily the hulk grabbed the axle of a cart, ran to the bridge over the Volchov and defeated the army of Novgorod. He went berserk to such an extent that his godfather, the kalika Ondronich Piligrimitch was called from the Cyrillos abbey nearby to negotiate. Perhaps Vasili would sign a peace treaty in return for a dish of pearls, a dish of silver, and a dish of gold. The monk was refused. Finally Vasili's mother was called and she persuaded her son to accept peace. Novgorod accepted Vasili Buslayev as mayor.

Commentary

Early Russian history, shows that in a cultural sense, Novgorod can be viewed as a St John type of herald for the city of Kiev, representing Christ in a cultural and mythological sense. With regard to the historical Kiev Rus, this seems to be based on the fact that both its exoteric historical culture (the sound of the Slav-Rurik Call and the Varangian Answer to it, and everything related to this, up to and including the foundation of the historical Kitezh), as well as its esoteric mythological culture, its Grail culture, which arose in the creation of the bylini and the legends about Kitezh, and is described in them, are based in the culture of the historical Novgorod. With regard to the future Kiev Rus, this was based on the fact that from the time of the Tartar domination, the bylini and the Kitezh legends were sung only in and around Novgorod, where they evolved as a sort of witness to the people. Together with all sorts of individual witnesses and in relation to a future Slav-Rurik Call and future Varangian Answer to it, this is the kernel of a Russia that in principle already exists, which was conceived in early Russian history and will one day be brought to light.

What becomes apparent is that Novgorod as a cultural centre outside Kiev represents more or less the same element of (Michael) St John that Ilya Muromets represented within Kiev in spiritual terms and as an individual in the Grail mysteries and everything related to them. This idea should be viewed in relation to the two apparently mutually contradictory statements to be found in Boris Raptschinsky's often quoted book, *Russian Heroic Sagas and Legends* about the historical nature of Ilya Muromets.

In the Novgorod cultural area in particular the character of Ilya Muromets was absolutely unknown (pp. 36-7). According to the thirteenth-century Scandinavian Wilking saga, Ilya Muromets is a Varangian, the second son of Hertnit of Scandinavia. Ilya's (Ilias') mother was a Greek, and through her he was supposedly a brother of King Vladimir of Kiev. Thus with regard to the later as well as the earlier relation in time of Michael to both Israel and Greece, the Jewish Elijah–Naboth character not only forms the basis for the character of Ilya Muromets, but also an aspect of the Greek Odysseus character.

Hertnits's first son Voldemar, by a non-Greek wife, became King of Poland and Russia, and Ilya became King of Greece (pp. 37 and 38 of the above-mentioned book). We will not examine here Raptschinsky's interpretation of these statements, but will indicate the following basic patterns concealed in these facts.

1) When Voldemar was King of Poland *and* Russia, the pattern emerged for Rurik's subsequent arrival in Novgorod: the pattern of a Call and Answer. This meant that the city would later fulfil an external cultural function as a St John type of herald for Kiev. This concerns a pattern in which Ilya is unknown. In addition, it is also the pattern by which the Liwik nephews later deceived Roman Mstislavich, and the pattern by which the pseudo Dmitri Ivanovich became the ruler of Russia.

2) The pattern of Ilya's later unique position in the Grail Christianity of Kiev emerged when Ilya was king of Christian Greece. He took up a position next to King Vladimir, his brother (in spirit). This is also the pattern of the subsequent individual and spiritual element of St John, as contained in everything that Ilya Muromets represented in Kiev after Christianity spread from Greece to Russia.

These two patterns complement each other. This is both because of what emerged from the two patterns, and because of the fact that Voldemar and Ilya were brothers. Conversely, this fact supports the idea expressed above about the symbolic significance of Novgorod. This idea, which was expressed in the summary of early Russian history, as well as the contents of the Wilking saga, particularly the aspect of the cultural function of Novgorod as a St John type herald, is expressed in a specific mythological way in the four Novgorod bylini, which actually arose in Novgorod and were both exported there. This has a particular outline that requires an elaboration on the subject of the evolution of the earth, as mentioned in the Introduction to the Kitezh legend.

The first part of the evolution of the Earth, up to the fifth Aryan cultural era, is described in terms of 'the early Mars development of the Earth'. This concerns that part of the evolution of the earth in which man assimilates the inheritance of earlier worlds in the law 'an eye for an eye, and a tooth for a tooth'. However, from the fifth Aryan cultural era it developed towards spiritual freedom and a demonstration of love and peace. The commentaries on the first three bylini outline how — from the Slav point of view — this occurred under the auspices of the Father mysteries, and under the leadership of certain mythological heroes (mythical bogatyri).

In a more historical sense, Elijah–Naboth (again the same character) became a leading figure in this Mars evolution and in the Father mysteries, so that they could later be renewed. This historical fact is also echoed in the later heroic bylina, 'Ilya Muromets and Sviatogor'. To be precise, Elijah was the most martial leader in this development. As such, he prepared the Jewish culture for the coming of Christ (perfectly in keeping with the past), the prince of peace and bringer of freedom, and the strength of the future of the world.

It is clear that the first two genuine Novgorod bylini about the extremely martial bogatyr Vasili Buslayev and his military exploits relate to that early Mars evolution of the world, and therefore indirectly also to Elijah, its most martial leader. After all, there are no two bylini which emphasize so clearly this martial element and describe the way in which it is related to Christ and Christianity in such detail as these two.

The second part of the evolution of the Earth, from the fifth Aryan cultural era onwards, is described in terms of 'the present and future Mercury development of the Earth'. It concerns that part of the evolution of the Earth in which mankind participates in the Grail mysteries, linked to Christ's 'law of love', by fulfilling it, in order to arrive at spiritual freedom and an increasing demonstration of that love. As described above, this serves the Rosicrucian ideal and the Rosicrucian and Manichean ideals together.

The Introduction to the Kitezh legend and the commentary on the preceding bylini outlined how this occurs (and occurred as a preparation for the future), and how it will occur. That commentary pointed out in particular how Elijah–Naboth was again a leading figure in and from the Slav culture for the (future) Mercurius evolution, this time in the character of Ilya Muromets. Having a special character of Self, he was the most Mercurial in the sense described above, also on the basis of his incarnation as Raphael and Novalis in the Latin and Germanic cultures. The transformation of the martial Elijah character into the Mercurial Ilya character took place when the character concerned was rejuvenated as St John the Baptist by St John the Evangelist to become a character like Raphael or Novalis. This was described in the commentary on the bylina 'The cure of Ilya Muromets'. The transformation consists of this rejuvenation.

It is clear that the second two real Novgorod bylini about the extremely Mercurial bogatyr Sadko and his acquisition of excesses in everything, are related to this future Mercurius evolution of the world, and therefore indirectly to Ilya Muromets — at least to the concealed Raphael and Novalis aspect of his character. Because of this, he is the most Mercurial leader of that development. There are no two bylini that describe in such direct terms the Mercurial element of Christ's words, 'Hold onto that love and all shall be well.'

In relation to the function of Novgorod as a cultural herald, we can now conclude that:

223

1) The two bylini about Vasili Buslayev express this culture mythologically by revealing and referring back to a hidden connection with the former Mars evolution of Earth (as a complement to what Ilya Muromets represents both as an individual, and spiritually in Kiev). In particular they refer back to and lead this development towards an early Jewish martial Elijah character.
2) The two bylini about Sadko (see p. 227-32) express this culture in mythological terms, in a reference to the present and future Mercurius evolution of the Earth, and particularly to the contemporary Western European Mercurial Raphael-Novalis character leading this evolution.

Therefore the cultural function of Novgorod as a St John type of herald, as revealed in early Russian history (and in the Wilking saga) is identified in the four true Novgorod bylini as both a martial Elijah-herald culture and a mercurial Raphael-Novalis culture.

As indicated, Sadko and his world seem to be an extension of Raphael's painted world of joy, and above all, of Novalis's fairytale world portrayed in his novel *Heinrich von Ofterdingen*.

Looking at the content of the first bylina about Vasili Buslayev, a very brief comment can be made. The hero's name, like that of Vasilisa, means 'royal' (Basil). He is the son of the rich merchant Buslay and his wife Mamelyfa Timofeyevna. (Vasili's grandmother on his mother's side appears to have the same name as his grandfather on his father's side.) Vasili's father dies very soon, and at the age of seven the boy is the 'son of a widow', just like Dobrynya Nikitich. This means that Vasili expresses the earlier Elijah aspect represented in him in the present, the aspect of the Father mysteries with the help of his own Self force, quite separately from the effect of the mysteries.

The bylina describes how Vasili assembles a band of Novgorod youths, testing them with certain martial initiation criteria. He takes over Novgorod in stages, using terrorist means, leading his band and together with his friends, Kostya Novotorzianien (which means 'steadfast' like the 'New Tarzan', the Mars force *par excellence*), and Potanya the Cripple (which means 'the fifth', 'the Pentecostal force', the broken Mars force, the Mars force which is already aimed at the mercurial future). This terrorism is based on the martial initiation processes, which require great courage and a great capacity for perseverance, also on the part of the people of Novgorod, who suffer a great deal because of the martial initiatives of Vasili and his band. The following bylina will show that these initiatives simply lead to a turning towards Christ and Christianity.

After a time Vasili becomes the mayor of the city of his birth, simply through his power. He increases its sphere of influence with the help of its wealth and the continued use of his own power. Eventually this is to the benefit of Kiev.

The Death of Vasili Buslayev

Travelling down the great rivers of Russia, Vasili and his band subjugated the Finns, the Mongols and most of the people around the Caspian Sea. They returned after a victorious campaign lasting many years. With Kostya Novotorzianien at the rudder, and Potanya and Foma at the bows, their ship entered the port of Novgorod via Lake Ilmen and the Volchov. Vasili looked grave. He set foot on land and went straight to his old mother. He wished to do penance for all his former violent acts, even if they sometimes served a good purpose.

He announced: 'My next trip will first lead to the grave of the Lord and then to the Jordan to cleanse me of all my sins. Finally I will climb Mount Tabor to gain an insight into what must happen both to me and to Novgorod.' Obviously Mamelyfa Timofeyevna gave her blessing for this excellent plan. She even predicted that the earth would no longer tolerate her son if he continued to plunder and murder.

The next day Vasili and his band sailed away from the port of Novgorod to Jerusalem. For a month they saw no one, for everyone fled from them. Then sails appeared on the horizon; they appeared to belong to a pair of trading ships. Vasili sailed alongside and informed the frightened merchants that he was no longer a robber. Could they show him the shortest route to Jerusalem? The merchants pointed out that there was a route across the Caspian Sea that only took seven weeks, but they added: 'That sea was recently blockaded. Robbers have occupied the Cumin Island. We advise you to take the detour through the western seas, which takes a year and a half.'

Vasili did not feel like this at all. Once again he allowed his temper to get the better of him, he sailed to the largest landlocked sea in the world, and soon landed on Cumin Island. There he again challenged the robbers to tell him the shortest possible route to Jerusalem. They were rather intimidated, and decided not to overpower the colossus and his helpers straightaway. They decided instead to subject Vasili to a test. If he was able to drain a flagon of wine containing a bucket and a half in one gulp after raising it to his lips with one hand, and if he was able to endure a blow to the head with a club of 10 poed without falling down, they would send a pilot along with him.

However Vasili succeeded and endured, all this without difficulty. After the blow wth the club he mocked: 'Have I been stung by a mosquito?'

After a journey of seven weeks with the pilot, the ship reached Mount Tabor. They moored, and climbed the mountain. Halfway to the top Vasili stumbled on a skull. He cried out: 'Speak, you desiccated death's head. Are you the head of a scoundrel, a robber, a Tartar or a Christian?' In his conceited way he kicked it right into the clouds. When it fell back to earth, the skull lamented: 'Why did you do that, Vasili Buslayevich? I am the head of a Christian crusader, braver than you. Because of the dishonourable way you have treated me, your head will soon fall on this spot and be covered in dust.'

Vasili jeered at the skull, and climbed to the top of the Tabor with his band of men. He then climbed down again and hastened to Jerusalem. In the cathedral in that city he had a Mass sung for himself and for his old mother, prayed for forgiveness for all his former sins, and gave generous gifts to the priests. Then he went to the Jordan to bathe with his 29 followers. Vasili bathed naked. An old woman saw him and called out: 'Why are you bathing naked, Vasili Buslayev? Only our Lord Jesus Christ could do that when he was baptized by John the Baptist. Oh brave band of men, know that you will soon lose your leader.'

Suddenly filled with fearful premonitions, Vasili led his men back to Mount Tabor so that they could all pray for forgiveness for his mockery of the skull. Where the skull had been, the hero now found a rock 40 vadem long and 20 vadem wide, with the following words hewn into it: 'Anyone who has the courage to jump over me will not stand up alive.' Once again Vasili felt challenged. He jumped, stumbled and hit his head against the ground. Dying, he sent his band of men back to his mother with the request not to spend any money in his memory. His friends buried him, sailed back to Novgorod, and told Mamelyfa Timofeyevna of the death of her son. She gave all her possessions away to monasteries so that the priests would pray incessantly for the peace of Vasili's soul.

Commentary

This bylina outlines how the former Mars-like element of the world is eventually Christianized and assimilated in the herald culture of Novgorod.

After conquering all his enemies, the Finns (Varangians), Western European nations and the Mongols, Vasili repents for his acts of violence. His repentence is also the result of the unconscious knowledge that the Mars-like pattern by which Russia must defeat her enemies is not based in any way on attack, but on defence and on a subsequent unexpected God-given conquest — a conquest through a fortunate turn in destiny. In the past this had regularly applied to the Israelites who prepared the Slav Manas culture.

Vasili makes a pilgrimage to Israel. In the first place he desires astral purification (to be made humble like Christ) by baptizing himself in the Jordan. This is a self-baptism to indicate that Vasili, though acting on the basis of his own Self force and independently of the Father mysteries, nevertheless has certain martial initiation capacities because of what he represents. Secondly, he wishes to Christianize these capacities (on the basis of his already awakened Self) by climbing Mount Tabor, the mountain of Christian initiation.

In order to achieve these two things, Vasili makes peace with his former seafaring enemies. Against the advice of some of them, he takes the shortest route to Palestine, a route controlled by pirates. These pirates subject Vasili to the initiation test that he had used to assemble his band of men in his youth. In other words, they represent the criterion for assessing whether Vasili is still the person he was, and therefore whether he truly has the right to fulfil his mission in Palestine. Vasili passes the test.

Because of his energy and skill, he and his men do not reach Palestine in the usual way via the Jordan, the symbol of baptism, catharsis, and death of the Self, but via Mount Tabor, the symbol of enlightenment in Christ — in other words, the Christianization of individual ability — or via that which follows upon baptism, catharsis, and death of the Self. This is avenged. The lack of respect for 'the Tabor's commands' makes him despise the value of the death of his Self and makes him kick into the air the skull of a crusader who had once preceded him in the death of the Self.

As Vasili did not achieve anything on the Tabor the first time, he went to the Jordan with his band of men. He bathed naked, revealing his contempt, and baptised himself with his own strength. (Only Christ could bathe naked, and even he was baptised by another.)

When he kicks the crusader's skull into the air, this results in a death of the Self in a literal and physical sense, and when he relies too much on his own martial strength by jumping over a rock after being warned against this, a fatal accident befalls him. It leads to his stumbling over the skull, the symbol of the true spiritual death of the Self that he had held in contempt. After his death it is his mother, Mamelyfa Timofeyevna, a symbol of the astral processes, who assimilates the martial inheritance (Elijah's inheritance) from the past, and which Vasili himself had brought into the present — into the herald culture of Novgorod.

How Sadko Became a Rich Merchant

All the lively young Sadko possessed in the world was a goesli. He played the instrument perfectly, and was therefore invited to all Novgorod's celebrations. However, after a few years he was tired of his social life and left for Lake Ilmen. On the beach he played such heartbreakingly beautiful music to the plants, the flowers, the birds, and the fish, that all of nature responded to his music. Sunshine and storms alternated rapidly. When he finished playing, the king of the lake rose up from the waves, and to reward him for his music he advised him: 'Make a bet with the merchants of Novgorod. Tell them that there is a species of fish here with golden fins, and challenge them to catch one. You'll see what will happen next.'

During a great ball, Sadko uttered this challenge. He bet his head against nine clothes shops in the trade collective that there was a species of fish with gold fins in Lake Ilmen. The fishermen of the town succeeded in catching some of these strange gold fish. Sadko bought the catch, dumped it in his cellar, and called the merchants. But when they appeared, the fish had changed into a pile of silver coins, a pile of silver and gold coins mixed together, and a pile of gold coins. The fishermen had witnessed the fact that all this money had been fish moments before. The merchants were convinced, and gave the musician his nine clothes shops.

Sadko prospered with his shops, married a beautiful lady from Novgorod, and proposed a second wager to the merchants. He would buy up all the goods in the city three times, paying cash every time. If he did not succeed, the town would have the right to demand three hundred thousand roubles from him. Sadko won the bet. At the third sale he was still able to pay for some broken pots with money from his own purse. Henceforth he was known as Sadko Syntinich (Sadko the Rich).

According to another version of this story, Sadko lost the second bet. He honourably admitted defeat, paid his debt, and said: 'I, Sadko, am rich, but Lord Novgorod the Great is even richer.'

Commentary

Rimsky-Korsakov wrote an opera called *Sadko*, based on the content of this bylina and the following one, just as he did with the Belski version of the Kitezh legend.

The bylina does not say anything about Sadko's origins, although he represents the future of the world in a very special way. His name means: 'The Satisfied'. Like Dobrynya Nikitich, Sadko is an excellent singer and goesli player, and like Solovei Budimirovich of Venice he is also a great merchant. He plays his goesli (initially the only thing he owns) so well that nature and the spirits of nature cannot but respond to his art. Sadko awakens nature with his goesli playing, so that he can learn from it.

He then learns how he and Novgorod can achieve an abundance in a cultural sense within the Mercurial Christian development. He learns this from the phenomenon of abundance characteristic of nature, especially since Christ shed his blood to awaken and rejuvenate nature (*inter alia*, so that the earth will be able to endure man's future pollution). This abundance of nature, based on a new life force that springs from Christ, is symbolized in the bylina by the fish with gold fins in Lake Ilmen.

Cultural abundance is symbolized by the piles of silver and gold in Sadko's cellar, which were created from the golden fish. Obviously cultural abundance is created by natural abundance. The story does not describe exactly how Sadko mobilizes the abundance of nature with his goesli playing, nor exactly how this abundance is transformed into a cultural abundance. This concerns a veiled, twofold secret of Christ (secret of Mercury), as well as a secret of the higher (Christ) Self.

However, it is clear that this mobilization concerns the power of the creative word and the transformation of a cultural abundance comparable to the so-called 'Cup of Love', which becomes fuller and fuller as more is poured out. Pouring from the Cup of Love refers to the correct Mercurial maintenance of the ideals of the French Revolution, the ideals of liberty, equality and fraternity. In ancient Israel, the martial Elijah — it could be no other — prepared for this Mercurial manifestation of love and the related cultural abundance by temporarily turning a small supply of oil and flour into an inexhaustible supply for the widow of Sarfat.

The esoteric idea that Mercurial Christian love is never finished when it is poured out, but increases and improves the quality of every area of life, is reflected in trade, often described as the lower Mercury symbolizing the higher Christian Mercurius, in the principle of profit. This also applies in this bylina. On the basis of the principle of profit from never-ending love and cultural abundance — founded on the above-mentioned twofold secret of Christ — Sadko and Novgorod become richer and richer, increasingly Mercurial, and increasingly Novgorod becomes the St John-Raphael-Novalis herald for Kiev in the cultural sense.

Sadko and the Sea King

For 12 years Sadko sailed the seas with his merchant fleet of 30 ships. One day the leading ship ran aground in the middle of the sea during a storm which arose from an unclouded sky. Sadko understood that this bad luck was because he had never paid tribute to the Sea King. He had a barrel of silver thrown into the sea, but it did not have any effect. Even a barrel of gold and a barrel of pearls could not succeed in softening the Sea King's heart. The rich merchant suggested that every member of the crew, including himself, should engrave his name on a block of wood and throw it over board. Anyone whose block sank had committed a deadly sin and would sacrifice himself to the Sea King in order to liberate the boat.

Sadko did not trust himself, and certainly did not wish to drown. Therefore he surreptitiously exchanged his block of wood for a feather. But the feather sank. To make sure, he did the test again, and this time exchanged his block surreptitiously for a piece of steel weighing 10 poed. Of course, the piece of steel sank. Sadko admitted that this was what he intended. He conquered his fear of death, grabbed his goesli, asked the crew to send his wife his last respects, and leaped overboard. Meanwhile the leading ship sailed off, went to the head of the fleet, and led the ships westwards.

Sadko sank down and came to the palace of the King and Queen of the sea. Sitting on their double throne, they were arguing and initially did not see the approaching stranger. Sadko bowed deeply before them and interrupted their argument: 'Hail father and mother of the watery kingdom of the sea. Why did you call me, Sadko of Novgorod?' The Sea King answered: 'My wife and I are arguing about which is more valuable to the people of Holy Russia, iron or gold. My wife believes that iron is more valuable, but think that you value gold more highly.' The visitor explained: 'King and Queen of the sea, this is the truth. Iron and gold are the same price, but we, the people of the earth, cannot do without iron, though we can, if necessary, do without gold.'

This answer showed the King that he had been wrong. He drew his sword and wanted to throw himself on his guest. However, quicker than a flash, the young merchant took hold of his goesli and played so beautifully that the Sea King immediately forgot his rage and started to dance through his palace. He danced more and more quickly, more and more wildly.

Then the Sea Queen whispered: 'Sadko, stop! Destroy your goesli. My husband's dancing is a pleasure to us, but above us he is creating spring tides and storms. The earth will be destroyed.' Sadko finished his playing with a strident chord which caused the strings to break. The water calmed down.

To reward him for his playing, the Sea King offered the musician the most beautiful mermaid of the kingdom. The Sea Queen whispered again: 'Sadko, three times three hundred beautiful virgins of the sea will pass by you. Let them go. Do not choose any for your wife. The procession will be followed by a small and scrawny girl. Marry her, but do not kiss her or make love to her. It is only if you choose her, and yet never touch her, that you will see Novgorod again.'

To the Sea King's displeasure, Sadko let all the three times three hundred enchanting mermaids go, and chose the ugly duckling for his bride. On their wedding night he did not touch her. The next morning, to his utter astonishment, the hero woke up on the banks of the River Volchov. In the distance he saw his fleet approaching, more richly laden with goods than ever before. The astonishment of his men was almost greater than his own. When he arrived home, his wife asked him to abandon the sea in future, for the sake of herself and their child. Richer than ever, Sadko agreed.

Commentary

Like the previous bylina, this one outlines how the present and future Mercury development of the world affects the herald culture of Novgorod, and conversely, how this culture gives form to that development.

The story begins by describing how Sadko sails the seven seas of the world for 12 years with his fleet of 30 ships. This means that the Slav-Novgorod herald culture as a Mercurius culture has become a global culture under the leadership of Sadko, particularly on the astral plane. In this bylina the culture is not merely characterized with the Mercurial characteristic of the mobilization of natural abundance and its transformation into a cultural abundance, but also with the spiritualization of the astral body into Manas, as mentioned above. This occurs on a global level, and in a sense it can be characterized as the reverse or mirror image of the first Mercurial characteristic.

The King and Queen of the Sea, the living nuclear forces of the astral element, want Sadko to tell them (logically it must be him) what is more valuable to the people of Novgorod-Russia, iron or gold — the lower or higher Self consciousness. They wish to know this particularly because despite Sadko's special and profound relationship with nature (astralis), expressed in his goesli playing, he has never paid tribute to nature. In other words, he has never revived nature with gold, silver and pearls (spiritual, astral, and soul force) as Christ did (and does). He restricts himself to the transformation of that nature into culture.

However, the Mercurial element described in the previous bylina, the mobilization of natural abundance and its transformation into cultural abundance, takes place on the basis of the secret capacities of the higher Self (gold), but it 'broadens out' through the cultural activities of the lower Self (iron). In contrast, the Mercurial characteristic described in this bylina — the spiritualization of the astral body into Manas — takes place on the basis of Self control, the death of the lower Self (iron), though it proves itself via the higher Self (gold).

On the basis of the principle that the Rose (the higher Self, Manas), which also adorns the Garden (of the world), this Mercurial characteristic contributes to the renewal of nature. This (astral) nature tests through 'the iron or gold question' which Mercurial characteristic has precedence over the other, which is the most fundamental. In other words, what is the primary concern of the Mercurial culture of Novgorod — the transformation of nature into culture, or the revitalization of nature?

For Sadko, one is no less important than the other. However, he points out to the Sea King and Queen that man cannot live without culture (iron). If man is to develop as Manas mankind, bringing life to nature — i.e. working with gold — he will first have to establish a culture which culminates in self-control, in the death of self-interest. The use of nature for the purpose of culture can be seen as a means of adding new life-force to nature.

It is because Sadko arrived at this wisdom that he is destined to visit the Sea King as soon as he uses his skills to bring life to nature — as soon as he pays his tribute to the Sea King. Having the right view is expressed in the way that Sadko's little block with his name on (a symbol of the Self), which is apparently as light as a feather or as heavy as lead, has exactly the right weight to sink down in the sea towards the Sea King.

(Astral) nature, particularly its male positive aspect, (the Sea King), obviously has a greater need to be revitalized than the transformation. This is in accordance with the words of St Paul that the whole of creation is stretching out towards the coming of the children of God, the Manas people, in order to be cured. Sadko's answer to the question about which Mercurial characteristic is fundamental in relation to the other does not please the Sea King. He wishes to kill Sadko. It is only by means of the power of sound (the Word), the force that mobilizes the forces of nature, that Sadko is able to calm the Sea King down.

However, his goesli playing gives rise to unrest and storms in the material world (the reflection of the astral world). At the Sea Queen's suggestion, he stops playing his goesli. The Sea King offers Sadko three times three hundred beautiful and enchanting mermaids for his art. These are all the forces of the soul: those of the soul of perception, those of the soul of emotions and intellect, and the soul of consciousness. In relation to the spiritualization of the astral body into Manas, they lead to victory over sexuality and death, primarily in an astral, imaginative sense.

In reality only one of all these forces of the soul leads to the particular goal, and only one of them forms the foundation for the immortal soul. This soul force is modesty, the devotion that cannot be reflected or touched by definition. It is represented as a scrawny mermaid whom Sadko may take as a bride but may not approach. The scrawniness of the mermaid is reminiscent of the scrawniness of the horses of Mikoela Selyaninovich and Ilya Muromets, which were really very strong — the image of the physical/individual element.

Sadko marries the ugly duckling, and then does not touch her. He wins her by means of (astral or soul) death and sees his mother country once again. It is even richer and more culturally developed than previously, and in addition it gives life to nature.

The most important non-historical bylini were explained in the commentary to the bylina 'Sadko with the Sea King'. This chapter concludes with a final consideration of these bylini, a consideration that comprises a) an overall summary of the mythology described, as well as a brief presentation of the genealogy of the Varangian Order Answer; b) an introduction to the next chapter, which deals with the history of and the historical bylini about Dmitri Donskoi and Dmitri Ivanovich.

Reflections on the Bylini

The explanatory outline of Russian mythology on p. 234, which ties in with other explanatory outlines in this chapter, is an illustrative summary of most of what was covered in the commentaries to the bylini. The diagram is not so much a mental construction; it evolved from the content of this chapter in an organic way, when it had been written. The diagram as a whole represents mythological Kiev Rus as a 'world grail' in which Novgorod encompasses Vladimir's sun-shaped Kiev in the form of a moon permeated by the Western European sense of Self.

In his series of lectures, 'Die Sendung Michael', Rudolf Steiner presents the Sun encompassed by the Moon as the cosmic image of the Holy Grail. It is intriguing, but probably not surprising, to see how the upper half of the diagram, the sun part, representing the star of Venus encompassed by the serpent dragon, as well as the square and the Sophia-Rose-Sun, which overlap the star — the part that stands for Kiev — represents theosophy's emblem of fraternity and the Lectorium Rosicrucianum, thus literally showing everything that spiritual science teaches about the development of human Manas.

It is also intriguing, though not surprising, to see how the lower point of the diagram, the lunar part, with the Self (the five-pointed star of the soul), enclosed by the Small Guard on the Threshold (as well as the Christ Self, the twofold St John Self, and the 'Arthur sun' which overlap that star), i.e. the part that represents Novgorod and Western Europe, depicts the emblem of Self consciousness that Rudolf Steiner designed for his fourth anthroposophical mystery drama (in this way literally depicting everything contained in spiritual science about the development of the Self).

For example, the twelve letter text, *Ich erkennet Sich* ('I recognize the Self'), which occurs in this context in the twelvefold nature of King Arthur's Round Table, particularly in the *Ich* and *Sich* which overlap each other, conceals the subtlety of the independent duo, Parsifal and Gawain, in this Round Table, as described above.

This explanatory diagram can be viewed as the counterpart of the table of 'The Genealogy of the Varangian Order Answer to the Slav-Rurik Call', an abbreviated version of which is given again on p. 235 for the sake of clarity. The diagram presents the (earthly) spiritual building pattern, the Grail pattern of the earlier, strictly mythical Kiev Rus, and therefore it also serves as a building pattern for the apocalyptic, mythical aspect of the future Kiev Rus. The diagram illustrates the material building pattern of historical and mythical-historical Kiev Rus, and therefore also serves as a building pattern for the chronological-material aspect of the future Kiev Rus.

Therefore there is a double pattern, leading both towards the past and towards the future, in the way in which there is a spiritual, invisible man concealed behind every physical visible man. This was indicated in the General Introduction, and is merely examined in greater detail in this and previous chapters. The following brief comment should be added. Both patterns must exist; they complement each other, and eventually coincide in the context of a higher reality of life and in the context of a lower one. The patterns must also coexist because they complement each other. Initially they were distinguishable, and they first came together at the start of Russia's early history in certain characters such as Oleg/Volga and Vladimir the Holy/Vladimir the Red Sun, just as spiritual man initially only touches material man, who is separate in a sense, at particular points (in the chakras/hormonal glands).

The two patterns coincide completely in the manifestation of historical Kitezh (of Georgi of Pskov/Yuri of Kitezh), as well as in the manifestation of the future Kitezh. They coincide in the context of a higher reality, a

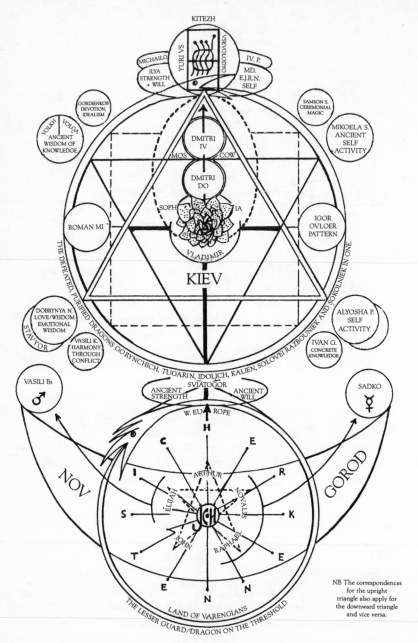

KITEZH

YURI VS · VSEVOLODOKOL

MICHAILO
ILYA
STRENGTH
+ WILL

IV. P.
MD.
E.J.R.N.
SELF

GORDIENKOB
DEVOTION,
IDEALISM

SAMSON S.
CEREMONIAL
MAGIC

VOLKH · VOLGA
ANCIENT
WISDOM OF
KNOWLEDGE

MIKOELA S.
ANCIENT
SELF
ACTIVITY

DMITRI
IV

MOS   COW

DMITRI
DO

SOPHI   IA

ROMAN MI

IGOR
OVLOER
PATTERN

VLADIMIR

KIEV

THE DEFEATED, PURIFIED DRAGONS GORYNCHICH, TUGARIN, IDOLICH, KALIEN, SOLOVEI RAZBOUNIEK AND SOKOLNIEK IN ONE.

DOBRYNYA N.
LOVE/WISDOM
EMOTIONAL
WISDOM

ALYOSHA P.
SELF
ACTIVITY

STAVYOR

VASILI K.
HARMONY
THROUGH
CONFLICT

IVAN G.
CONCRETE
KNOWLEDGE

SVIATOGOR

ANCIENT
STRENGTH

ANCIENT
WILL

VASILI Bs
♂

SADKO
☿

W. EU   ROPE

H

C   E

NOV

I   R

ARTHUR

ELIJAH   NOVALIS

GOROD

S   K

JOHN   RAPHAEL

T   E

E   N

N

LAND OF VARENGLIANS

THE LESSER GUARD/DRAGON ON THE THRESHOLD

NB The correspondences
for the upright
triangle also apply for
the downward triangle
and vice versa.

KIEV RUS
(MYTHOLOGICAL)

THE WORLD GRAIL

234

Table of the genealogy of the Varangian Order Answer to the Slav–Rurik Call (abbreviated)

1380	Dimitri Donskoi defeats the Tartars at the Battle of Polye on the Don. A brief repetition of the former Order established in Russia by the Varangians.
	↑
1263–1380	Tartar domination — Moscow develops as Russia's most important principality.
	↑
1240–63	Alexander Nevsky, ruler of Novgorod, officially avoids Tartar domination, though in fact Novgorod pays tribute to the Tartars. Start of the songs about the Poljanje bogatyri of Kiev by the Slavjanje bards of Novgorod. For the second time, Novgorod serves as an inner herald for Kiev.
1237–40	Khan Batu conquers the whole of Russia, the end of Kiev Rus, the end of the Varangian Order Answer to the Slav–Rurik Call. Russia is in chaos and subject to the Mongol Orda. Only Novgorod to some extent resists the Tartars.
1236/37	Khan Batu destroys Little Kitezh. Ascension of Great Kitezh under its ruler and his son Prince Vsevolod. The end of Russia's esoteric order.
1168–1236	The flowering of Kitezh, to achieve the zenith of the esoteric order of Kiev Rus.
1174–1212	Reign of Vsevolod III, Boljoje Gniezdo of Vladimir Suzdal. During his reign his great-great nephew Georgi (Juri) Vsevolodovich, the ruler of Pskov (1165–8), founds Great Kitezh as a Christian communist city, the social conclusion of the Round Table of Kiev.
1157–74	Russia's order in the external areas of life comes to an end under Andrei Bogolyubski of Vladimir–Suzdal, while the esoteric order of the country continues.
1125–57	War of succession between Vladimir M's (grand)sons. Fourth period of disorder.
	↑
1113–25	Vladimir Monomach gathers together all the (exoteric) individual orders and harmonizes them.
1054–1113	War of succession between Jaroslav's (grand)sons. Third period of disorder.
	↑
1019–54	Jaroslav establishes a legal order in Russia. (To some extent he is a fifth cultural person.)
1015–19	War of succession between Vladimir's sons. Second period of disorder.
	↑
980–1015	King Vladimir consolidates Olga's exoteric religious order. Kiev Rus is established.
988	Start of Russia's esoteric religious order: foundation of Kiev's Round Table as a preparation for Kitezh as a Christian communist city state.
973–80	Jaropolk fights for Russia's throne. First period of disorder, prior to Russia being overrun by the Tartars.
	↑
962–73	Sviatoslav consolidates Rurik's individually established orders.
945–62	Olga establishes order in Russia in an exoteric religious sense.
912–45	Igor expands Russia so that order will be established over a larger area.
879–912	Oleg establishes order in Russia's untamed nature. (Identification of Oleg with Volga S.)
862–79	Rurik of Rus establishes a social, political and military order in Russia. Start of the Varangian Order Answer to the Rurik Call (initially exoteric). Novgorod first serves as external herald for Kiev.

Left-margin brackets: Kingdom of Kiev — Kingdom of Kiev — Republic of Novgorod — Kiev Rus

↑

KIEV RUS
(historical or historical-mythological)

The Varangian Answer of Order
to the Slav Rurik Call.

Christian communist reality, just as spiritual and physical man will also eventually coincide in this context as a result of initiation.

However, both patterns also completely coincide in the context of a lower reality, the reality of the later Tartar-Tsarist-Soviet Communist Russia, culminating in non-Christian communism. This was completely predictable, and is no more than the spirit of the new age, the propulsive force of the emerging historical process that devours all mythology and sprang from the conscious soul culture of the West. Evidently this took place on the basis of the end of the coincidence of these patterns as a result of the downfall of Kitezh in the context of the higher (historical) reality.

This happens because the ultimate Kitezh as the social conclusion of an ultimate Kiev Rus will have to become the music of the future in its essential aspect of Manas reality (rather than Manas preparation). It happens — because there is no real alternative — simply as a stronger and double intensification of the icon aspect that characterized historical Kiev Rus. While historical Kiev Rus, including the historical Kitezh with its higher reality, served as an icon of the ultimate Kiev Rus (including the ultimate Kitezh, again with its higher reality), the Tartar-Tsarist-Soviet Communist Russia ('Moscow-Russia'), in its turn serves as the icon culture of Kiev.

As such, Moscow-Russia simply refers back to the earlier culture (A), and then, with the increase of the conscious soul culture in Western Europe, it anticipates the future Kiev Rus and its Manas culture (B). In the case of (B), Moscow-Russia does the same as the historical Kiev Rus, but it does so indirectly without being in any sense a Grail nation. To summarize: Moscow-Russia, in which the mythical and historical elements or patterns coincide in the context of a lower reality, unites the historical and future Kiev Rus. In its social highpoint (the cities of Kitezh), these elements or patterns coincide in the context of a higher reality.

What is described under (A) was achieved by Dimitri Donskoi, who repeated the historical Varangian Order Answer for Russia. What is described under (B) was achieved by Dimitri Ivanovich, who indirectly anticipated the future Varangian Order Answer for that Russia in a particular way. These characters and their underlying motivation were mentioned in the General Introduction. In the following chapter those references and the ideas mentioned here will be explored and expounded. In particular, at the end of the chapter there is a more detailed consideration of the relationship of these characters to the double pattern outlined above, when the Kitezh legend is examined in the light of the Demetrius question.

Finally, the names of these Dimitri figures were included in the Explanatory Outline of Russia's mythology and given a particular place in the schedule of the Varangian Order. The next and final chapter outlines their history and their bylini, with a commentary, in order to explain why they have been included in that particular place, and to indicate how these characters behaved and united the historical Kiev Rus with the future via Moscow-Russia, as stated above.

Epilogue

A great deal of the two versions of the Kitezh legend has to remain unexplained in this first volume, particularly everything related to Kitezh as a Utopia compared with other Utopias

Having come almost to the end of this book, I would like to refer again to the character of Ilya Muromets, particularly with regard to the paradox mentioned in the commentary on the bylina 'The three journeys of Ilya Muromets' that the correct (future) Varangian Answer to the Slav-Rurik Call is undoubtedly something that present and future Russia really needs, while it is also something that Russia already has wholly and completely in one sense (in its early history, particularly the mythology related to that history, and the Kitezh legend).

Certainly Russia already has the (future) Varangian Order Answer (in the guise of the past), but it has this in the same way in which the strong external Self forces and spiritual science are repressed behind its own weak Alyosha Self. This applies in the first place to the strong Self of Ilya Muromets.

As a result, the establishment of a future Varangian Order in Russia, the sounding of a new Varangian Answer for establishing an Order, will not be very different from carrying out the request of Zamyatin, and many other individual witnesses succeeding the virtually silent Novgorod collective of people. This request was to return to the Russia people its history, early Russian history and the related mythology and Kitezh legend, as well as their meaning, though not the history of the Tartar-Tsarist-Soviet Communist Russia (apart from the history of the two great Demetrius figures). In fact, it does not even refer so much to the history of the Slavophile movement of figures like Alexei Chomyekov, and later on, Tolstoy, Dostoyevsky, and Soloviev.

In returning this history, the spirit of the archangel Michael — Michailo Ivanovich Potyk — and the Self of Ilya Muromets — i.e. the St John Self will become effective in Russia. In addition, knowledge will be acquired through spiritual perception, the Aparoksha (Apraxia) and the knowledge of the rebirth of the soul (symbolized by the Natasha figures).

In returning this history, the Western-oriented Self and Eastern-oriented Manas of people of goodwill will strengthen each other and unite in an alchemical way; a new Kiev Rus will emerge as the basis for determining a world Manas culture. In returning this history, the ultimate Demetrius character will arise in Russia, anticipated in broad terms by the Slavophile movement. In returning this history, the new Kitezh will arise from the Svetli Jarr in Russia, the Manichean Christian communist state of Salvation. All these things will take place in an interrelationship described in this book in order to relieve the Soviet communists standing guard.

We conclude this publication with a unique twentieth-century bylina which describes the return of Russia's bogatyri.

How the Holy Mountains Released the Mighty Russian Bogatyri from Their Rocky Graves

(Taken from *The Origin of Russia* by Hermann von Skerst and from a verse translation from German by M.N.)

When your understanding of reason is no longer enough
Turn your ear to the voice of silence.
It will tell you what was decided
In highest heaven — for she is Sophia.
She silently answers anyone who wishes to know.

I

When Russia's earliest bogatyri
Defeated the Hunnenheir on The Sarfat,
They boasted about it. They were mad with success.
They had no wisdom and they called out:
'We think that now we could even
Defeat armies of spirits.'
At once two fiery spirit knights appeared.
Alyosha slew both, but it did not avail;
Not two, but four of these spirit knights now appeared.
Alyosha slew them, but to no avail.
It seemed that eight figures rose up
Where the four had fallen.
After being hit by Ilya Muromets,
After being struck by Vasili Buslayev,
After being smashed by Ivan Gostiny,
The enemy numbered 64 spirits.

240

Side by side, in serried ranks,
Russia's finest soldiers stormed the enemy,
Smote and pierced — but the fiery Hunnen
Multiplied more than twice every time
The knight struck them.
Prince Vladimir's heroes fell —
Fled to the safe foot of Sviatogor,
The steadfast early hero, now the Holy Mountain,
Under cover of those who were striking, smashing, hitting.
When Ilya of Myrom begged him for protection
For the weak, for the strong, for himself,
The giant rock raised his eyes;
Bottomless lakes appeared.
He knit his brow, and his eyebrows
Transformed into forests.
His enormous lips parted slightly;
The earth tore apart, simmered, shuddered,
And for a moment Russia became an abyss.
Slowly he stretched himself, touched the clouds,
Stared at Ilya in utter astonishment,
And then he recognized his younger brother
In spirit. How sombre he seemed.
Swinging his arms, Sviatogor picked him up,
As in the past — put him in his pocket with his horse —
As in the past — put his brothers in as well and went to sleep.

II

In the window of Sviatogor's bedroom
The young ones had no choice
But to keep guard endlessly together
For although their eyes can see little in the dark,
Sviatogor slept deep and black,
They heard with spirit ears how the
Lies rattled loudly over all of Russia.
In the hands of the Lying Prince.
Turning to the Russians, the Prince said:
'I can stand up to any power here,'
While he gloated maliciously,
'I gladly compare myself to Jesus Christ.'
The Russians in their holy land
Were dismayed by his voice and his boasting.
Suddenly, the peasant's son cried out and shattered
The darkness into a thousand pieces with his scream.

241

Yes, his heart was a pure cry, a cry for help,
His heart was on his tongue: a gong between his lips.
Mother, Mother Earth!
Do not blame me, the youngest of your sons,
For being imprisoned with all my brothers
For their former boasting,
Sitting in the dark, in a thousand shadows,
For a thousand years, of which each is a cruel thorn.
When you can and may, when the time has come,
Awaken Sviatogor, the Holy Mountain, then we will be free.
Give us a free will. We wish to acquire
Perfect modesty to serve the Holy Earth,
Which you bore, rejuvenating yourself,
Which your bore before bringing us into the world.
We wish to save Russia and the Russians
From the evil spirit of lies.
Oh hear me, Mother Earth!

III

Ilya's Call was reproduced
Through the mountain, as though boring through it.
It flew up and reached the heaven
Of the fixed stars, far above the mass of clouds,
Then fell back slowly as a cloud of rain,
A still cloud at the feet of Sophia.
Wisdom saw the cloud, and heard
Ilya's Call, which was so loud and then so still. She wept.
She rose from her throne and walked
To the throne of Jesus Christ, her beloved son,
Even more beloved than Vladimir's knights.
Wisdom knelt, Wisdom interceded for the heroes,
And asked forgiveness for their former boasting.
The stars described new orbits.
The rain became sheets of white snow.
The saviour spoke: 'Most highly blessed Lady,
Who intercedes for sinners, great and small,
Your mercy redeems them. It is good.
I will help those crazy, excited Russians.
Christ ordered the silent St Michael
To mobilize the forces of heaven.
Then, as the Seraphim's trumpets sounded,
And the choirs of the Cherubim hummed,
The dragonfly wings of God's messengers

And the butterfly glow of the angels
Moved under Mother Wisdom,
To place her down on Earth.
Those in high places, the lords of the world,
Automatically raised their eyes to heaven.
The trumpets of the Seraphim continued to sound,
The humming of the Cherubim did not cease,
The angel messengers penetrated the realm of gold crystal.
They penetrated the heaven of the fixed stars,
They penetrated the spheres of the planets,
Past Saturn, Jupiter, Mars and the Sun,
Past Venus and Mercury and beyond the Moon.
Wisdom arrived on Earth as Mother Earth,
And she said: 'Oh, my highest Holy Mountain.
Split your sheer height, break your breadth.
Free the youngest of my children at last.
Release Vladimir's heroes today.
Their former pride is forgiven them.
Their boasting of the past has disappeared.
Come, awaken, ancient mountain of time, awaken!
Ancient mountain of time, awaken, awaken, awaken!
Release the youngest of my children at last.
Holy Russia — my beloved youngest sister —
Needs them, needs them, needs them!

IV

At the word of Mother Earth
The Mountains of the world broke apart.
The Carpathians groaned, thundered and cracked.
The piled up ice and stones wrote the message of life
In the granite.
Fresh air entered the ancient abysses.
Sviatogor sprang up from the deepest cave,
The oldest of the ancient bogatyri,
Himself also a Holy Mountain.
From the dark, Russia's other younger bogatyri
Stepped out to meet Aurora:
Bare-headed, side by side, in renewed glory,
Ilya of Murom, a peasant's son, appeared at last.
Dobrynya Nikitich, the boyar's son,
Alyosha Popovich, the priest's son,
Ivan Gostiny, the merchant's son,
Vasili Buslayev, the son of Novgorod.

They all made the sign of the cross,
Bowed to the west, north, east, and south,
And left on their horses to the Sarfat.
At the water's edge they pitched their tents,
Prayed to Sophia and to God,
And went to sleep.
But Ilya, the peasant's son — tired or not —
Continued to stand guard . . .

Appendix

The Histories of Dimitri Donskoi and Dimitri Ivanovich with a Commentary

(An analysis of the 'Demetrius question' in relation to early Russian history, the two versions of the Kitezh legend and one bylina. The Polish Kitezh legend)

This Appendix is the final chapter (V) in the original Dutch edition, and the 'apotheosis' of the book. It retells and explains the bylina of Dimitri Ivanovich, probably the only historical bylina. This bylina is introduced here as the bridge between the past and future fulfilment of the mythical and historical bylini, and especially of both Kitezh legends. In consultation with the author, we decided to publish it as an appendix because of the deep esoteric analysis.

Edgar Cayce on Russia

The great hope of the world will be Russia's religious development. The nation or group of nations that have the closest ties with Russia will benefit most from this during the gradual changes and in what is finally established. This is how the world is governed. (3976-10)

(From a speech made during the great stock market crash, 29 October 1929)

The hope of the world lies in Russia. Not in that which is called communism or bolshevism, but in freedom — freedom! And in every man living for his fellow man. This principle arose there. It will be years before it has crystallized, but the hope of the world will once again spring from Russia. How will it be directed? Through friendship with that nation which has the words 'In God we trust' on its coins.

(Is this the ideal in your own heart when you pay the debts you owe? Do you have it in your prayers when you send your missionaries to other countries? Do you say: 'I give what I have, for in God we trust'?

(1554-3) There is a rebirth in Russia leading to a new understanding . . .

(3976-19. Answer 5.) As we indicated before, the tortured people will be granted a new understanding. But as a result of the yoke of oppression, desire for an easy life and hedonism, something extreme has developed in Russia. The land will be troubled until freedom of expression is established, as well as the right to worship according to one's religious persuasion.

245

(3976–12.) The basis for a greater worldwide religious idea or movement may come from Russia.'
(From the Edgar Cayce readings [22])

As indicated, Dimitri means 'son of the mother'; in a Slav context it means 'the son of Mother Russia'. The Demetrius that Dimitri Donskoi and Dimitri Ivanovich were named after was the patron saint of Thessalonika, which had often been besieged by the Slavs before the time of King Vladimir the Holy. Later on this Demetrius — the prototype of what was described in previous chapters as 'the son of the widow' — was worshipped in Russia as the patron saint of soldiers. His saint's day was celebrated there on 26 October.

In the Kontakion of that day, 26 October, it says: 'With your blood, Demetrius, God has submerged the Church in purple after you had turned it with the strength of your belief into an invincible fortress and a city dedicated to me.'

'. . . And the lords spoke: 'Let us give up the principle of domination which we were forced to use, and for so long. Let us serve each other.' And their servants loved them and called them 'Father . . . Mother . . .'

From *Notes from memory on conversations with Dr. R. Steiner*, by Count Ludwig Polzer Hoditz, 1/1/1924, in translation.

Introductory note
One of these conversations (from which this quotation is taken) was about a group of fanatical Varangians, the Jesuits of the sixteenth and seventeenth centuries, who were urging the establishment of an unasked for 'spiritualist-materialist' order in Russia, which would take the place of the Tartar Order and prevent the future Varangian Order Answer from being asked. The Jesuits wished to establish an order in Russia, as described in the Utopia, *La Città del Sole*, by Tomasso Campanella, an order based on the image of Christ by Ignatius de Loyola.

The Jesuits hoped to convert Russia to Catholicism despite Dimitri Ivanovich. Because this Jesuit attempt did not yet play a role in the arcane mysteries, and because they support this attempt, Steiner endeavoured to unravel the Dimitri question, and pointed out that Frederick Schiller had started to do this in his 'Demetrius fragment'. (M.N.)

Then there was a discussion of the activities of the Roman Catholic and Western Freemasons' lodges. Steiner solemnly emphasized that it is of the greatest importance for the future to solve the following three questions:

1) The question of the two St Johns.
   (To some extent Steiner himself answered this question in his commentaries on the Gospels and his *Letze Ansprache*. In addition,

most anthroposophical studies of the lives of Elijah, Raphael, and Novalis contribute to solving this question. And the commentaries in this work on the bylini about Ilya Muromets also contribute in this way. (M.N.)

2) The question of who Demetrius was. (The subject of this chapter. M.N.)
3) The question of where Kaspar Hauser came from. (This question was largely solved by P. Tradovsky in his work *Kaspar Hauser*. M.N.)

For all three problems it is of particular importance not to focus too much on the death and the circumstances related to the death of the characters concerned, but on the context of their birth, where they came from, and what their missions were. The character of Kaspar Hauser was an inspiration for the Rosicrucian movement from the very beginning. He was born on 29 September 1812, the son of the Grand Duke Karl Ludwig of Baden and his wife Stephanie de Beauharnais. He fulfilled an important mission for esoteric Christianity in his lifetime and after it.

For the Russians the image of Demetrius emerges [text missing] . . . as the archetypal Christopherus who died and rose like Christ, coming from outside to replace the king of vengeance and to rule as everyone's servant, abolishing evil with goodness, and in this way establishing a true communal kingdom on earth . . .

This is the image which was kept in Kitezh but was turned into a more Luciferian image as a result of the Tartar influence on which the Greek Orthodox Church is based. It is this (archetypal and transformed) image which the Western occult school, the Jesuits, wished and still wish to diminish and replace by Loyola's image of Christ, tinged by Lucifer and Ahriman, which represents Jesus as an earthly superman and just tyrant.

This was the subject portrayed by Schiller in his unfinished play *Demetrius*: the introduction of the false Western imitation of Jesus from Poland and the Catholic Church into the East, behind Dimitri's back.[23]

Blavatsky was also involved in this conflict between the western and eastern Asiatic camps. Indeed we are all involved in this. It is not of essential importance who Demetrius was as a mortal, or who Kaspar Hauser was as a mortal. Posed in this way, the question must lead away from the facts behind the scenes of what apparently happened. It is not important who Demetrius or Kaspar Hauser were, but what they wanted. This is what should concern us, and looking in this direction we will find a key to understanding many difficulties.

Alexander Nevsky of Novgorod had granted his son Dani'il the still insignificant city of Moscow, with the permission of the Tartars. From 1304 to 1320 this son successfully fought for the city against the lords of Tver. Then he became the first ruler of the city of Moscow, which began to replace Vladimir–Suzdal as the capital of Russia.

Dimitri, a great-great-grandson of Dani'il, was the fifth ruler of Moscow from 1359 to 1389, and therefore unofficially the ruler of the whole of

Russia. (Officially the kingdom of Muscovy became a single state only in 1462, as a result of the ambitious plans of Ivan III, Dimitri's great-grandson.) Dimitri succeeded in defeating the divided Tartar hordes in the Battle on the Don. This is why he was called Dimitri Donskoi. The account of his deeds is a historical bylina.

Dimitri was a very kind-hearted ruler. For example, he would pay from his own pocket for the funerals of soldiers who had died in his service. What this means only becomes clear when one remembers that Dimitri's army on the Don comprised 150,000 men, and virtually the whole army had fallen. Dimitri's victory was a Pyrrhic victory in the most literal sense, to such an extent that several years later Dimitri was unable to assemble enough soldiers to counter a Tartar revenge attack. Khan Tochtamysh again overran Russia, though this time without explicitly taking Moscow.

Nevertheless, the Battle of the Don was catastrophic for the Tartars, particularly in a psychological sense. In 1476 they were no longer able to force Ivan III to pay tribute. Without much more conflict, the Tartar yoke was removed from Russia for good, at least in an official external sense. Ivan III emerged as Russia's new khan, and with him began 'Tsarist Russia'.

Dimitri Donskoi was made of different metal from his great-grandson. After his conquest on the Don, he tried to restore the democracy based on the former Varangian Order Answer in Russia in the form of the ancient kingdom of Kiev: he established a democractic monarchy in Moscow.

That he did so is clear from the following observations. After his defeat of the Tartars, the Grand Prince of Moscow had the icon of Our Lady of Vladimir brought to Moscow. According to the legend about this icon, sometimes known as the Russian Paladium, the Grand Prince Dmitri and the people of Moscow hoped in this way to protect Moscow against foreign attacks, through the power of Christian non-violence which results from a just style of government and order in society (as established in Kitezh via Kiev).

As stated above, Vladimir means 'famous ruler'. The icon of Our Lady of Vladimir, simply known as the Vladimirskaya, therefore symbolizes the wisdom that repulses enemies, with which a nation is ruled in the right way, in the style of Kitezh.[24] Indeed, all icons of Our Lady (Mary) symbolize wisdom or the Sophia, i.e. Manas, or to be more precise, a particular aspect of this. Therefore, as stated above, the Vladimirskaya represents the wisdom to rule according to the just, Manichean practice of Liberty, Equality and Fraternity, as had taken place in Kiev Rus, particularly in Kitezh.

This wisdom was then introduced into Moscow by Dimitri Donskoi in the form of an icon, or a sort of remembered synopsis, following the past practice of the historical Varangian Order Answer — at the time between that Answer and a similar future Answer. This once again underlines the absolute icon character of the bygone Kiev Rus. In this way Dimitri Donskoi and some of his contemporaries performed the mission mentioned in the Introduction with a corresponding morality (which will be discussed further below). In other words, he introduced the Varangian Order to Moscow as a remembered culture.

For a while he was successful in this. When new hordes of Mongols, led by Timur Lengk, threatened to overrun Moscow after his death in 1395 (which Khan Tochtamysh had failed to do earlier), they retreated after a short siege, for reasons which are not clear. It is believed that the Vladimirskaya was responsible for fending off the aggression.

Up to now, Moscow, in the sense that it is the memory of the icon culture of the former Kiev icon culture, has not been overrun. Just as Great Kitezh has not been overrun. However, in real terms, Moscow certainly did eventually collapse from the inside, from the moment that Ivan III became the Tsar of all Russians. This was inevitable, like the fall of Kiev Rus. Dimitri Donskoi was no more a self-conscious Manas man than the rulers of Kiev and Kitezh, and as the bearer of an icon, this could not be expected of him.

As stated above, historical Kiev Rus as an icon culture anticipated and served as a basic for the incarnation of a future Kiev Rus. The question arises, how could the Moscow icon culture (as an icon of the Kiev icon culture) anticipate it and serve as a basis for its incarnation? This question can only be answered on the basis of the history of Dimitri Ivanovich, and by comparing it with the two Kitezh legends.

Serge of Radonesh, who was a close friend of Dimitri's, founded monasteries throughout Russia, which were copies of the monasteries described in the Slav Church version of the Kitezh legend. In this way he created a representation of the Christian communism of Kitezh, and in a way reintroduced the peak of the religious aspect of the Varangian Order Answer (where Dimitri Donskoi himself reintroduced the social and military aspect, particularly with regard to his soldiers). In a sense, this religious instruction of the faithful hero seemed invincible, like Kitezh and Moscow, for of course it was also under the aegis of the Vladimirskaya — it acted as a stimulus for the religious life of later Tsarist Russia. However, as it was based on asceticism (Sergei was basically an ascetic) rather than on Manichean Self-consciousness, it was also susceptible to degeneration from the inside, again like Moscow. In fact, it was a temporary matter, like all the icon culture not based on Manas. In this connection the most famous monastery built by Sergei in 1340, the monastery of the Holy Trinity just outside Moscow, is considered as the mother of all the Tsarist Russian monasteries.

Furthermore, it is no coincidence that it was precisely during a culture which was an icon culture in two senses, that Russian icon painting reached its peak in Andrei Rublev. He founded the Moscow school of icon painting, finally giving form to the archetypal images that are used in the icons. Conversely, this peak is also reflected in what is illustrated by the twofold icon character of Dimitri Donskoi's Moscow.

As mentioned above, this Moscow began to come to an end with Dimitri's death in 1389. Increasingly, post-Tartar and pre-materialistic

Western European influences affected Moscow. Russia's dictator, Ivan the Terrible, a distant great-great-grandson of Dimitri Donskoi, died in 1584. Under him these influences had become firmly established in Russia. This was followed by the so-called 'Time of Troubles' in Russia, and the emergence of the second great Demetrius figure in Russian history. Confusion reigned supreme.

Some years before his death, Tsar Ivan IV, who was in some ways a genius but also insance, had beaten his oldest and only able son to death in a fit of rage. In order to secure the succession, on his deathbed he elected a number of boyars as regents for his second son Fyodor, who was unfit to rule. One of these was Fyodor's brother-in-law, the Tartar Boris Godunov, an able regent who was not descended from Rurik. After Ivan IV's death Godunov took his chance, and soon seized power after Fyodor's succession. He ruled over Russia as First Regent until Fyodor's death in 1598. He promoted his best friend, the priest Hiob, to become patriarch of the Greek Catholic Church, so that the latter would crown him Tsar in 1598, following the advice of the Zemski Sobor — the council of boyars — who had been prepared for this. He thus brought to an end the Varangian dynasty which had begun with Rurik.

As a regent Godunov had wisely undone a great deal of the injustice which Ivan IV had inflicted on his people. However, this was not always a permanent success, and he seemed destined to be punished by fate. When he became Tsar, Godunov foolishly surrounded himself with Tartar members of his family, and sent his former co-regents back home. This was another reason for his lack of success. They started to hatch intrigues against the new Tsar, and this turned him into more and more of a tyrant. He saw everything as a threat to his (stolen) position, and particularly pursued the Romanovs, Fyodor's relations on his mother's side. He saw all of them, and particularly his brother-in-law Michail Romanov, as pretenders to the throne. There is a piece of Russian history about Boris Godunov, or a historical bylina about him, which reveals that he had already removed the threat of another pretender to the throne at an earlier stage.

Immediately following Fyodor's successions, Ivan's third son Prince Dimitri, aged three at the time, was exiled with his mother Maria of Nagoye and all her family to the small principality of Uglich. Maria was Ivan's seventh wife, and according to the law of the Greek Catholic Church her son was not eligible for the Tsar's crown, because that law prohibited having more than three wives.

From 1591–1605 the following strange rumours circulated in Russia:

1) It was said that the young Dimitri had died in 1591. According to one version of this rumour, he had been murdered. It was said that on the initiative of his father Godunov, the young son of Boris Godunov's representative stabbed Dimitri with a knife while they were playing.

According to another version, he caused a fire in which Dimitri died. These versions were circulated by Dimitri's mother because she hated Boris Godunov. According to another version of this rumour, Dimitri, who was an epileptic like his father, had a fit while he was playing with the representative's son, and fell on his own knife. Obviously this version was the official one released by Boris Godunov.

2) It was not young Dimitri who had died, but the son of his wetnurse, who was believed to have been burnt. This fire had been lit by someone who wished to abduct Dimitri for unknown reasons, to create the impression that the boy had died in Uglich. This did not work, for although the burnt body of a boy was found, it was not Dimitri's, and he remained lost. This rumour circulated from 1601.

3) The young Dimitri had certainly lost his life in a fire in 1591. The son of his wetnurse was abducted, so that in future he could replace Dimitri Ivanovich (and Godunov) for the benefit of a particular power faction. The second rumour was also accompanied by the idea that something like this could be behind the abduction of Dimitri Ivanovich. The third rumour and the supposition accompanying the second rumour were prevalent from 1604 because of the following event which took place in Poland.

In 1604 an anonymous monk appeared there. According to some, he was the adventurous monk Grigory Otrepyov, once an orphan who had been adopted by the Otrepyov family. [25] He said he was Dimitri Ivanovich, and did have some of the physical characteristics and features that Dimitri had had as a child. The Polish Woiwods (nobility) and Jesuits, as well as some of the Russian boyar regents who had been betrayed by Godunov and had escaped to Poland, were remarkably quick to accept the claim of the foreign monk to the throne. On condition that he became Catholic, they honoured his request to mobilize an army with which he would be able to fight against Boris Godunov. Meanwhile, he became engaged to Marina von Mnischek, the daughter of a leading nobleman George von Mnischek, who was in contact with the Pope in Rome.

In his 'Demetrius fragment' Schiller describes this engagement in extremely dramatic terms, and it coincides with the identification of the stranger as Dimitri Ivanovich, on the basis of the above-mentioned physical characteristics and features. He described George and Marina von Mnischek as 'intriguers'. In his book *Dimitri* (1966, Houghton Mifflin Co., Boston, USA), Ph. L. Barbour incidentally remarks that on her wedding day later in Moscow, Marina's future act in relation to Dimitri was described by Polish insiders as a sacrifice.

The monk, hereafter referred to as Dimitri, soon marched east with the army he had assembled, consisting of officers from the Polish nobility, Jesuit advisors, Polish peasants, and later also Russian peasants. In the context of the second rumour, Boris Godunov blamed the boyar regents who had remained in Moscow for the new pretender to the throne from Poland, and said that they had encouraged his claim. He sent the whole Russian army against Dimitri. That army was victorious because of its superior strength. However, the boyar generals were divided among themselves, and the most influential boyars joined Dimitri not long after the victory, so that the victory was reversed. Boris Godunov died what was probably a natural death in 1605, a disappointed man.

In Russia opinion was divided about Dimitri. The first rumour was no longer very relevant, except that it complicated later rumours. The people, especially the boyars, either believed rumours 2 and 3, or they ignored them — especially the common people — and regarded Dimitri as Ivan's son, in the hope that he would resolve the chaos in the land.

Dimitri made himself acceptable to everyone, possibly even to Godunov's daughter Axinia, the Tartar fiancée of Michail Romanov, who was to found the Romanov dynasty many years later, and for whom he had a soft spot, according to Schiller. Nevertheless, he married Marina. Supporting the second rumour, it was said that Maria of Nagoye, after being liberated from her exile by Dimitri, recognized him as her son, or considered doing so. Following the third rumour, several boyars, led by the city ruler Zusky, who had ambitions to become Tsar himself, planned a revolt against Dimitri and his Polish advisors. However, this failed. Then Dimitri demonstrated his greatness of heart by transmuting Zusky's death sentence into exile. Zusky soon regained his freedom.

After several months Dimitri ascended the Russian throne. He was unlike anyone who had ever ruled over Moscow, full of consciousness of the lower and higher Self, the conscience. He was highly gifted, educated (because of his training as a monk), brave, and radiated total success. Marina van Mnischek ascended the throne together with him. Strangely, she was crowned Tsarina even before the coronation of Dimitri, with remarkable Polish honours (Ph. L. Barbour: 'Dimitri', chapter 15). At her request, neither she nor Dimitri went to communion, as celebrated by the Greek Orthodox Church, after the coronation, although they were expected to do so and were actually obliged to do so (Ph. L. Barbour: 'Dimitri', chapter 15).

Whether or not he was the true son of Ivan the Terrible, shortly after his coronation one or more Polish advisors circulated the second rumour about Dimitri among the people and his close associates in an extreme way. According to Schiller, this took place with regard to Dimitri in a shock procedure which disoriented his Self, so that Zusky and his men could be remobilized. According to Barbour, this took place by means of a lobbying process which achieved the same results. This event can be explained when we assume, in accordance with rumours 2 and 3, that a Polish Jesuit power faction wished to establish influence in Russia through Dimitri (whether or not he was the true Dimitri), or wished to give an unjust and unasked for Varangian Order Answer in Russia, and that the manipulated Dimitri escaped from their leadership and the tie with Marina von Mnischek.

Not long after the celebrations for the coronation in 1607, chaos reigned. Zusky and his men locked Dimitri in the Kremlin, claiming that they were protecting him from the rebellious people, but in fact in order to murder him. Dimitri was assassinated. Zusky had the victim identified as a false Dimitri, an imposter, and he had the true Dimitri sanctified. He stated that in contrast with what was generally suggested, Maria von Nagoye had not officially sworn that the murdered Tsar had been her son. Zusky became Tsar.

In the same year, 1607, the second Dimitri appeared, probably prompted by the Poles, who obviously still wished to achieve their goal. He was recognized by some of the Russians for a short while, but was soon rejected, and died in 1610. Zusky's stance against Poland, to whom he had become indebted, was considered too weak and he was deposed. The group of Russians who had recognized the second Dimitri for a while then offered the Tsar's crown to the son of King Sigismund of Poland. Others wished to have Zusky's cousin as Tsar. In 1611 a third Dimitri emerged, but after a number of small successes he was condemned in Moscow in 1613.

Finally, the Poles were banished from Moscow, including the Von Mnischek father and daughter. A state assembly elected Michail Romanov as Tsar, and with him the dynasty of the Romanovs was founded.

Commentary

The search for a solution to the Demetrius question, which was encouraged by Rudolf Steiner so that the (Slav) future could be prepared in the right way, was seen in anthroposophical circles as a search for the origin and mission of the Demetrius character on the basis of Schillers 'Demetrius fragment'. Generally speaking, this was also the mission of Demetrius himself. Steiner had indicated that in this work Schiller was on the way to finding a solution to the problem.

As Dimitri Ivanovich is explicitly presented as a false Dimitri in Schiller's work, and not as the son of Ivan the Terrible, it was increasingly considered in anthroposophical circles that the solution of the Demetrius question would be discovered in the detailed historical description and spiritual examination of the ideas expressed by Schiller (and supported by Steiner, it was thought). In his lecture, 'The fate of Russia and its future culture', given by P. Tradovsky at the Conference for International Understanding in October/November 1983 in Witten (D), he referred to a sort of conclusion of the search in this direction, and to an examination and provisional solution of the Demetrius question.

In this lecture he summarized as follows: 'Perhaps the thrust of Schiller's drama can be formulated briefly as follows: the modern age, also for Russia, began in about 1600. In this age spiritual impulses are no longer engendered by the forces which live in heredity and in the blood, but on the basis of Self force and imminent Manas development. In Russia the previous age concluded with the death of Ivan the Terrible, and the new age began with his legitimate successor. This legitimate successor was Dimitri, who was not Ivan's son by blood. He proved his right by acting as Tsar in Moscow in accordance with the demands of the new age, as a merciful ruler: spiritually he was the true Dimitri Ivanovich (A).

Obviously his nature and his right were part of his destiny, his karma (B). There is little to add on this point here. He was able to come into his own and be the true Dimitri Ivanovich in spirit precisely because he was *not* in blood. In blood he was the false Dimitri Ivanovich (C).

In this context Dimitri's mission to prepare for the new age in Russia can be formulated in the form of the following conclusion, although it is in itself such a general and meaningless formulation that it hardly requires any support to be recognized. It was his mission to introduce into Russia at a historical level the principle of mercy and brotherly love, which is independent of blood. This is at the expense of the blood-related (Tartar) principle of the sword, represented by his father (1); for this he indisputably required the turn of fate which made it possible for him to be accepted as Dimitri Ivanovich without actually being this character (2) (D). (A Polish Jesuit power faction, which wished to convert Russia to Catholicism, and thereby deprive it of its future Manas development, to some extent met the conditions under (A), (B), (C), and (D), intervened, complicated and distorted Dimitri's destiny until he escaped from their influence (E).

Tradovsky's description of Dimitri's mission (D), particularly the appositional clause (2) on which the main premise (1) hinges, is obviously entirely dependent on the a priori premise given under (C): 'What works as Self force and Manas cannot be based on what works in the blood.' It is only when that a priori statement applies that the main premise (1) follows from the appositional clause (2). If it does not, that statement may also be true, but does not necessarily follow from it.

In the latter case, Tradovsky's description of Dimitri's mission remains fairly separate from his life (destiny). This description says little, as it can easily be supported by a general statement such as that in Russia the Self era started in 1600 (quite irrespectively of the specific Dimitri character). The value of Tradovsky's solution of the Demetrius problem therefore depends on the truth of the above-mentioned a priori statement. What can be said about that?

That a priori statement may be true — it sounds logical and attractive, and if it is true, statement (D) (1) follows from the appositional clause (D) (2), and Tradovsky's solution is both reasonable and elegant. However, the a priori statement may not be true. For what is the significance of the idea that the birth and mission of Christ as the world's permanent Self-bearer and Manas developer were based on what works through blood (via a process lasting centuries)? Does this mean Moses's blood purifying law of retribution? Christ's law of love replaced Moses's law of retribution, though not without initially being supported by it. Jesus Christ was certainly Mary's true son. Simply the possibility that the a priori statement concerned is not necessarily applicable, means that Tradovsky's solution of the Demetrius problem as a description of Dimitri's mission in life is less meaningful.

The question of Dimitri's identity remains open. The above analysis of Tradovsky's lecture, 'The state of Russia and its future culture', was based on the fact that modern Demetrius research tends to assume that Demetrius was Ivan IV's son by blood (Ph. Barbour, 'Dmitri', p. 250 ff.) Because of this, as well as the fact that the above-mentioned a priori statement is not necessarily applicable, anthroposophical research into the Demetrius question, which is based on Schiller's Demetrius fragment, has come to a dead end. The main objection to this research, which clearly explains its fruitless character, is that the Demetrius question is viewed against too narrow a background. In its interpretation it is too much directed towards Schiller's fragment, and what Steiner supposedly said about this.

As indicated earlier, I believe that the solution of the Demetrius problem means that it should be seen against the background of Russian history and mythology, as an organic whole, as outlined and commented on in this work, particularly against the background and in the light of certain bylini (those about Roman Mstislavich), the history (historical bylina) about Dimitri Donskoi, and the two versions of the Kitezh legend. In this respect it is certainly the case that Schiller's assumption that Dimitri was a false Dimitri by blood, and that Steiner's evaluation of Schiller's fragment should be interpreted differently and in a wider sense than has been done up to now. The history and mission of Dimitri Ivanovich should be viewed together with the above-mentioned idea that future Russian history will repeat early Russian history at a higher level, and that Dimitri Donskoi repeated and synthesized that early Russian history in the form of icons, between the two historical periods in the (Tartar-Tsarist-Soviet Communist) interim period, thus starting to unite the past with the future.

In Russian history Dimitri Ivanovich's place should be seen in the light of the fact that the organic, mirror-like character of that history as a whole requires that there must be a counterpart to Dimitri Donskoi, and what he achieved: a character to succeed him, who brings not only the past, but also the future, into the present. This is someone who anticipates the eventual Russia of the future, in the present (in the context of Moscow's twofold icon culture).

early Russian history ⎤ ⟶ present Russian history ⟶ ⎡ future Russian history
⎦ D. DONSKOI/D. IVANOVICH ⟵⟶ ⎣

Where Schiller, Steiner, Barbour and others suggest that in general it was Dimitri Ivanovich's task to prepare for Russia's Manas future, it is logical to view this second Dimitri as Dimitri Donskoi's counterpart. Moreover, it is also logical in the context of Russia's historical mirror-image character to derive certain specific aspects of Dimitri Ivanovich's life and mission from particular aspects of Dimitri Donskoi's mission.

Above all, it should be remembered that in order to achieve this mission, i.e. to express his Self, Dimitri Donskoi brought the Vladimirskaya into Moscow. This was the icon of the Sophia relating to the correct style of government as performed in historical Kiev Rus, particularly in the historical Kitezh. (With regard to the Vladimirskaya, it should be remembered that it has a characteristic twofold element: as a representation of the Sophia, it refers to the Slav-Manichean character, and as a symbol of the right style of government, it refers to the Varangian Self character.) If this is viewed as a mirror image, Dimitri Ivanovich should also have introduced something like a Vladimirskaya into Moscow in order to achieve his mission, and express his Self. In fact, he did so, or tried to do so. However, because he was manipulated and misled, he introduced into Moscow a caricature of something rather like the Vladimirskaya.

What sort of Vladimirskaya should Dimitri Ivanovich have introduced into Russia? Not one like that which Dimitri Donskoi introduced into Moscow, not a magic amulet as the 'dead' representation of the Sophia or of the Manas (the ruling aspect), which serves as a reference to Russia's pseudo-Manichean past. It should have been a Vladimirskaya like a magic queen of flesh and blood, a living anima image of that Sophia or that Manas (the ruling aspect), which belonged at that time to Russia's true Manichean future. In order to prepare for Russia's future, Dimitri Ivanovich should have introduced the Sophia or Manas (ruling aspect) into Moscow in the form or the figure of a woman who could have permanently fulfilled her 'anima-identification role' with regard to him, just as Isolde had done for Tristan of Lyonnesse and Sophie von Kühn would later do for Novalis. (In both heroes there was a strengthening of the Self, and above all, a preparation for development of Manas resulting from this, from which everyone around them benefited.)[25] In this respect he should have followed in the footsteps of characters such as Ilya Muromets, Michailo Potyk, and above all, Vsevolod Yurivich of Kitezh, and continued these tracks of Russia's interim period in the direction of Russia's future destiny.

What sort of Vladimirskaya did Dimitri Ivanovich introduce into Moscow? It was the Princess Marina von Mnischek, the image of the Polish Jesuit Black Madonna, the image of the false Sophia, the false Manas (ruling aspect); a woman who may be assumed, on the basis of Schiller's suggestions and Barbour's research, to have forced herself on Dimitri as a pseudo-anima, a sacrifice presented by her father, George van Mnischek and the Jesuits. She was a woman controlled by her background in a way that Latygorka of the Latyr Sea and Avdotya Lichodjevna had never been (not to mention Fevronia).

It was Marina's mission to prevent Dimitri Ivanovich from preparing for the development of Manas, a development of Manas through 'pure' anima experience like that of Ilya, Michailo or Vsevolod. As a result, he would not achieve his mission in Moscow, so that there would be an opportunity to convert Russia to Catholicism, and in this way sever it from its Manas future. Just as certain Freemasons (related to the Jesuits) succeeded in stagnating the Self development of Kaspar Hauser, 'the Child of Europe', the ultimate Varangian, by depriving him of development in thought, speech and education in childhood, the Jesuits deprived Dimitri Ivanovich of the right anima experience during the years of his puberty and adolescence. This meant that his preparatory Manas development stagnated, and therefore indirectly his Self development as well.

Dimitri Ivanovich was predestined to experience this as the true Dimitri, irrespective of whether or not he was so by blood. Misrepresented, and united with (the image or representative of) the false Sophia, he appeared to be, and actually was a false Dimitri. In my opinion, when this point of view is taken, the presentation of this specific deceit is Schiller's contribution to the solution of the Demetrius problem, a contribution which was greatly valued by Steiner, though it was later interpreted oversimply strictly in terms of Self.

In the light of this solution to the Demetrius question, it may be argued that although it is based on the strong a priori premise of the mirror-image structure of Russian history, and therefore appears to be true, this does not necessarily mean that it is true. To support the solution, one might like to know, for example, who should have been the true anima Queen for Dimitri Ivanovich. Perhaps it was the Tartar Axinia Romanov, to whom Dimitri was clearly attracted. Or perhaps she was forced by the Tartars to make herself acceptable to Dimitri. On the other hand, possibly Dimitri sought in her — though in vain — the right anima that he was lacking.

These questions will be difficult to answer, for in the context of this solution, the Polish Jesuit power faction was concerned above all with keeping such an anima character away from Dimitri Ivanovich. Therefore the insolubility of these questions cannot really be used as an argument against their solution. Further thoughts on this matter are given at the end of this chapter. With regard to the idea that the sort of solution outlined here does not have to be correct, there are two points which support it. The first is concerned with Western Europe, or the Varangian culture. In spiritual-scientific circles it is often pointed out that the appearance of Dimitri Ivanovich in Eastern Europe coincided with the appearance of the Rosicrucian writings of Johann Valentine Andreas in Western Europe. This is particularly true with regard to the appearance of the work *The Alchemical Wedding of Christian Rosenkreuz*, which was written in 1603, disseminated among those who were interested in 1604, and printed in 1614. The other works *De Fama Fraternitatis* and *De Confessio* were written later, after the death of Dimitri Ivanovich.

This coincidence means that Dimitri Ivanovich should probably have taken the liberating influence of these writings with him to Russia, instead of taking the compulsive Polish Jesuit influence and the related decadent lifestyle. Then he could have arrived at a pure lifestyle himself. However, it should be specified in relation to the appearance of Andreas' books: Dimitri Ivanovich should have allowed himself to be inspired to have this experience, and everything related to it, with the help of the work *The Alchemical Wedding of Christian Rosenkreuz*. This work deals with the alchemical wedding between the spirit (the higher Self) and the soul (the Manas), which is foreshadowed by the correct anima experience. If he had done so, on the basis of anticipating the correct future Varangian Order Answer to strengthen his Self in a preparatory sense — in the sense of the anima experience for which he was predestined — he could have developed Manas in himself and in his people (anticipating the Manas culture of the future Kiev Rus).

The second point is concerned with the East European Kitezh legends. The concluding comments on the bylini pointed out that the historical and mythical element in both the historical and future Kitezh coincide in the context of what was called 'a higher reality'. They also do so in the context of a so-called lower reality in the Russia of the present, the time of a Tartar–Tsarist–Soviet Communist Russia, or the Moscow Russia of Dimitri Donskoi, and that of Dimitri Ivanovich. In this respect the twofold Moscow Russia, and the twofold Kitezh Russia, had similar characteristics. This general pattern of comparisons can be described in a surprisingly new light if we compare:

the Moscow of Dimitri Donskoi and his history with historical Kitezh or the Slav Church version of the Kitezh legend, particularly the passages relating to Georgi Vsevolodovich of Pskov; the Moscow of Dimitri Ivanovich and his history with the anticipatory outline of the future Kitezh, or the Belski version of the Kitezh legend, particularly the passages about Vsevolod Yurivich and Lady Fevronia.

As regards the first comparison, it should be pointed out that while Dimitri Donskoi introduced the icon (or 'dead' image) of Vladimir's Mother of God into fourteenth-century Moscow in the context of the lower reality referred to here, Georgi Vsevolodovich tried to introduce the icon (or the 'dead' image) of Fyodorovsk's Mother of God, the Fyodorovskaya, into twelfth-century Little Kitezh in the context of the higher reality referred to here.

The ancient Kitezh legend goes as follows: 'All the inhabitants of this town (Little Kitezh) asked the true believer Prince Georgi to take the image of the saint, the icon of the Holiest Mother of Fyodorovsk, which could work miracles, to their town . . . When the Prince wished to carry the statue of the saint into the town, he was unable to move it from its place.' (He saw this as the will of the Mother of God.)

The name Fyodor (Theodorus) means 'God's gift'. Therefore the Fyodorovskaya is the ('dead') image in the form of an amulet of the Sophia, of Manas as God's gift. Therefore Georgi Vsevolodovich wished to introduce this icon into Little Kitezh at the request of the people of the town.

However, he was unable to do so, for the icon could not be moved. The Manas as an undivided gift of God is clearly different from the Manas in one of its aspects, particularly the Manas as an aspect of ruling based on the Varangian Self. Manas as God's gift has two aspects of the New Jerusalem descending from heaven: a) it cannot be lifted up like an amulet, whenever required; b) it belongs in Great Kitezh, the city of Manas, and not in Little Kitezh, which precedes it.

The Fyodorovskaya was prevented by God from entering historical Little Kitezh. Nevertheless, this twelfth-century Kitezh incident anticipated the pattern — crossing over from the Theodorus principle to the Vladimir principle — of Dimitri Donskoi's introduction of the Vladimirskaya into later fourteenth-century Moscow, anticipating the introduction by God of a (cultural and root race) Manas in the Great Kitezh of the future.

As regards the second comparison, it should be pointed out that in the context of the above-mentioned lower reality, Dimitri Ivanovich should have introduced into seventeenth-century Moscow his true anima as a living image of the ruling aspect of Manas, i.e. the queen N.N. who never appeared. However, in the context of the above-mentioned higher reality, Vsevolod Yurivich does (or did) introduce his true anima as the living image of Manas and as God's gift or Queen Fevronia — the twentieth-century anticipation of the future Great Kitezh. Therefore this concerns the Belski version of the Kitezh legend.

Fevronia means 'the bringer of blessings' (from the Greek *pherenikè*); in relation to salvation, the blessing of Great Kitezh on the Tartars, the name also refers unambiguously to the concept of 'God's gift'. The name also means 'Vera', iconic.

Earlier in this chapter it was shown how Dimitri Ivanovich introduced the living image of the Polish Black Madonna into Moscow, instead of the living anima image of the undivided Sophia. Now it is possible to say that just as God prevented the Fyodorovskaya from entering historical Little Kitezh, Satan prevented the living image of the Sophia from entering seventeenth-century Moscow. Nevertheless, this seventeenth-century Moscow incident clearly anticipates the pattern (crossing over from the Vladimir principle to the Theodorus principle) of the introduction of Lady Fevronia via Vsevolod Yurivich into the Kitezh of Belski's version of the legend, and anticipates the Christian communist rule through service of the Kitezh of the future. Comparisons a) and b) (above) can be illustrated as follows:

These patterns and the way in which Dimitri Ivanovich's appearance coincides in time with the Rosicrucian works of Johann Valentine Andreas reinforce the beginning of a solution to the Demetrius problem in the direction proposed in this work.

In this way the Kitezh legend is first related to the mythical and heroic bylini by means of a review of early Russian history as an organic whole, showing that Kitezh forms the social conclusion of a Grail development in

259

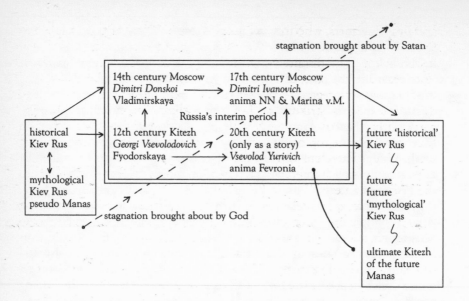

stagnation brought about by Satan

14th century Moscow	17th century Moscow
Dimitri Donskoi ⟶	*Dimitri Ivanovich*
Vladimirskaya	anima NN & Marina v.M.

Russia's interim period

12th century Kitezh	20th century Kitezh
Georgi Vsevolodovich ↗	(only as a story)
Fyodorskaya ⟶	*Vsevolod Yurivich*
	anima Fevronia

historical Kiev Rus

mythological Kiev Rus pseudo Manas

stagnation brought about by God

future 'historical' Kiev Rus

future future 'mythological' Kiev Rus

ultimate Kitezh of the future Manas

Kiev, both in a historical and a future context. Furthermore, it is also now related to the two most important historical bylini, or Russia's present history. This relation showed that historical Kitezh (the 'old' Kitezh legend) clearly determined the pattern for the first of these two historical bylini, and that conversely, the second of these clearly determined the pattern for the 'new' Kitezh legend.

We would like to conclude this chapter by returning briefly to the bylina about Roman Mstislavich, the bylina in which a Polish political military pattern of action is described as the archetypally incorrect Varangian Answer to the Slav-Rurik Call, particularly as the archetypal attitude of the Polish Jesuit power faction to Dimitri Ivanovich, which was described above. It is also the bylina which shows how the ultimate Demetrius can fulfil the mission of his life, thanks to the imaginative and inspirational capacities of a father of a different calibre from Ivan IV. In my view, the first part of this bylina unmistakably refers to the conduct of Dimitri Ivanovich, while the second part is a reference to the coming of an ultimate and final Demetrius.

How and as whom should this character be interpreted? It is a person (or a force) that will introduce into Russia in the future the age-old Demetrius principle at the physical and historical level — i.e. Manas (in an individual cultural and root race sense) as a Christian communist principle of government. As this was also the mission of Vsevolod of Kitezh (and indirectly also that of his father, Georgi — a father of a different calibre than Ivan IV), assessed as future hero(es), it is logical to equate this Demetrius to him (them) as an individual and/or as a force, leaving aside how this is done, and to what extent.

To a lesser extent, this comparison applies to the (future) King Vladimir

260

and Ilya Muromets, who initially introduced the Demetrius principle into Russia (or will introduce it) at the mythological (ethereal) level, as shown in the bylina 'The dispute between King Vladimir and Ilya Muromets'. With regard to the past, this sort of comparison undoubtedly also applies in some way with regard to the two earlier great Demetrius characters. In this context it is striking to note how these figures come together, particularly Dimitri Ivanovich and Vsevolod Yurivich (but also Ilya Muromets), at the top of the upper part of the diagram of Kiev Rus as a world Grail. Therefore the bylina about Roman Mstislavich, with the description of Polish intervention in Russia, indirectly relates, *inter alia*, to the Prince of Kitezh.

In this context, it is relevant to note that a Kitezh legend also arose in Poland, which was later transcribed as a ballad by Polish poet Adam Mickievich, and used in a composition by Chopin in his Opus 38 in F. This legend refers to a Polish-Lithuanian lake in which the clash of arms could be heard at night. The castle of Svitesh or Kitezh was once drowned in that lake. A descendant of the former lord of that castle and the surrounding area went to investigate and met a beautiful woman. She told him about Kitezh, about his ancestors, the Tuhan dynasty, and how Kitezh had been attacked by the Russians (Tartars), but sank into the ground, creating a lake. This had happened because the daughter of the last Lord of Tuhan had prayed to God for help to save the women remaining behind in the castle from being dishonoured. God changed the women and children of Kitezh into flowers (immortal souls). Anyone who picked them died. The beautiful storyteller (no one other than the daughter of the story) withdrew back into the lake, and never appeared again.

The woman who told this legend, or the princess of the submerged Polish Kitezh, can clearly be compared with Lady Fevronia of the Russian Kitezh legend. Her story corresponds to Fevronia's letter to Griska Kuterma, but it serves more as an answer and a way of passing information than as an appeal which Fevronia made to the Russian Sower of Confusion to repent, and it is addressed to one of her descendants rather than at a guilty sinner. This Polish Fevronia serves as the counterpart of the Polish Black Madonna.

It is possible to speculate on the following question. Should not a representative of the Polish Fevronia have served as the anima for Dimitri Ivanovich instead of Marina van Mnischek as a representative of the Black Madonna? (Or, if he had remained in Russia, a representative of the Russian Fevronia?) Whatever the answer to this question, Lady Fevronia herself is soon united, as the Sophia and the Rose of the soul, with Prince Vsevolod of Kitezh, or the third Demetrius.

Notes

On Ignatius de Loyola's image of Christ:
See his 'Spiritual Exercises'. This concerns the exercise in which one concentrates on the image of the battle of Armageddon. From Jerusalem,

the army of Jesus — the Jesuits — prepares to defeat the army of Satan in order to subjugate the whole world to Jesus as the lord of the world. Meanwhile the army of Satan is also preparing in Babylon to subjugate the world, this time to Satan.

On Rudolf Steiner's view on Dimitri Ivanovich and Schiller's 'Demetrius fragment':
I. and R. Engelen: Rudolf Steiner über Russland (collected texts).

On the restricted development of the Self of Kaspar Hauser and his death:
P. Tradovsky: Kaspar Hauswer.

On the Polish (Svitesh) Kitezh legend based on A. Mickievich and Chopin's opus 38 in F:
Höweler's Encyclopedia of Music.

Glossary

Ahriman: Together with Lucifer (q.v.) the representation of Evil in Anthroposophical belief. Ahriman was originally a Persian god.

Alkonost: Russian sacred bird.

Atman: Sanskrit term. First and highest member of the higher self; the transformed phsyical body.

Bogatyri: Russian hero-figure roughly equivalent to a Western knight.

Book of Hermits: Medieval Russian apocryphal text.

Book of Jerusalem: Medieval Russian apocryphal text.

Book of the Holy Mountain: Medieval Russian apocryphal text.

Boyar: Member of a Russian noble family.

Buddhi: Sanskrit term meaning second member of the Higher Self; the transformed ethereal body.

Bylini: Russian heroic songs.

Doppelgänger: Anti-human double, as described in Stephenson's famous novel *Dr Jekyll and Mr Hyde*.

Durma: a Council of advisors drawn from military and aristocratic families.

Filioque: Literally 'and the Son'. This clause, inserted into the Creed at the Third Council of Toledo (AD 589), asserts that the Holy Spirit proceeds from the Father and the Son. The clause is rejected by the Orthodox Church and is the subject of much debate between Eastern and Western Christians.

Goesli: A musical instrument.

Hypertrophy: Sudden growth or development.

Icon: Incarnation-bed (like 'river-bed') for the sake of an outpouring of energy or of an idea originating from the spiritual world. Popular meaning: image.

Kaliki: A mendicant monk generally perceived as belonging to an older, heroic era.

Kundry: The name of the Messenger of the Grail in various medieval texts. Also known as 'the Loathly Lady'.

Logres: A name for the inner kingdom of Arthurian Britain.

Lucifer: In Christian teaching the Angel of Light who fell after an unsuccessful struggle with the archangel Michael. In Theosophical terminology synonymous with Evil.

Manas: Sanskrit term. Third member of the Higher Self, the transformed astral body.

Monaskik: Medieval Russian apocryphal text.

Poed: Measurement of weight roughly equivalent to one-and-a-half pounds.

Polienietsa: Female Bogatyr (q.v.).

Root race: A term used in Theosophy and Anthroposophy to refer to the division of the human race into a number of basic racial archetypes which have appeared at different times and through successive ages of development.

St Nikola the Holy: Nicholas, i.e. Santa Claus.

Sardes culture: Our present-day Western European culture, in which man develops his Self and his Higher Self.

Senoriat: Governing Body/Parliament.

Skazitila: A minstrel.

Skomoroch: A wandering minstrel of pre-Christian origin.

Verst: Measurement of distance roughly equivalent to about two-thirds of a mile.

Vetsches: Municipal town-councils.

Zubr: Auroch, i.e. ancient prehistoric creatures something like gigantic cows.

Notes

[1] For an understanding of his article on Kitezh, Valentin Tombert assumes that his readers have a knowledge of Anthroposophy, for many of them subscribe to the Anthroposophical Journal in which the article was published. Therefore Tomberg did not explain all the concepts he used; furthermore, he was not in the habit of using references. In general, he referred to Anthroposophy as a whole. Therefore we must assume a knowledge of some of the concepts used here (and in the following chapters). However, some of the least well known concepts will be explained either in these notes or in a subsequent list of notes, or in most cases a reference to the relevant literature will be given.

[2] On the other hand, Sviatogor represents the exponent of Atman man, as mentioned in the introduction, as he first appears in the sixth Manichean root race. This is when the Self becomes manifest as the Atma. (The ultimate complete Atman man will only exist on earth after the seventh root race era.) What Sviatogor represents in a (root) racial context is represented by Ilya Muromets in a cultural context. He is the Atman man of the Manas culture. In addition, he also represents the Self man in this culture, together with Alyosha Popovich, as will be explained in greater detail below.

[2] As mentioned in the introduction, Mikoela represents both man in pre-history and man in the sixth or Slav root race, as the bearer of the Self; as the archaic bearer of the Self, he is the precursor and prototype of the present Self man.

[4] (Alyosha Popovich, and later Ilya Muromets, do the same as the tenth century man, and man in the sixth Slav cultural period.)

[5] At the time of the future Slav culture, the bogatyr Dobrynya Nikitich will fulfil this role. This is explained in greater detail in later bylini.

[6] Therefore Volga's kingdom is the (Russian) kingdom of assimilation.

[7] It is said about the six-pointed star of Venus, the star of 6, the 6th period, the 6th cycle, the 6th era, that it shines above the future Slav culture, and the new Slav era following this, the Slav root race. That culture and that era are a culture and an era of the 6. (Before the Middle Ages this star was known as the Star of Mercury, which is now the five-pointed star. Later it became as described here.)

[8] This will one day result in the older bogatyri and the younger bogatyri coinciding, as mentioned earlier.

[9] Particularly the soul of perception which has a twelvefold structure like the astral body. See also the Epilogue.

[10] With regard to this polarization, see also the commentary on the bylina about Solovei Budimirovich.

[11] With regard to this polarization, see also the commentary of the bylina about Solovei Budimirovich.

[12] However, in the early mysteries this applied to a lesser extent than it does today. The present Self man, represented here by Alyosha and Ilya, cannot be regarded as being the same as before, nor as early man, either in or out of early mysteries (both represented by Mikoela Selyaninovich).

[13] This is obviously seen from the point of view of the future. The future Ilya Muromets refers back to the historical one.

[14] The influences of the past and the effect of the Father Mysteries in a sense extended as far as the Middle Ages. This is why there is a process of shifting time in some of the bylini.

[15] On the other hand, it is Ilya's companion and counterpart, Michailo Ivanovich Potyk, who corresponds to Gawain in this pattern. He liberates his anima/*femme fatale* as a world Grail messenger of her demonic drive in the same way as Gawain frees Lady Ragnell from this as an individual Grail messenger. He transcends Ilya in this way and complements him. (See also the bylina about him.)

[16] One of the following bylini deals with this.

[17] See the commentary on the last two bylini about Ilya Muromets.

[18] The process of death is described by the Manichean brothers as the 'Endura'; the process of the transformation of body and soul as the 'Transfiguration'. These two processes are united in each other.

[19] See J. van Ryckenborgh, *The Alchemical Wedding of Christian Rosenkreuz*, the commentary to *The Third Day* (Rozenkruispers, Haarlem).

[20] This is rather different when the earth (as a world Grail) is viewed as a developing sun which will one day replace the present sun.

[21] Also see the outline summarizing Russian mythology on p. 234.

[22] The numbers indicate the relevant readings, which each consist of a question and an answer.

[23] On this subject, also see Mussorgsky's opera *Boris Godunov* and Ph. Barbour's biography *Dmitri*.

[24] Great Kitezh was also spared from being overrun, because it was ruled in the right way. However, with regard to both Moscow and Great Kitezh, which are both icon cultures, it should be said that it is only true to a certain extent, for Great Kitezh is no longer visible, and Moscow became anti-Varangian from the inside.

[25] For the anima theme, see the commentaries on the heroic bylini of Kiev.

Further Reading

Consult the Dutch original of this book for a complete bibliography in which the author renders account for his quotations and references.

Allen, P.M., *A Christian Rosenkreutz Anthology* (Rudolf Steiner Publications, Blauvelt, New York, 1968).

Bailey, A.A., *The Treatise on the Seven Rays* (5 vols) (Lucis Press, 1936).

Barbour, Ph. L., *Dimitri* (Houghton Mifflin Co., Boston, 1966).

Blavatsky, H., *Isis Unveiled* (Theosophical Publishing Society, London & Benares, 1910).

——, *The Secret Doctrine* (Theosophical Publishing Co. London, 1880).

Campanella, T., *The City of the Sun* trans. A.M. Elliott & R. Millner (The Journeyman Press, London & West Nyach, 1981).

Ivanits, L.J., *Russian Folk Belief* (Armonk, New York, M.E. Sharpe. Inc. 1989).

Komorovic, V.I., *Kitezkaja Legenda* (Moscow, 1936 (in Russian)).

Lievegoed, B.C.J., *Mystery Streams in Europe and the New Mysteries* New York (The Anthroposophic Press, 1982).

Matthews, C., *Sophia: Goddess of Wisdom* (Mandala, London, 1991)

Novalis, *Heinrich von Ofterdingen* (Fredrick Ungar Pub. Co. New York, 1982).

Raptschinsky, B., *The History of the Russian People* (W.J. Thieme, Zutphen, 1927).

——, *Russian Hero Sagas and Legends* (W.J. Thieme, Zutphen, 1932).

Rijckenborgh, J.V., *The Coming New Man* (Rose Cross Press, Amsterdam, 1985).

Schiller, F., *The Demetrius Fragment* (in) *Original Poems*, trans. C. Hodges (Trench, Tubner, London, 1836).

Steiner, R., *The Apocalypse of St John* (Rudolph Steiner Press, 1977).

——, *Christ and the Spirit World, The Search for the Holy Grail* (Rudolph Steiner Press, 1963).

——, *Esoteric Christianity and the Mission of Christian Rosencrutz* (Rudolph

Steiner Press, 1984).

——, *The Fifth Gospel* (Rudolph Steiner Press, 1968).

——, *The Gospel According to St John* (Rudolph Steiner Press, 1982).

——, *The Gospel of St Luke* (Rudolph Steiner Press, 1964).

——, *The Gospel of St Mark* (Rudolph Steiner Press, 1986).

——, *The Gospel of St Matthew* (Anthroposophical Press, 1985).

——, *Karmic Relationships* (Rudolph Steiner Press, 1975).

——, *Knowledge of the Higher Worlds* (Rudolph Steiner Press, 1969).

——, *Luciferian Past and Ahrimanian Future* (in) *The Influences of Lucifer and Ahriman* (Rudolph Steiner Press, 1954; and *The Ahrimanic Deception* Anthroposophical Press, 1975).

——, *Four Mystery Plays* (Rudolph Steiner Press, 1988).

——, *Occult Science* (Rudolph Steiner Press, 1979).

——, *The Priest Apocalypse* for private circulation only, 1924).

——, *The Search for the New Isis, the Divine Sophia* (Mercury Press, New York, 1983).

——, *The Temple Legend* (Rudolph Steiner Press, 1985).

——, *Theosophy* (Rudolph Steiner Press, 1970).

——, *World History in the Light of Anthroposophy* (Rudolph Steiner Press, 1977).

Stegmann, C., *The Other America* (privately published, n.d.).

Tomberg, V., *Meditations on the Tarot* (Amity House, New York, 1985).

Volkoff, V., *Vladimir the Russian King* (Honeyglen Publishing, Bath, 1984).

Zenkovsky, S.A., *Medieval Russia's Epics, Chronicles and Tales* (E.P. Dutton, New York, 1974).

Index

271